MARXISM
Philosophy and Economics

by
THOMAS SOWELL

Quill
William Morrow
New York

It is the policy of William Morrow and Company, Inc., and its imprints and affiliates, recognizing the importance of preserving what has been written, to print the books we publish on acid-free paper, and we exert our best efforts to that end.

Library of Congress Cataloging-in-Publication Data

Sowell, Thomas, 1930-
    Marxism: philosophy and economics.

    Bibliography: p.
    Includes index.
    1. Marx, Karl, 1818-1883. 2. Marxian economics.
    I. Title.
HX39.5.S6539 1986   335.4   85-31800
ISBN 0-688-06426-4 (pbk.)

Printed in the United States of America

9 10 11 12 13 14 15

BOOK DESIGN BY JAYE ZIMET

PREFACE

This slim volume distills more than a quarter of a century of research and thought on the economic and philosophic doctrines of Karl Marx. Over this long span of time, it has been possible to separate the essential from the non-essential in the theories of Marx and Engels, and thus to say in a small book what would otherwise take several volumes. The most non-essential—indeed, intellectually counterproductive—aspect of Marxism has been the elaborate jargon and stylized rhetoric in which its substance has been discussed, especially by followers and interpreters. Marxists, non-Marxists, and anti-Marxists alike have become bogged down in turgid words, when the real subject is "the blaze of ideas," to use Marx's own phrase.[1]

Wherever possible, I have quoted the original words of Marx and Engels. But passage-quoting is not enough. For Marxian writings that fill many volumes and span several decades of changing circumstances and evolving doctrines, *context* is crucial. Interpretation is a demanding responsibility that cannot be discharged merely by stringing quotes together. However, it is not necessary to believe the doctrine that one can "prove anything" by lifting quotes from Marx. On the contrary. Much recent interpretive literature, especially in economics, inadvertently demonstrates that various interpretations of Marx *cannot* be supported by quotes from his writings. Even articles in learned journals and scholarly books have solemnly and extensively analyzed particular "Marxian" doctrines *without a single citation of anything ever written by Karl Marx*. Often this "Marxism" bears no relationship to the work of Marx or Engels. In this way, particular doctrines and whole systems have emerged that might more accurately be called Samuelson-"Marxism" or Sweezy-"Marxism," etc. These modern concoctions have acquired a life of their own through sheer repetition, citation, and inertia.

While this book will not spend much space on refuting the secondary literature, there will be points at which the original Marxian analysis and doctrines will be contrasted with more recent fabrications bearing similar labels. Because the main purpose of this book is interpretation, its critical evaluation of Marxism will be saved until the last chapter.

A stylistic note may be in order. Because of Marx's penchant for italicized words, it should be noted here that all emphases are in the original, unless specifically stated otherwise.

My own philosophic, economic, and political orientations have ranged widely across the spectrum from the time of my undergraduate honors thesis on Marx at Harvard in 1958, through various articles on Marx in scholarly journals in the United States, Britain, and Canada during the 1960s, to the present work. What is gratifying is to be able

PREFACE

to read back over these earlier efforts and see how little difference my own changing viewpoints have made in the purely interpretive analysis.

Compared to my earlier writings on Marx, the present book draws on additional knowledge, later scholarship by others, newly unearthed facts and more recently translated works—notably Marx's *Grundrisse*. But this has largely meant putting flesh and blood on a skeleton that has not changed essentially in form. What has become possible today is a more three-dimensional look at one of the most intellectually and morally challenging visions of the modern era, and one which this and succeeding generations will have to confront in one way or another.

Thomas Sowell

The Hoover Institution
September 3, 1982

CONTENTS

9

Chapter 1

ECONOMICS AND PHILOSOPHY

Philosophy and economics were not simply separate interests of Karl Marx. His philosophy provided the intellectual framework and the very language in which Marx discussed economics. That language must be understood in order to understand Marxian economics, regardless of whether or not the economic substance is logically independent. The philosophy is also important in itself as the driving force behind a vision that has come to dominate a major part of the globe and of the human species.

Marxian philosophy and economics derive from many sources, as well as bearing the unique imprint of Karl Marx and his lifelong friend and collaborator, Friedrich Engels. The towering figure of G.W.F. Hegel stands out among the philosophers influencing Marx's thought, but other elements of his philosophy go as far back as Democritus, Epicurus and Lucretius in ancient times, Helvetius and

MARXISM

Holbach in the eighteenth century, and Feuerbach among the contemporaries of the young Marx. In economics, the analysis and terminology of David Ricardo provide much of the background for Marx's *Capital*, but the intellectual predecessor of both men was Adam Smith, patron saint of *laissez-faire* capitalism.

A sharp distinction must be made between saying that the *form* of Marxian thought was shaped by some predecessor and saying that the substance was similar. The difference may be illustrated by comparing Hegel's description of a certain period of history with Marx's description, which was quite similar in form, but utterly different in content. First Hegel:

> These three events—the so-called Revival of Learning, the flourishing of the fine Arts and the discovery of America and of the passage to India by the Cape—may be compared with that *blush of dawn*, which after long storms first betokens the return of a bright and glorious day.[1]

Then Marx:

> The discovery of gold and silver in America, the extirpation, enslavement and entombment in mines of the aboriginal population, the beginning of the conquest and looting of the East Indies, the turning of Africa into a warren for the commercial hunting of black-skins, signalised the rosy dawn of the era of capitalist production.[2]

Marx was quite open and frank in declaring himself "the pupil of that mighty thinker," Hegel, and deliberately used "the modes of expression peculiar to him," in writing *Capital*.[3] But he also sharply distinguished "the method of presentation" from the substantive inquiry.[4] To say that Hegelianism was the language in which Marx expressed

12

many concepts is not to say that Marx's substantive statements repeat Hegel. It does say, however, that understanding the peculiar language and intellectual framework of a Hegel or a Ricardo is necessary for understanding the economics of Marx. As the distinguished economist J. A. Schumpeter once observed: "This is all the more important because the necessity for it does not show on the surface." That is, words like "alienation" or "contradiction" (from Hegel) or "wages" and "value" (from Ricardo) can be taken in their ordinary senses and Marx interpreted coherently—but incorrectly, and completely missing the point of his arguments. Marx's business cycle theory, for example, has been grossly misunderstood by interpreters who have seized upon the word "contradiction" in its ordinary (non-Hegelian) sense. Marx's predictions about wage levels under capitalism have likewise been greatly distorted by interpreters unfamiliar with the peculiar Ricardian concepts of "rises" and "falls" in wages.

Marxism is not inherently difficult to understand, in either its philosophic or economic aspects. It has, however, been made difficult by a number of circumstances. One was Marx's method of presentation, especially in his massive classic, *Capital.* Other sources of difficulty are the numerous and diverse interpretations by writers who have not troubled themselves to study the philosophic and economic framework of Marx's ideas. Schumpeter listed a formidable set of prerequisites for studying Marx[5]—and these can also be read as a list of reasons why so few interpreters have understood Marxism. Much of the modern economic literature, for example, sidesteps the whole problem of interpretation by taking what is commonly believed about Marxian economics as a starting point, and then elaborately analyzes and critiques the implications of these "Marxian" doctrines—often without a single reference to anything actually written by Karl Marx.[6]

Another source of interpretive difficulty is that the classic writings of Marx and Engels were polemics written against competing doctrines. Many of these competing doctrines were prominent at one time but have now disappeared into obscurity, so that later interpreters have not fully understood what it was that Marx and Engels were arguing against—and therefore have not always understood the real thrust and limits of their words.

In addition to its own peculiar problems of interpretation, Marxism shares a common danger in the history of ideas—the tendency to interpret earlier writers by reading back into them later ideas and events. Thus Keynes' ideas have been read back into Malthus, and fascism into Pareto. To avoid this fatal trap, Marx's communism (with a small c) will be distinguished from twentieth-century Communism as the doctrine of a particular set of parties or governments. The degree of correspondence between the two is an empirical question to be investigated at the end of the analysis, not a foregone conclusion to be assumed at the outset.

Finally, there are claims made by some scholars that Engels did not really understand Marx's ideas, and that much that is taken as authentic Marxism in Engels' writings is incorrect or misleading.[7] This would be unfortunate, if true, for Engels' writings are often much clearer than Marx's, and a valuable source of clarification would be lost. Nevertheless, this claim will be examined in later specific discussions. For now, it may suffice to point out that Engels and Marx collaborated for four decades, exchanged letters with great regularity,[8] and each wrote part (or all) of some writings that appeared under the other's name,[9] in addition to their explicit co-authorship of many writings. It is no small task to intellectually separate Marx from Engels, nor has this task been seriously undertaken by those who depict Engels—an intelligent and well-read man—as misunderstanding a friend whose ideas he was more familiar with than anyone else in the world.

In short, there are difficulties of interpretation due to the original sources, the intellectual background, and a prior interpretive literature that obscures more than it clarifies. These are the author's problems. The reader's problem is whether the Marxian ideas—once disentangled—are excessively complex in themselves. They are not. That should become apparent in the chapters that follow, as we examine first the philosophy, then the economics, and finally the historical legacy of Karl Marx.

The approach here will be neither an uncritical exposition of Marxism nor a continuous sniping at the Marxian ideas in the process of explaining them. Rather, the exposition and the critique will take place in separate chapters.

Chapter 2

THE DIALECTICAL APPROACH

Out of the massive and complex writings of the philosopher G.W.F. Hegel, and the derivative writings of the neo-Hegelians who flourished in Germany during Marx's youth, certain key concepts of Marxism developed. Then and now, these concepts have produced an arcane language of their own,[1] less an expression than an obfuscation of the underlying ideas. "Dialectical materialism" is perhaps the most comprehensive of these arcane terms—though not a term used by either Marx or Engels. It is a general label for Marxian philosophy, expressing the simple fact that Marxism uses the approach called "dialectics" by Hegel and is also in the centuries-old philosophic tradition known as materialism. These two aspects can be examined separately and then their interaction seen in the Marxian theory of history in general, and of capitalism in particular. This will be done in Chapters 2–4.

DIALECTICS

Marx and Engels emphasized the dialectical *method* of Hegel[2]—the way he looked at and analyzed the world—rather than the elaborate philosophic system erected in his books or the "mystifying"[3] language in which he expressed it. What Marxian philosophy derived from Hegel was that the way to understand the world was not to see it as a collection of *things* but as an evolving *process.* An acorn or a caterpillar could not be understood as a fixed and isolated thing, without seeing that it was a transitory stage of an ongoing process that would eventually turn one into an oak tree and the other into a butterfly. Social analogies to metamorphoses in nature abound in the writings of Marx and Engels.[4]

Dialectics in Plato referred to the counterpoints of an argument. Dialectics in Marx referred to opposing forces in reality—internal and inherent forces whose mutual conflicts produce metamorphoses. It is not the shaping of clay by an external force for an external purpose, but the unfolding of internal forces—each intrinsic to the thing itself —that transforms it into some other thing, predetermined by what went before. Acorns do not become butterflies nor caterpillars become oak trees. Each unfolds according to its own inner pattern. Understanding that pattern is understanding the essence of the thing itself. Seeing only a particular phase of it as it exists empirically at a given moment is being deceived by appearances.

The distinction between the inner *essence* and the outward *appearance* is one which runs throughout Marxian philosophy and Marxian economics.[5] An "appearance" is not simply a delusion without foundation. It is quite real, however incomplete and therefore misleading. The blind men who felt different parts of an elephant were not simply imagining what they felt, but were nevertheless quite

17

mistaken in their inferences about the nature of an elephant. A distorting mirror produces an appearance quite different from the reality, but wholly based on the reality and systematically related to the reality. A given stage of metamorphosis is quite real, but an acorn, a caterpillar, a tadpole, or an apple blossom may be a completely inadequate and misleading representation of what will ultimately develop.

The dialectical approach rejects uncritical acceptance of existing empirical appearances, and seeks instead the inner pattern from which these appearances derive and evolve. There are both methodological and ethical consequences to this approach.

METHODOLOGY

If one wishes to understand the essence, and all that is visible is the appearance, then one must abstract from what is visible, analyze the abstraction, and then reason systematically from there in order to get back to a truer understanding of empirical reality. Although, superficially, common sense might suggest that one "commence with the real and concrete," yet "on closer consideration," according to Marx, this approach "proves to be wrong."[6] What is "the scientifically correct method" is to proceed by simplifying the concrete into an abstraction—an "imaginary concrete" which becomes "less and less complex," until "we get at the simplest conception." Then, by systematically adding complicating factors, we "start on our return journey" toward empirical reality, "but this time not as a chaotic notion of an integral whole, but as a rich aggregate of many conceptions and relations."[7]

In short, Marx was a believer in abstraction, systematic analysis, and successive approximations to a reality too complex to grasp directly. It was precisely the complexity and ever-changing phenomena of the real world that made

THE DIALECTICAL APPROACH

systematic analytical procedures—science—necessary. As Marx expressed it: "All science would be superfluous if the appearance, the form, and the nature of things were wholly identical."[8] The same point was made both in Marx's correspondence and in the third volume of *Capital.* [9] Marx based his approach on the Hegelian "method of advancing from the abstract to the concrete," while disapproving the way Hegel presented it.[10] Abstract deductive analysis is necessary because "every-day experience," according to Marx, "catches only the delusive appearance of things."[11]

Marx's economic analysis, especially in *Capital*—was constructed in this pattern of systematic, successive approximations. In the preface to the first volume of *Capital,* Marx asserted:

> In the analysis of economic forms . . . neither microscopes nor chemical reagents are of use. The force of abstraction must replace both.[12]

In the first volume of *Capital,* Marx also referred to various puzzling economic phenomena which could not be dealt with at the level of abstraction there, under the many simplifying assumptions of that volume, but which would be explained later in the third volume,[13] where many of these assumptions were eliminated. This echoed the approach in his earlier book, *Critique of Political Economy,* where at the beginning Marx warned that there would be no "anticipation of results" which depended on later stages of the argument.[14] Conversely, at the beginning of the third volume of *Capital,* after all the preparatory analysis that went before, Marx said that the phenomena to be discussed now would "approach step by step that form which they assume on the surface of society, in their mutual interactions, in competition, and in the ordinary consciousness of the human agencies in this process."[15] The analysis

19

had advanced from the inner essence to the outward appearance.

Marx's methodological criticisms of the classical economists underscored the importance he attached to successive approximations—and to consistently operating at one level of abstraction at a time. Of Adam Smith he said:

> On the one hand, he traces the inner connection between the economic categories—or the hidden structure of the bourgeois economic system. On the other hand, alongside this inner connection he sets up also the connection as it is manifested in the phenomena of competition, and therefore as it presents itself to the unscientific observer as well as to the man who is preoccupied and interested from a practical standpoint in the process of bourgeois production. These two modes of approach in Adam Smith's work not only run unconstrainedly side by side, but are interwoven and continuously contradict each other: the one penetrating to the inner relations, the physiology as it were, of the bourgeois system; the other only describing, cataloguing, expounding and bringing under classifying definitions the external phenomena of the process of everyday life in their outward manifestation and appearance.[16]

Even the more analytically rigorous David Ricardo did not escape similar criticisms from Marx. For "while Ricardo is accused of being too abstract, the opposite accusation would be more justified—i.e., lack of the power to abstract," to stay on one level of abstraction without bringing in factors belonging on a different level.[17] For example, Marx considered it a "mistake" on Ricardo's part to have discussed the modifications of his value theory before reaching the stage of the argument where the modifying factors had been analyzed.[18]

Marx credited the "classical economists"—a term he coined—with delving below the surface, however inconsistently. He coined another term, "vulgar economists," for those whose analysis "deals with appearances only" and "seeks plausible explanations of the most obtrusive phenomena."[19] As Marx outlined his own projected work on *Capital* in a letter to Engels, he pointed out that only in the third volume would he reach the "forms of *appearance* which serve as the *starting point* in the vulgar conception."[20]

As Marx was preparing to publish the first volume of *Capital,* Engels pointed out that "the philistine is not accustomed to this sort of abstract thought"[21] and that "the points here established dialectically" might better be presented some other way, in order to avoid some "terribly shallow" objections that would be made.[22] Marx replied that changing the presentation in order to silence all objections based on misunderstandings of his abstract approach would "ruin the whole dialectical method of development." Some people would indeed misunderstand, he agreed, because "only the immediate form in which relationships appear is always reflected in their brain, and not their *inner connection.* " If it were possible to see directly the inner connections (the essence), then "what would be the need for a *science* at all?"[23] After *Capital* was published and the objections predicted by Engels began to appear, Marx said of one reviewer:

> . . . as against the disclosures of the inner connection, he proudly claims that in appearance things look different. In fact, he is boasting that he holds fast to the appearance and takes it for the last word. Why, then, any science at all?[24]

Ethics

In the early days of Marx and Engels, when they expected revolution at any moment, they were preoccupied with polemical writings in anticipation of a new society. Decades later, after many disappointments, there was time for leisurely discussions of basic philosophic questions. By this time, Marx was physically spent and unable to complete his magnum opus, *Capital.* It was, however, one of Engels' most fruitful periods, continuing on past Marx's death, so that much of the philosophical—including ethical—writings of Marxism are by Engels. This raises the question already alluded to in Chapter 1, whether or to what extent Engels' writings at this period distort the basic ideas of Karl Marx.

Fortunately, Engels' most extensive discussions of ethical issues occurred in his *Anti-Duhring,* a book whose manuscript he read to Marx in its entirety, and to which in fact Marx contributed a chapter.[25] The issue of a possible deviation by Engels is thus minimized for this particular work, one of their last joint writings, though published solely under Engels' name. Perhaps more to the point, the ethical views expressed in *Anti-Duhring* are completely consistent with other views expressed by Marx and by Engels in other writings.

In a lecture delivered in 1865, Marx declared: "What you think is just or equitable is out of the question." According to Marx, the question is: "What is necessary and unavoidable with a given system of production?"[26] Later, in the first volume of *Capital,* Marx asked, "what avails lamentation in the face of historical necessity?"[27] Though he made the criticism of capitalism his life's work, Marx also saw a "transitory necessity for the capitalist mode of production".[28] The individual capitalist had to be judged morally within the framework of this stage of history:

> My stand-point, from which the evolution of the economic formation of society is viewed as a process of natural history, can less than any other make the individual responsible for relations whose creature he remains, however much he may subjectively raise himself above them.[29]

THE DIALECTICAL APPROACH

Engels provided a systematic exposition of the principles behind such statements. "The great basic thought" of Hegel, according to Engels, was that "the world is not to be comprehended as a complex of ready-made *things,* but as a complex of *processes.* "[30] Once this central notion of dialectics is grasped, "the demand for final solutions and eternal truths ceases."[31] Engels said:

> Each stage is necessary, and therefore justified for the time and conditions to which it owes its origin. But in the face of new, higher conditions, which gradually develop in its own womb, it loses its validity and justification. . . . For it (dialectical philosophy), nothing is final, absolute, sacred.[32]

Historical justification is thus the only justification—the supreme ethical principle—in Marx and Engels. The concept of historical justification runs throughout their writings.[33] Even slavery and incest were considered to be historically justified—at given stages of history.[34] Adam Smith's method of economic reasoning, though severely criticized by Marx, was nevertheless considered by him to be historically justified:

> He is justified in doing this because—if we except a few of his special enquiries such as that into money—his task was in fact a double one: on the one hand, to attempt to penetrate to the inner physiology of bourgeois society: on the other, partly for the first time to describe the living forms in which this inner physiology manifests itself outwardly, to show its relations as they appear on the surface, and partly also to find a nomenclature and the corresponding abstract ideas for these phenomena, and therefore partly also for the first time to reproduce them in language and in the process of thought. The one task interests him as much as the other, and as both proceed independently of the other, the result is a completely contradictory way of looking at things—one

23

that more or less directly expresses their intrinsic relations, the other with equal justice and without any internal relationship—with no connection at all with the other way of examining the subject—expressing the relations in their outward appearance.[35]

But because Adam Smith was considered to be historically justified in 1776 does not mean that his followers in the middle of the nineteenth century were still justified in continuing these inconsistencies.[36] Similarly, early socialist writers like Robert Owen, Fourier, and St. Simon were highly praised by Marx and Engels,[37] while the latter-day disciples of these "utopian socialists" were unmercifully castigated.[38] Scathing Marxian criticisms of later utopian socialists among their contemporaries have misled some modern interpreters into concluding that Marx and Engels had "contempt" for Owen, Fourier, and St. Simon. Nothing could be further from the truth. As Engels said:

> If in Saint-Simon we find the breadth of a genius, thanks to which almost all of the ideas of later socialists which are not strictly economic are contained in his works in embryo, in Fourier we find a critique of existing social conditions, which, typically French in its wit, is nonetheless penetrating.[39]

Robert Owen was likewise "a born leader of men,"[40] according to Engels, Utopian socialists "were Utopians because they could be nothing else at a time when capitalist production was as yet so little developed."[41] They were historically justified. In looking back on them, it is possible to "delight in the inspired ideas and germs of ideas which everywhere emerged through their covering of phantasy."[42]

In much the same vein, the *Communist Manifesto* spoke of the original utopian socialists as "revolutionary" but of their latter-day followers as "mere reactionary sects."[43] In *The German Ideology*, Marx and Engels spoke of Fourier's "masterly observations" on education[44] and of his theories in general as containing "a vein of true poetry" but dismissed his "orthodox disciples" as "the antipodes of Fourier."[45] By the middle of the nineteenth century, utopian socialism was no longer considered historically justified.

DEVELOPMENT AND ALIENATION

In the dialectical vision of an unfolding reality, the key concept is development—meaning not simply quantitative growth but qualitative transformation. Development was defined by Marx as the "transition from one form to another."[46] These transformations occur through inner pressures and stresses—"contradictions" in Hegelian jargon[47] —which realize the potential essence. Again, metamorphosis exemplifies this process. Marx said:

> Milton produced *Paradise Lost* for the same reason that a silk worm produces silk. It was an activity of his nature.[48]

In neither case was this production simply a matter of one-way causation. The producer transforms himself in the act of production. In the Marxian vision, the humanity of man is historically unfolded and transformed through his own productive work.[49] Communism, as envisioned by Marx, was to be "a society in which the full and free development of every individual forms the ruling principle,"[50] a society "in which the free development of each is the condition for the free development of all,"[51] a society that seeks for its members "the completely unrestricted development and exercise of their physical and mental faculties."[52] This was even more important than the material standard of living.[53] Capitalism was condemned as repressing such development: "If the silk worm were to spin in order to continue its existence as a caterpillar, it would be a perfect wage-worker."[54] It was not material poverty that Marx saw as the basic tragedy of the workers under capitalism, but their stunted development. The assembly-line worker under capitalism, through "life-long repetition of one and the same trivial operation," has been "reduced to the mere fragment of a man" and must in a future society be replaced "by the fully developed individual" who is given "free scope to his own natural and acquired powers."[55]

Because the inner potentialities of man are not allowed to unfold freely, according to Marx, they do not simply vanish. They appear in strange forms, unrecognized by man as his own essence. For example, the thwarted human desires for more humane, just, and loving relationships among men reappear as the characteristics of the gods, who are then perceived as independent beings rather than as projections of an unfulfilled human essence. This perception was called "religious self-alienation."[56] To correct it was not merely an intellectual problem, but more fundamentally a question of creating social conditions in which these unfulfilled human desires can be more directly achieved in the real world. "Alienation" implies not only that something human has been falsely perceived as belonging to a mere product of humans, but that that man-made product then assumes ascendancy or dominance over man, like the gods of religion or like Frankenstein's monster. Money was likewise seen as a man-made object representing wealth that dominates its own creator: "Money is the alienated essence of man's labor and life, and this alien essence dominates him as he worships it."[57]

Money originally had value only because it represented the real goods it could buy, but eventually goods appear to have value only because they can be sold for money. It is this "inversion of the original relationship" that is central to the concept of alienation.[58] As capital, "the object which

THE DIALECTICAL APPROACH

labour produces—labour's product—confronts it as *something alien,* as a *power independent* of the producer"[59]—something that can employ him or discharge him according to its own needs as capital, rather than according to his needs as a human being. In Marx's vision, "man's own deed becomes an alien power opposed to him, which enslaves him instead of being controlled by him."[60] Although Marxian communism was intended to end this condition, it was not considered a condition unique to capitalism.

> This crystallization of social activity, this consolidation of what we ourselves produce into an objective power above us, growing out of control, thwarting our expectations, bringing to naught our calculations, is one of the chief factors in historical development up till now.[61]

This Hegelian language of "alienation" tended to disappear from Marx's writings with the passing years, but the underlying concept remained.[62] In *Capital,* for example, Marx said: "It is no longer the labourer that employs the means of production, but the means of production that employ the labourer."[63] For producers in general, "their own social action takes the form of the action of objects, which rule the producers instead of being ruled by them."[64] Marx wrote of "the character of independence and estrangement which the capitalist mode of production gives to the instruments of labour and to the product, as against the workman."[65] Capital thus consists of "means of production that command the producer,"[66] and "the instrument of labour becomes the means of enslaving, exploiting and impoverishing the labourer."[67] This was inherent in capitalism, according to Marx:

> It cannot be otherwise in a mode of production in which the labourer exists to satisfy the needs of self-expansion of ex-

isting values, instead of on the contrary, material wealth existing to satisfy the needs of development on the part of the labourer. As in religion, man is governed by the products of his own brain, so in capitalistic production, he is governed by the products of his own hand.[68]

That these were expressions of "alienation" without specific use of the term is further supported by Marx's *Grundrisse*, an earlier draft of the book that was ultimately to become *Capital*. Here the explicit Hegelian notion of alienation abounds in passages whose substance later reappeared in *Capital*.[69]

MARXIAN VERSUS HEGELIAN DIALECTICS

The reality of Hegelian philosophy is less relevant, for present purposes, than the perception of it by Marx and Engels, and the way the latter distinguish their philosophy from it. In addition to the methodological and ethical conclusions derived from the dialectical approach, Marx and Engels also referred to various Hegelian generalizations or "laws." Here as elsewhere, the Marxian conception derived from, but did not merely repeat, that of Hegel.

The ever-evolving world as conceived by Hegel and Marx undermined not only fixed ethical conclusions but also fixed categorical definitions, particularly of opposites. The notion of "fixed lines of demarcation and distinctions" was rejected, along with "polar antagonisms put forward as irreconcilable and insoluble."[70] As Engels observed in his *Anti-Duhring*:

> The recognition that these antagonisms and distinctions are in fact to be found in nature, but only with relative validity, and that on the other hand their imagined rigidity and absoluteness have been introduced into nature only by our

THE DIALECTICAL APPROACH

minds—this recognition is the kernel of the dialectical conception of nature.[71]

It bears repeating here that *Anti-Duhring* was read to Marx in its entirety before being published, so that this cannot be regarded as one of Engels' alleged deviations. Moreover, Marx in *Capital* likewise spoke of a "unity of differences," that poles are "necessarily" both "connected" and "opposite,"[72] that in the real world, "contradictions are reconciled."[73] This was completely consonant with what Engels said, that dialectics is concerned "precisely with the inadequacy of all polar opposites" as concepts,[74] that dialectics "reconciles the opposites."[75] In modern Marxism, this principle is often referred to as the "interpenetration of opposites" but such jargon neither clarifies nor advances the argument.

One of the polar opposites repeatedly rejected by Marxian philosophy—and Marxian economics—is that between "necessity" and "accident." A particular event may be largely accidental and yet be part of a pattern that has a certain necessity behind it. The temperature on a given day in September may be accidental, in the sense that no one could have said on the same date of the previous September what it was going to be. And yet the fact that temperatures are generally higher in September than in January is not accidental, but follows necessarily from the structure and movements of the solar system. In much the same way, Marx considered it a general necessity, under capitalism, that commodities exchange in proportion to their respective costs of production, but it was at the same time accidental whether this actually happened at a particular juncture:

The economists say that the *average price* of commodities is equal to the cost of production; that this is a *law*. The

29

anarchical movement, in which rise is compensated by fall and fall by rise, is regarded by them as chance. With just as much right as one could regard the fluctuations as the law and determination by the cost of production as chance. . . . But it is solely these fluctuations, which, looked at more closely, bring with them the most fearful devastations and, like earthquakes, cause bourgeois society to tremble to its foundations—it is solely in the course of these fluctuations that prices are determined by the cost of production.[76]

This same conception of price (and resource allocation) as being both necessary and accidental under capitalism runs throughout the economic writings of Marx, from his youthful notes of 1844[77] to his most mature work, *Capital.*[78] Engels merely made more explicit the thinking behind it when he said that "the accidental is necessary,"[79] that there is a "regularity inherent in these accidents,"[80] that there is an "external necessity, in the midst of an endless series of seeming accidents,"[81] and referred to "Hegel's account of the inner connection between necessity and chance."[82] Inherent in this approach is a rejection of determinism:

In opposition to this view, there is determinism which passes from French materialism into natural science, and which tries to dispose of chance by denying it altogether. According to this conception only simple, direct necessity prevails in nature. That a particular pea-pod contains five peas and not four or six, that a particular dog's tail is five inches long and not a whit longer or shorter, that this year a particular clover flower was fertilized by a bee and another not, and indeed by precisely one particular bee and at a particular time, that a particular windblown dandelion seed had sprouted and another not, that last night I was bitten by a flea at four o'clock in the morning and not at three or five o'clock, and on the right shoulder and not on the left calf—these are all facts which have been produced by an irrevocable concatenation of cause and effect, by an unshatterable necessity of such a nature indeed that the gaseous sphere, from which the solar system was derived, was already so constituted that these events had to happen thus and not otherwise.[83]

Determinism results when cause and effect are taken literally and as categorically distinct opposites. But the dialectical approach rejects that set of polar opposites in favor of causation in the form of reciprocal interaction, including interaction among conscious, independent beings. Engels spurned "the common undialectical conception of cause and effect as rigidly opposite poles, the total disregarding of interaction." Of those who reasoned that way, he said:

What these gentlemen all lack is dialectic. They never see anything but here cause and there effect. That this is a hollow abstraction, that such metaphysical polar opposites only exist in the real world during crises, while the whole vast process proceeds in the form of interaction . . . and that here everything is relative and nothing is absolute—this they never begin to see. Hegel has never existed for them.[84]

How, then, did Marx differ from Hegel? Hegel made ideas, whether of men or of God—the driving force of history.[85] This Marx rejected.[86] More fundamentally, however, Marx and Engels took various Hegelian "laws" as empirical generalizations about the real world, rather than as mystical forces unfolding historically. Those who saw in Marx only the application of Hegelian formulas were surprised at his empiricism—which to Marx was an integral part of his own general approach. According to Marx, a contemporary reviewer of *Capital* "is naive enough to say that I 'move with rare freedom' in empirical matter." Marx

31

added: "He hasn't the least idea that this 'free movement in matter' is nothing but a paraphrase for the *method* of dealing with matter—that is, the *dialectical method.*"[87] In a similar vein, Marx quoted another reviewer who referred to Marx's "strictly scientific manner"[88] and his "realistic" approach[89] by saying, "what else is he picturing but my dialectical method?"[90] Yet because the Marxian analysis was presented with Hegelian categories, "it may appear as if we had before us a mere *a priori* construction."[91]

But as Marx observed in a letter to Engels, to bring an analysis "to the point where it can be dialectically presented is an altogether different thing from applying an abstract ready-made system."[92] Repeatedly, Marx distinguished his actual method of *inquiry*—empirical and methodologically "scientific," in his view—from his method of *presentation.*[93] This theme of empiricism runs through the Marxian writings, dating from Marx's youthful manuscripts of 1844, where he declared that his results were achieved by "a wholly empirical analysis based on a conscientious study of political economy."[94] Engels returned to the same theme three decades later, against a critic who "committed the blunder of identifying Marxian dialectics with the Hegelian."[95] For example, the Hegelian notion of "negation of the negation" was mentioned in Marx's *Capital,*[96] and the critic saw this and other Marxian statements as examples of forcing reality into Hegelian molds.[97] Engels replied:

> But what role does the negation of the negation play in Marx? On page 834 and the following pages he sets out the conclusions which he draws from the preceding fifty pages of economic and historical investigation. . . .[98]

References to the negation of the negation were incidental:

> In characterising the process as the negation of the negation, therefore, Marx does not dream of attempting to

THE DIALECTICAL APPROACH

prove by this that the process was historically necessary. On the contrary: after he has proved from history that in fact the process has partially already occurred, and partially must occur in the future, he then also characterises it as a process which develops in accordance with a definite dialectical law. That is all.[99]

In short, Marxian dialectics was "a guide to study, not a lever for construction after the manner of the Hegelians."[100]

SUMMARY

Marxian philosophy looks at the world as a set of processes whose unfolding must be analyzed theoretically, not as a set of things that can be understood as isolated observable facts. What must be understood about a process are the inner tensions that provide the driving force behind its transformations. These intrinsic conflicts—called "contradictions" by Hegel and Marx—are the source of "development," meaning not merely quantitative growth but qualitative transformation. A tadpole does not simply become a bigger tadpole but also changes *from within,* by its own forces, to become a frog.

Metamorphosis in general illustrates the Marxian approach to social and historical phenomena. Marx and Engels were not really seeking to explain a given state of being (the empirical "appearance") but rather the intrinsic pattern of potentialities for change (the "essence"). In the language of biology, they were not explaining anatomy but evolution. In the language of physics or economics, they were not explaining statics but dynamics. In the language of sociology, they were not explaining structures but processes—and in particular, the way that processes change structures.

This kind of change from within must be distinguished from externally created change, as when a block of marble is shaped by a sculptor to form a statue. The distinction in concept is more than a theoretical fine point. It has profound implications for Marx's conception of a *revolution* generated by relationships and tensions inherent in a given society, as distinguished from a *coup* engineered by those who wish to shape a society as a sculptor molds clay or chisels marble. Freedom is at least possible with the first conception, but dictatorship and terror may be necessary with the second. Either action can of course be taken in Marx's name, but whether it follows Marx's conception is another matter.

If Marxian philosophy emphasizes development, it also recognizes its opposite, alienation. Alienation, in Marx's sense, is not simply a general malaise but more specifically a misconception of reality growing out of thwarted development—an inversion in which human reality and human needs are made subservient to artificially created things, to the imaginary gods of religion or to the financial institutions of capitalism. For Marx, ending alienation requires not just an intellectual process to dispel misconceptions but a social process that allows development to proceed without the frustrations that underlie these misconceptions.

Causation, in Marx and Engels, is a matter of interaction rather than a one-way mechanism. Thus there is neither pure determinism nor pure chance, but instead a stream of events reflecting both "accidental" factors and underlying forces whose necessary relationships shape the general tendency of these events as a whole. A given day's weather cannot be predicted with certainty, but that winter will be colder than summer is much more predictable.

The manner in which Marx and Engels sought to investigate causation was by seeking underlying patterns of internal tensions, which by definition cannot be seen directly by collecting concrete facts. Rather, the overwhelming complexities of empirical reality must be reduced to manageable proportions by abstracting those features considered essential and focussing the analysis on these. After determining the relationships and conflicts inherent in these essential features, a fuller and richer approximation to reality can be achieved by then considering some of the features initially put aside in the name of simplicity. This systematic and intellectually disciplined approach was for Marx the hallmark of scientific procedure that distinguished it from mere aimless fact-gathering. Science did not dispense with facts, but used them in a systematic way.

The dialectical approach was seen by Marx and Engels as a useful way to investigate the real world, not a mysterious force imposing its own will on humanity or on history. Pat formulas like "thesis-antithesis-synthesis" express interpreters' stereotypes rather than Marx's own procedure —or the procedure of Hegel, for that matter.[101]

There were ethical as well as causal implications to the Marxian approach. If what is possible at one stage of social metamorphosis is very different from what is possible at another stage, then the observed performance of those bound by the limitations of their time must be judged accordingly, whether as a moral or an intellectual performance. Marx and Engels themselves judged historical figures in this way. The pitfalls of this approach will be considered in later chapters.

Chapter 3

PHILOSOPHIC MATERIALISM

Two entirely different and unrelated concepts are designated by the word "materialism." In its popular sense, materialism refers to preoccupation with material possessions—greed, in a word. This has nothing whatsoever to do with *philosophic* materialism, the tradition to which Marxian philosophy belongs.

Among the earliest materialists in ancient times were Democritus, Epicurus, and Lucretius—all of whom lived before Christ, and all of whom regarded the material world as the ultimate reality. In their view, there were no gods or other spiritual forces behind the material reality. The ethical norms of the materialists were based ultimately on human happiness.

THE MATERIALIST TRADITION

Democritus, a Greek philosopher who lived in the fourth and fifth centuries before Christ, originated the theory of

PHILOSOPHIC MATERIALISM

atoms, too small to be seen, as the source of the innumerable phenomena of the material world. The same theme was elaborated in the writings of another Greek philosopher, Epicurus, in the third and fourth centuries B.C. Epicurus was an empiricist who said that "we must not conduct scientific investigation by means of empty assumptions and arbitrary principles, but follow the lead of phenomena."[1] Yet the purpose of seeking scientific explanations of natural phenomena was not science for its own sake but human tranquility: "If we were not troubled by the phenomena of the sky and about death . . . we should have no need of natural science."[2] Epicurus said that "we must not suppose that any other object is to be gained from the knowledge of the phenomena of the sky than peace of mind and a sure confidence,"[3] for the "principal disturbance in the minds of men" comes from fears of spiritual beings in the heavens and of "some everlasting misery, such as is depicted in legends."[4]

Epicurus did not deny the existence of gods, but did not attribute to them either natural phenomena or the fate of men.[5] According to materialism, "death, the most terrifying of ills, is nothing to us, since so long as we exist, death is not with us; but when death comes, then we do not exist."[6] In Epicurus' view, "good and evil consists in sensation, but death is deprivation of sensation."[7] Contrary to the modern or popular concept of an "Epicurean" life, Epicurus himself said:

> When, therefore, we maintain that pleasure is the end, we do not mean the pleasures of profligates and those that consist in sensuality, as is supposed by some who are either ignorant or disagree with us or do not understand, but freedom from pain in the body and from trouble in the mind. For it is not continuous drinkings and revellings, nor the satisfaction of lusts, nor the enjoyment of fish and other

37

luxuries of the wealthy table, which provide a pleasant life, but sober reasoning, searching out the motives for all choice and avoidance, and banishing mere opinions, to which are due the greatest disturbance of the spirit.[8]

According to the ethics of Epicurus, "No pleasure is a bad thing in itself: but the means which produce some pleasures bring with them disturbances many times greater than the pleasures."[9] Yet he rejected greed. "The wealth demanded by nature is both limited and easily procured: that demanded by idle imaginings stretches on to infinity."[10]

Wealth was not intrinsically evil, but a free spirit "cannot acquire many possessions, because this is not easy to do without servility to mobs or monarchs."[11] But, regardless of how it was attained, wealth was not the prime goal of Epicurean materialism: "It is better for you to be free of fear lying on a pallet, than to have a golden couch and a rich table and be full of trouble."[12]

Nor were the pleasures of the flesh a prime goal. For Epicurus, "the pleasures of love" were likewise all right in principle, provided that "you do not break the laws or good customs and do not distress any of your neighbors or do harm to your body or squander your pittance," but in reality "it is impossible not to come up against one or other of these barriers" and a man is "lucky" if he comes to no harm pursuing sex.[13]

To Epicurus, philosophy, like science, had humanistic goals: "Vain is the word of a philosopher which does not heal any suffering of man."[14] Much the same spirit pervaded the work of Lucretius, a Roman materialist philosopher of the first century B.C., who praised and followed the Epicurean philosophy with which "the terrors of the mind are dispelled."[15] Lucretius thought that human beings were "crushed down under the weight of religion"[16] because they "take unto themselves hard taskmasters, whom they poor wretches believe to be almighty."[17] Often "that very religion has given birth to sinful and unholy deeds."[18]

Lucretius' attempt at scientific explanations of natural phenomena were, like those of Epicurus, intended to "release the mind from the fast bonds of religious scruple."[19] Lucretius likewise did not deny the existence of gods but simply denied them a role in the affairs of nature or man. Gods were conceived as "withdrawn from our concerns." Nature "free at once and rid of her haughty Lords seemed to do all things spontaneously without the meddling of the gods."[20] Lucretius' classic, *On the Nature of Things,* proposed that "solid bodies of matter fly about for ever unvanquished through all time."[21] In Lucretius' vision, "living things are begotten from senseless things,"[22] and the mind is a material organ, "no less part of the man, than hand and foot and eyes."[23] Therefore, "the nature of mind and soul is bodily"[24] and is the body's "partner in death as well."[25] Thus "we have nothing to fear after death."[26]

A totally materialist conception of nature and man implies determinism—an implication faced by Lucretius. If human thinking and feeling are nothing but mechanical responses to external stimuli, which are themselves determined by the laws of physics, then all of life and history are predetermined. Lucretius postulated that particles of matter "at quite uncertain times and uncertain spots" must "swerve a little"[27] in order "to break through the decrees of fate."[28] Epicurus before him had rejected determinism as more oppressive than religious beliefs (since gods could at least be placated or appealed to for help)[29] and ridiculed the determinists,[30] but had never faced up to the implications of a thoroughly mechanical conception of materialism. Lucretius' resort to an arbitrary postulate of unpredictably swerving atoms indicated one of the sore spots of the materialistic system of philosophy. Centuries later, Marxian materialism would avoid determinism by rejecting mechanical causation in favor of a dialectical conception of causation as interaction among thinking beings with some measure of autonomy.

While the focus of the ancient materialists was the individual and his achievement of personal tranquility and a moral and rewarding life, the focus of the materialists who flourished in the eighteenth century was society and its reformation. Holbach was the central figure among the eighteenth-century materialists whom Marx regarded as his predecessors.[31] Their social philosophy was an egalitarian one which stressed that individual and class differences in behavior and outlook were due to differing social environments. According to Holbach, evil is not due to human nature,[32] but to preventable social disorders and injustices:

> So many crimes are witnessed on the earth only because every thing conspires to render man vicious and criminal; the religion he has adopted, his government, his education, the examples set before him, irresistibly drive him on to evil: under these circumstances, morality preaches virtue to him in vain. In those societies where vice is esteemed, where crime is crowned, where venality is constantly recompensed, where the most dreadful disorders are punished only in those too weak to enjoy the privilege of committing them with impunity, the practice of virtue is considered nothing more than a painful sacrifice of happiness. Such societies chastise, in the lower orders, those excesses which they respect in the higher ranks; and frequently have the injustice to condemn those in the penalty of death, whom public prejudices, maintained by constant example, have rendered criminal.[33]

Men in general suffer from "chains which tyrants, which priests have forged for all nations."[34] The evils of the world derive not from the nature of man but from his oppression by those who are powerful and designing:

> It is errour, consecrated by religious enthusiasm, which produces that ignorance, that uncertainty in which man ever finds himself with regard to his most evident duties, his clearest rights, the most demonstrable truths. In short, man is almost everywhere a poor degraded captive, devoid either of greatness of soul, of reason, or of virtue, whom his inhuman gaolers have never permitted to see the light of day.[35]

According to this view, nature "does not make man either good or wicked"[36] but his actions are predetermined by environmental forces. He "never acts as a free agent" for "even his will is moved by causes independent of himself."[37] Man was repeatedly referred to by Holbach as a "machine"[38]—one with "complicated motion"[39] but nevertheless an automatic respondent to external stimuli. Man "is purely passive in the motion he receives" and those who are "wicked are never more than men who are either drunk or mad."[40] It is possible to "engrave ideas on the brain of man"[41] and "education is nothing more than the *agriculture of the mind.*"[42] This mechanical and deterministic materialism of the eighteenth century went far beyond that of ancient Greece and Rome, and was later ridiculed by Engels, as noted in Chapter 2, for predetermining the very time and place of every flea bite.

MARXIAN MATERIALISM

Marx, like Engels, was not uncritical of his materialistic predecessors.

> The materialist doctrine that men are products of circumstances and upbringing, and that, therefore, changed men are products of other circumstances and changed upbringing, forgets that it is men that change circumstances, and

41

that the educator himself needs educating. Hence this doctrine necessarily arrives at dividing society into two parts, of which one is superior to society. . . .[43]

This philosophical point was to prove to be of historic importance in twentieth-century Communist societies, as well as in some other societies. If the mechanistic conception of materialism is applied, and human beings viewed as mere raw material to be shaped and molded, then a totalitarian kind of thought control is implied, based on the inconsistent assumption that there are those who have so transcended bad environmental influences that they can undertake this superhuman task. If a *dialectical* conception of materialism is applied, then the world is much less deterministic, and a mutual "education" through evolving experience is more appropriate, implying greater freedom and less unilateral direction of others' thinking.

Marx was quite conscious of being within the materialist tradition. His doctoral dissertation was on Democritus and his first book written in collaboration with Engels in 1845 contained a summary of eighteenth-century materialist philosophy.[44] More immediately, Marx was influenced by the contemporary materialist philosopher Ludwig Feuerbach, who enjoyed his greatest influence during the 1840s, the intellectually formative years of Marx and Engels. Feuerbach rejected the purely mechanistic conception of the eighteenth-century materialists—for example, the notion that ideas were simply passive responses of the brain to external stimuli ("an excrescence of the organism"), when in fact ideas might play a profound role, such as in motivating other people to heroic sacrifice.[45] Feuerbach's historic contribution was his view that man projected his ideals onto supernatural beings, whom he regarded as existing independently and having varied relations with each other and with human beings. What religious man was worshiping, according to Feuerbach, was his own alienated essence.[46] This idea was to reappear in Marx's *Capital,* where the relationship of commodities to each other in the marketplace was taken as an alienated appearance concealing the underlying essence that human beings were relating their respective isolated economic efforts to each other without being aware of it. Both Feuerbach and Marx used the term "fetishism" to describe the use of external objects (religious and economic, respectively) to express human relations which were not consciously understood.[47] According to Marx, in a complex capitalist economy the isolated producers of different commodities essentially "work for one another"[48] but see the empirical appearances of the marketplace as showing "a social relation, existing not between themselves, but between the products of their labor." He said:

> ... it is a definite social relation between men, that assumes, in their eyes, the fantastic form of a relation between things. In order, therefore, to find an analogy, we must have recourse to the mist-enveloped regions of the religious world. In that world the productions of the human brain appear as independent beings endowed with life, and entering into relations both with one another and the human race.[49]

Because he saw in religion the projection of unfulfilled human ideals and longings, Marx did not advocate a prohibition of religion, but the creation of social conditions that would more directly satisfy such ideals and longings. His often misunderstood description of religion as "the *opium* of the people"[50] was not a call for religious persecution but was instead part of an argument that saw religion as a *"realization* of the human essence" in fantasy because it could not be realized in the real world as it existed.[51] He said: "The demand to give up illusions about its conditions is the demand to give up a condition that needs illusions."[52] The philosophic criticism of religion that ran through the whole materialist tradition was in Marx turned into a revolutionary criticism of existing society:

> The criticism of religion ends with the teaching that man is the *highest essence for man,* hence with the *categoric imperative to overthrow all relations* in which man is a debased, enslaved, abandoned, despicable essence. . . .[53]

More generally, Marx saw philosophic criticisms as vain unless they led also to social change: "The philosophers have only *interpreted* the world in various ways; the point, however, is to *change* it."[54]

MATERIALIST ETHICS

Materialism in Marx, as in earlier materialists, was a doctrine of humanistic ethics. In the words of Marx and Engels, materialism "coincides with *humanism*"[55] and forms "the *logical* basis of *communism.*"[56] Specifics of this logic were omitted. But in their first joint writing, the *Holy Family* (1844), Marx and Engels mentioned many ethical issues and took positions on them. They were quite conscious here of following the materialist tradition:

> If correctly understood interest is the principle of all moral, man's private interests must be made to coincide with the interests of humanity. If man is unfree in the materialist sense, i.e., is free not through the negative power to avoid this or that, but through the positive power to assert his true individuality, crime must not be punished in the individual, but the anti-social source of crime must be destroyed, and each man must be given social scope for the vital manifestation of his being. If man is shaped by his surroundings, his surroundings must be made human. If man is social by nature, he will develop his true nature only in society, and

44

the power of his nature must be measured not by the power of separate individuals but by the power of society.

This and similar propositions are to be found almost literally even in the oldest French materialists. This is not the place to assess them.[57]

As the last sentence suggests, Marx and Engels were not uncritical echoes of earlier materialists, any more than they were uncritical echoes of Hegel. Marx's rejection of the notion that some human beings would mold others by controlling their environment has already been noted. It was a theme that reappeared in Marx's writings from his early work of the 1840s to his mature work three decades later. In 1842, Marx said: "Who shalt decide on the bounds of scientific research if not scientific research itself!"[58] He rejected any concept of the state as "a children's home" or of the people as "a crowd of adults whose destiny is to be educated from above."[59] More than thirty years later, similar ideas appeared in Marx's *Critique of the Gotha Programme:*

Defining by a general law the expenditures on the elementary schools, the qualifications of the teaching staff, the branches of instruction, etc., and, as is done in the United States, supervising the fulfillment of these legal specifications by state inspectors, is a very different thing from appointing the state as the educator of the people! Government and church should rather be equally excluded from any influence on the school.[60]

Religious freedom was likewise basic: "Everyone should be able to attend to his religious as well as his bodily needs without the police sticking their nose in."[61]

Not only were Marx and Engels not prepared to carry materialism to the totalitarian extremes that might be implied by a mechanistic (as distinguished from dialectical) conception of causation; they were highly critical of the principle of manipulating or molding other people, even on the individual level. In *The Holy Family* they were scathing in their denunciations of the hero of a contemporary novel who tricked people into doing the right thing.[62] They rejected the notion that "a foul trick is not foul when it is done for *'good, moral'* motives."[63] They denounced the hero for destroying others' individuality in order to replace it with dog-like devotion to a cause.[64]

Although Marx and Engels rejected that aspect of materialism that was potentially totalitarian, they embraced other aspects which raised questions about the nature of freedom. Freedom was for Marx and Engels not simply the absence of deliberate constraints imposed by other human beings, but environmental freedom—the presence of viable options, "quite palpable material conditions."[65] This conception of freedom permeates their writings from the earliest to the latest. For example, in the *German Ideology,* written in 1845–46, Marx and Engels said:

> Only in community with others has each individual the means of cultivating his gifts in all directions; only in the community, therefore, is personal freedom possible.[66]

Freedom thus means environmental freedom—freedom *to,* not freedom *from.* Freedom from the constraints of others was regarded as a delusion. For example, in *The Holy Family* in 1845:

> Indeed, the individual considers as his *own* freedom the movement, no longer curved or fettered by a common tie or by man, the movement of his alienated life elements, like property, industry, religion, etc.; in reality, this is the perfection of his slavery and his inhumanity.[67]

PHILOSOPHIC MATERIALISM

Mere political freedoms were not, however, rejected:

> *Political* emancipation is indeed a great step forward. It is
> not, to be sure, the final form of human emancipation, but
> it is the final form *within* the prevailing order of things.[68]

Years later, in his *Capital,* Marx continued to distinguish
formal freedom from deliberately imposed constraints
from the more fundamental freedom in terms of available
options:

> . . . the "free" labourer, thanks to the development of capi-
> talistic production, agrees, *i.e.,* is compelled by social condi-
> tions, to sell the whole of his active life, his very capacity for
> work, for the price of the necessaries of life, his birthright
> for a mess of pottage.[69]

In this Marxian conception, the time which a worker is
free to sell his labor "is the time for which he is forced to
sell it," so that he is in reality "no 'free agent.' "[70] Capitalism is thus based on "exploitation of the nominally free
labour of others."[71]

Personal responsibility for harmful acts to others was
likewise viewed within this framework of dominating environmental influences. As already noted, the capitalist is a
creature of circumstances.[72] So too is the criminal. Like the
eighteenth-century materialists, Marx found crime to be a
product of social conditions, and tended to be critical of
punishment in general[73] and of capital punishment in particular:

> . . . it would be very difficult, if not altogether impossible,
> to establish any principle upon which the justice or expedi-
> ency of capital punishment could be founded in a society
> glorying in its civilization.[74]

MARXISM

The supposed *predictability* of the volume of various crimes was for Marx evidence that "the fundamental conditions of modern *bourgeois* society" are what "produce an average amount of crime in a given national fraction of society," that such criminal acts have "the regularity of physical phenomena."[75] He referred to "a necessity for deeply reflecting upon an alteration of the system that breeds these crimes, instead of glorifying the hangman who executes a lot of criminals to make room only for the supply of new ones."[76]

It is not clear how far Marx would carry this mitigation of personal responsibility. Certainly not to its logical extreme, given the reaction of Marx and Engels to some of their followers who had excused some capitalists who were "only children of their time":

> Unfortunately everyone is only a "child of his time" and if this is a sufficient excuse nobody ought ever to be attacked any more, all controversy, all struggle on our part ceases; we quietly accept all the kicks our adversaries give us because we, who are so wise, know that those adversaries are "only children of their time" and cannot act otherwise.[77]

Whatever the merits or demerits of this particular criticism of their followers' judgment, Marx and Engels had provided no *principle,* or even guidelines, by which to know what moral responsibility an individual should bear. The general ethical principles of materialism, and their emphasis on environmental influences, could be carried to the extremes of Marx's daughter Eleanor, who excused her continued liaison with a man whose unscrupulous and shameless character were well known, by saying:

> More and more I realize that wrong behavior is simply a moral sickness, and the morally healthy people like yourself

are not qualified to judge the condition of the morally sick, just as the physically healthy can scarcely realize the condition of the physically sick.

There are people who lack a certain moral sense, just as many are deaf or short-sighted or in other ways afflicted. And I begin to realize one is as little justified in blaming them for the one sort of disorder as the other. We must strive to cure them, and if no cure is possible, we must do our best.[78]

This is not to say that Marx would have condoned such behavior or such excuses. Marx did not in fact allow this particular scoundrel in his house.[79] The point here, however, is that his ethical philosophy provided no explicit limitation to the societal responsibility emphasized by the materialist tradition.

PHILOSOPHIC IDEALISM

Marxian materialism in no way precludes idealism in the popular sense of unselfish thought and action in the service of higher concerns. But "idealism," like "materialism," has both a popular and a philosophic meaning. Within each framework, idealism is opposed to materialism, but in very different senses.

If "idealism" is taken in the popular sense, "then every person who is at all normally developed is a born idealist, and how, in that case, can there still be any materialists?"[80] But as Engels well knew when he posed this rhetorical question, the *philosophic* issue between idealists and materialists was "that concerning the relation of thinking and being."[81] To the materialist, "the material, sensuously perceptible world to which we ourselves belong is the only reality."[82] To the philosophic idealist, our perceptions and ideas are the ultimate reality that we as human beings can know, and the material world is only an inference from these perceptions. We can know our perceptions of a thing but not the thing in itself. Engels dismissed this central premise of philosophic idealism:

> The most telling refutation of this, as of all other philosophical crotchets, is practice, namely, experiment and industry. If we are able to prove the correctness of our conception of a natural process by making it ourselves, bringing it into being out of its conditions and making it serve our own purposes into the bargain, then there is an end to the Kantian ungraspable "thing-in-itself."[83]

In short, empirical experimentation was the answer to philosophic idealism:

> . . . human action had solved the difficulty long before human ingenuity invented it. The proof of the pudding is in the eating. From the moment we turn to our own use these objects, according to the qualities we perceive in them, we put to an infallible test the correctness or otherwise of our sense perceptions.[84]

The practical application of our sense perceptions and their derivative conclusions was thus crucial for distinguishing mere subjective impressions from objective reality —that is, for establishing the reality of a material world as a basic foundation for further discussions. As long as the material world remained a mere object of *contemplation,* there was in Marx's words, a "defect in all hitherto existing materialism." But "human activity itself" in its practical applications established both "the reality and power" of our perceptions of the material world, while "the reality or non-reality of thinking which is isolated from practice is a purely *scholastic* question."[85]

Idealism in the philosophic sense is essentially *idea*-ism, a belief in the primacy of ideas. The varieties of philosophic idealism range from the Platonic "forms" which provide the patterns that material objects only imperfectly copy, to John Stuart Mill's theory that history is only an outward expression of the general progress of the human mind.[86] Marx specifically attacked the idea of "the general progress of the human mind" (without mentioning Mill by name) when he developed his own theory of history[87] based on philosophic materialism and the dialectic approach.

SUMMARY

Philosophic materialism and philosophic idealism involve issues entirely different from those implied by materialism and idealism in their popular senses. The philosophic issue is the ultimate reality known to human beings, which can serve as a foundation on which to build their reasoning. To the idealist, the phenomena of the human mind are the ultimate reality experienced by people. To the materialist, the physical world is the ultimate reality, and the fact that it is not directly experienced does not reduce the certainty of its existence or its properties. Marx and Engels regarded practice—both experimental and instrumental—as providing sufficient proof of material reality to serve as the basis of all reasoning. (Idealists, incidentally, do not deny the existence of matter but deny that it is the ultimate reality or the ultimate reality known to man.)

The materialist tradition in philosophy goes back many centuries as does the idealist tradition. Although the term "Epicurean" today conjures up an image of someone preoccupied with the pleasures of food, drink, material possessions and/or sex, the actual philosophy of Epicurus warned against all these things. From the moral isolation of the human race implied by materialist philosophy, Epicurus derived the ethical norm of human happiness as the ultimate good, but a happiness consisting more in tranquility than thrill-seeking. The theme of personal tranquility ran through the writings of the ancient materialists, including Lucretius who offered theories of natural phenomena for humanistic rather than scientific purposes.

Eighteenth-century materialism, which more directly influenced Marxism, was concerned with social rather than individual well-being, and sought to explain society rather than nature. Baron D'Holbach, who epitomized eighteenth-century materialism, saw human beings as shaped—indeed, utterly determined—by their social environment. From this he derived a hostility to all privileges and distinctions, including the distinction between criminals and noncriminals. More fundamentally, the evils of the world were not due to the nature of man or the inherent constraints of human existence, according to Holbach, but were a product of institutions whose removal would open boundless possibilities of happiness. Education in its broadest sense as social conditioning was the key factor needed to produce better people and a better world.

Marx saw the totalitarian danger inherent in the mechanistic conception of one-way causation—a conception that would have one human being molding another as a sculptor molds clay. A dialectical conception of causation involved more personal free will and also more political freedom. But the Marxian conception of "freedom" merged political freedom with social options as freedom *to* rather than freedom *from.* More fundamentally, Marxian ethics centered on society, with reduced responsibility for the individual. How much reduced is not clear.

Marxian materialism is the foundation not only of political and ethical doctrines but also of the Marxian theory of history.

Chapter 4

THE MARXIAN THEORY OF HISTORY

Marx's theory of history grew out of materialist assumptions and a dialectical approach. Men are products of their environments in general, and of their economic environment in particular. What is to be explained are not states of being, but the transformations of one form of society into another—feudalism into capitalism, or capitalism into socialism, for example. The classic expression of the materialist vision was in Marx's *Critique of Political Economy:*

> In the social production which men carry on they enter into definite relations that are indispensable and independent of their will; these relations of production correspond to a definite stage of development of their material powers of production. The sum total of these relations of production constitutes the economic structure of society—the real foundation, on which rise legal and political superstruc-

tures and to which correspond definite forms of social consciousness.[1]

The terms used by Marx take their meaning from his general philosophic framework. The "economic" structure of society, for example, does not refer to relations among commodities, interest rates, international trade balances, or money flows. These non-human phenomena are the superficial "appearances" of the economy. The underlying reality—the inner "essence"—are the human relations growing out of a particular way of organizing the people and technology of a given time and place for the purposes of production. In Marx's words: "Economic categories are only the theoretical expressions, the abstractions of the social relations of production." These "social relations" are the table of organization of people in production. They depend on the technology—the "productive forces" of the time and place. In Marx's terminology: "Social relations are closely bound up with productive forces."[2] They are, nevertheless, conceptually distinct:

> Machinery is no more an economic category than the bullock that drags the plow. The modern workshop, which depends on the application of machinery, is a social production relation, an economic category.[3]

It is the *people* and their relationships that make the workshop an economic category in Marx's sense. Slavery is a different economic category, because it is a different set of human relations.[4] Marx said:

> What is a Negro slave? A man of the black race. The one explanation is as good as the other.
>
> A Negro is a Negro. He becomes a slave in certain relations. A cotton-spinning jenny is a machine for spinning

cotton. It becomes *capital* only in certain relations. Torn from these relations it is no more capital than gold itself is *money* or sugar the price of sugar.[5]

CAUSATION

As expressed by Marx in *Critique of Political Economy*, the materialist theory of history might seem to imply one-way causation from the economic "foundation" to the legal and political "superstructure." But such a mechanistic conception is not in fact a part of the Marxian theory of history, for elsewhere Marx and Engels say that "circumstances make men just as much as men make circumstances,"[6] implying reciprocal interaction rather than one-way causation. Engels' later writings and letters make this even more clear. For example, "once an historic element has been brought into the world by other elements, ultimately by economic facts, it also reacts in its turn and may react on its environment and even on its own causes."[7] Engels depicts this not as a difference between himself and Marx but as a difference between earlier and later stages of their lives:

> Marx and I are ourselves partly to blame for the fact that younger writers sometimes lay more stress on the economic side than is due to it. We had to emphasize this main principle in opposition to our adversaries, who denied it, and we had not always the time, the place or the opportunity to allow the other elements involved in the interaction to come into their rights. But when it was a case of presenting a section of history, that is, of a practical application, the thing was different. . . .[8]

The historical writings of Marx and Engels—*The Eighteenth Brumaire, The Civil War in France, The Origin of the Family*, etc.—contain no one-way causation from economic foundation to political superstructure.[9] Engels was clearly correct on the dialectical conception of reciprocal interaction rather than one-way causation underlying his work and Marx's. He was, however, perhaps overly generous to Marx, whose tendency toward epigrammatic expressions produced formulations that appear to be one-way causation, not only in his early discussions in the *Poverty of Philosophy* in 1847 but even in *Capital,* twenty years later.

In the earlier book, Marx said that "the handmill gives you society with the feudal lord; the steam-mill, society with the industrial capitalist."[10] In *Capital,* Marx referred to "my view that each special mode of production and the social relations corresponding to it, in short, that the economic structure of society, is the real basis on which the juridical and political superstructure is raised, and to which definite social forms of thought correspond. . . ."[11] If read literally, these words suggest one-way causation and an explanation of given states of being rather than of transformations. But that is clearly inconsistent both with Marx's and Engels' own treatment of history and with the dialectical conception of reciprocal interaction. These words are perhaps best read as examples of Marx's achievement of brevity through epigrams—and of the dangers of misunderstanding inherent in that writing style. Yet, ironically, it is Engels who is blamed for "mechanistic" thinking by critics who claim to see a substantive difference between the two men.[12]

The Marxian theory of history did not attempt to explain the law and politics of a given era as deriving solely from the economic relations of that era. That would be explaining isolated states of being as if each era were hermetically sealed and began from nothing, rather than from the preceding era. What the Marxian theory attempted to explain were the *changes* from one era to another—the social

transformations or "development" in dialectical terms. As
Marx said in his *Critique of Political Economy:*

> At a certain stage of their development, the material forces
> of production in society come in conflict with the existing
> relations of production, or—what is but a legal expression
> for the same thing—with the property relations within
> which they had been at work before. From forms of devel-
> opment of the forces of production these relations turn into
> their fetters. Then comes the period of social revolution.
> With the change of the economic foundation the entire
> immense superstructure is more or less rapidly trans-
> formed. In considering such transformations the distinc-
> tions should always be made between the material
> transformation of the economic conditions of production
> which can be determined with the precision of natural sci-
> ence, and the legal, political, religious, aesthetic or philo-
> sophic—in short ideological forms in which men become
> conscious of this conflict and fight it out.[13]

Engels' *Anti-Duhring,* written in close consultation with
Marx, presents a very similar picture:

> . . . the ultimate causes of all social changes and political
> revolutions ought to be sought, not in the minds of men, in
> their increasing insight into eternal truth and justice, but in
> changes in the mode of production and exchange; they are
> to be sought not in the *philosophy* but in the *economics* of the
> epoch concerned. The growing realization that existing so-
> cial institutions are irrational and unjust, that reason has
> become nonsense and good deeds a scourge is only a sign
> that changes have been taking place quietly in the methods
> of production and forms of exchange with which the social
> order, adapted to previous economic conditions, is no
> longer in accord. This also involves that the means through
> which the abuses that have been revealed can be gotten rid
> of must likewise be present in more or less developed form,

in the altered conditions of productions. These means are not to be *invented* by the mind, but discovered by means of the mind in the existing facts of production.[14]

In short, it is the "solution" that creates the "problem." As history unfolds, men face in each epoch a set of constrained options, based ultimately on the existing state of technology. With new technological developments, the original social arrangements, which may have been optimal for the prior set of options, are no longer optimal. Historically, a problem or conflict now arises between those wedded to the existing set of social relations and those who see the new possibilities presented by technological changes. What was "right" before is no longer right. For Marx as well as Engels, the solution creates the problem:

> Therefore, mankind always takes up only such problems as it can solve, since, looking at the matter more closely, we will always find that the problem itself arises only when the material conditions necessary for its solution already exist or are at least in the process of formation.[15]

As Marx wrote to a friend:

> Men never relinquish what they have won, but this does not mean that they never relinquish the social form in which they have acquired certain productive forces. On the contrary, in order that they may not be deprived of the result attained, and forfeit the fruits of civilization, they are obliged, from the moment when the form of their commerce no longer corresponds to the productive forces acquired, to change all their traditional social forms.[16]

In short, according to Marx: "With the acquisition of new productive faculties, men change their mode of production and with the mode of production all the economic relations which are merely the necessary relations of this particular mode of production."[17]

Just how do historic social transformations take place, and what is the role of ideas and ideologies in these transformations? That is a large subject in itself.

IDEAS AND IDEOLOGIES

The Marxian epigrams about "superstructure" and "base" sketch bold conclusions without specifying the *process* by which these events unfold. That process is one in which human beings form ideas under the influence of circumstances (materialism) and then such ideas compel them to change the circumstances (dialectical interaction with the source of the ideas). As Engels said, "everything that sets men acting must find its way through their brains"[18] and "nothing happens without a conscious purpose, without an intended aim."[19] But, contrary to such mechanistic materialists as Holbach in the eighteenth century—and contrary to the interpretations of modern critics[20]—Engels did not regard ideas as mere predetermined responses to external stimuli. Human ideas were seen by Engels as a complex blend of the most varied concerns with "external objects, partly ideal motives, ambition, 'enthusiasm for truth and justice,' personal hatred, or even purely individual whims of all kinds."[21] Marx likewise saw the subjectively felt motivations as including "old memories, personal enmities, fears and hopes, prejudices and illusions, sympathies and antipathies, convictions, articles of faith and principles."[22] There is free will, according to Engels, but history is *not* simply the carrying out of these freely willed intentions:

> That which is willed happens but rarely; in the majority of instances the numerous desired ends cross and conflict with one another, or these ends themselves are from the outset incapable of realization, or the means of attaining them are

59

insufficient. Thus the conflicts of innumerable individual wills and individual actions in the domain of history produce a state of affairs entirely analogous to that prevailing in the realm of unconscious nature. The ends of the actions are intended, but the results which actually follow from these actions are not intended, or when they do seem to correspond to the end intended they ultimately have consequences quite other than those intended.[23]

In short, "what each individual wills is obstructed by everyone else, and what emerges is something that no one willed."[24] Theory attempts to predict results—"what emerges"—not intentions. Intentions may therefore be regarded as largely accidental and yet the results show a pattern with a certain element of necessity. From this perspective, "it is not a question so much of the motives of single individuals, however eminent, as of those motives which set in motion great masses, whole peoples, and again whole classes of people in each people; and this, too, not momentarily, for the transient flaring up of a straw fire which quickly dies down, but for a lasting action resulting in a great historical transformation."[25]

None of this implies a rationalistic, much less an economically motivated, set of ideas behind historic transformations. The theory of Charles A. Beard—who claimed that the Constitution of the United States reflected the economic self-interest of its writers—is far removed from the theory of Karl Marx, though the two have often been confused in the interpretive literature. Marx dismissed a similar theory of history in his own day as "facile anecdote-mongering and the attribution of all great events to petty and mean causes."[26] Marx saw a logic in the pattern of historical events, but did not impute this logic to the agents involved in these events, or to those who bring about historical transformations. Marx cautioned that "we must not form the narrow-minded notion that the petty bourgeoisie, on principle, wishes to enforce an egoistic class interest."[27]

The economic element in the Marxian theory of history is not a subjective preoccupation with economic self-interest by individuals or classes. Rather, it is that the economic relations—that is, the *human* relations growing out of production—shape the conflicting perceptions that lead to historic struggles and social transformations. A revolutionary class—whether the bourgeoisie under feudalism or the proletariat under capitalism—achieves that status by "undertaking the general emancipation of society."[28] Narrow self-interest would impede rather than promote such historic tasks. Marx saw France as more revolutionary than Germany precisely because political idealism was considered more prevalent in France.[29] Revolution, as depicted by Marx, was anything but a rationalistic process:

> Men make their own history, but they do not make it just as they please; they do not make it under circumstances chosen by themselves, but under circumstances directly encountered, given and transmitted from the past. The tradition of all the dead generations weighs like a nightmare on the brain of the living. And just when they seem engaged in revolutionizing themselves and things, in creating something that has never yet existed, precisely in such periods of revolutionary crisis they anxiously conjure up the spirits of the past to their service and borrow from them names, battle cries and costumes in order to present the new scene of world history in this time-honoured disguise and this borrowed language.[30]

Marx's theory of history was based on a principle later applied in physics by Einstein—that the position of the observer is an integral part of the data. The "economic structure" of society puts each class in a different position to observe and experience what is unfolding. Therefore, the "conception of eternal justice . . . varies not only with time and place, but also with the persons concerned."[31] A "selfish misconception" may cause the dominant class to ideologically eternalize existing social relations.[32] But conversely, those classes who either experience the special pains created by these social relations or who experience the new options and opportunities emerging despite the constraints of existing society, will more vividly perceive the advantages of change. In short, a rising class may think of its ideas for restructuring society as "the only rational, universally valid ones."[33] Were it purely a direct clash of opposed self-interest, perceived as such, some mutual accommodation could be worked out. But if each class perceives the situation *ideologically*—as a clash of fundamental principles and ideals, with the fate of society as a whole hanging in the balance—then the stage is set for a revolutionary fight to the finish.

But because the agents themselves are subjectively motivated by ideology does not mean that observers and analysts must accept ideology as the essence of the struggle:

> Just as our opinion of an individual is not based on what he thinks of himself, so can we not judge of such a period of transformation by its own consciousness; on the contrary this consciousness must rather be explained from the contradictions of material life, from the existing conflict between the social forces of production and the relations of production.[34]

Marx and Engels made a fundamental contribution to historical thinking with this distinction between the subjective motivations of historical actors and the transforming factors underlying the observable course of events:

> Whilst in ordinary life every shopkeeper is very well able to distinguish between what someone professes to be and

what he really is, our historians have not yet won even this trivial insight. They take every epoch at its word and believe that everything it says and imagines about itself is true.[35]

To accept what the historical actors say or believe as the actual cause of historical events in a given epoch is to *"share the illusion of that epoch."*[36] Thus, though ancient Greece and Rome may have been preoccupied with political philosophy and the Middle Ages with religion, "the Middle Ages could not live on Catholicism, nor the Ancient world on politics."[37] Both had first to earn a living, and the particular way that they organized to do that—"the mode in which they gained their livelihood"[38]—was their economic structure and the key element in their history, as seen by Marx. Engels repeated this theme in his speech at the graveside of Marx—provoking later critics to make yet another claim that he misunderstood his collaborator.[39] In Engels' words:

> . . . Marx discovered the law of development of human history: the simple fact, hitherto concealed by an overgrowth of ideology, that mankind must first of all eat, drink, have shelter and clothing, before it can pursue politics, art, science, religion, etc.; that therefore the production of the immediate means of subsistence and consequently the degree of economic development obtained by a given people or during a given epoch form the foundation upon which the state institutions, the legal conceptions, art, and even the ideas on religion, of the people concerned have been evolved, . . .[40]

This not only repeated Marx's emphasis on "the mode in which they gained their livelihood"[41] but made clear that how history *evolved* was the subject being explained. That is, the economic structure of a given era was not intended to explain the *state of being* of that era but rather the *changes* from the preceding era. As Engels said elsewhere, "economy creates nothing absolutely new *(a novo),* but it determines the way in which the existing material of thought is altered and further developed."[42] What Marx called the "tradition of all the dead generations"[43] continues to have an effect even at the moment of revolutionary crisis. The United States, therefore, "without any feudal past" has in Engels' words, nevertheless "taken over from England a whole store of ideology from feudal times, such as the English common law, religion, and sectarianism."[44] The capitalist economic system, for example, does not create a completely capitalist superstructure of ideas and institutions, according to Marx, for there are "traditional influences, influences not arising from the womb of bourgeois society itself."[45] Engels declared that "in all ideological domains tradition forms a great conservative force," but "the transformations which this material undergoes spring from class relations, that is to say, out of the economic relations of the people who execute these transformations."[46]

Because the Marxian theory of history is a theory of transformations, and not a theory of states of being, it is misleading to refer to the "weight" of the economic factor, vis-à-vis other factors in the Marxian scheme. What matters is which element is more of a source of *change.* It might be argued, for example, that the existence of family units is better explained by biological or psychological factors than by economic factors. But that is not the question which the Marxian theory addresses. The question it addresses is: Why have the family unit and family relations *changed* as they have from one era to the next? It suggests that this is due to economic changes. It does not attempt to explain the whole state of being—why there are families at all. Similarly, if urbanization tends to produce certain changes, then it may produce these changes in Japan as in Britain— but without Japan's ending up the same as Britain, for they started from different traditions. (In mathematical terms, Marx is explaining the derivative rather than the integral.)

IDEAS IN HISTORY

The ideas, and especially the morally charged systems of ideas—ideologies—behind historic clashes, were seen by Marx as class phenomena:

> Upon the different forms of property, upon the social conditions of existence, rises an entire superstructure of distinct and peculiarly formed sentiments, illusions, modes of thought and views of life. The entire class creates and forms them out of its material foundations and out of the corresponding social relations. The single individual, who derives them through tradition and upbringing, may imagine that they form the real motives and the starting point of his activity.[47]

The individual thus believes sincerely in his ideas as ideas. In Engels' words:

> Every ideology, however, once it has arisen, develops in connection with the given concept material, and develops this material further; otherwise it would not be an ideology, that is, occupation with thoughts as with independent entities developing independently and subject only to their own laws. That the material life conditions of the persons inside whose heads this thought process goes on in the last resort determine the course of this process remains of necessity unknown to these persons, for otherwise there would be an end to all ideology.[48]

Thus, although the law, for example, "only sanctions the existing economic relations,"[49] it must have an internal consistency and "independent historical development."[50] As Engels explained:

MARXISM

In a modern state, law must not only correspond to the general economic position and be its expression, but must also be an expression which is *consistent in itself,* and which does not, owing to inner contradictions, look glaringly inconsistent. And in order to achieve this, the faithful reflection of economic conditions is more and more infringed upon. All the more so, the more rarely it happens that a code of law is the blunt, unmitigated, unadulterated expression of the domination of a class—this in itself would already offend the "conception of justice."[51]

This reinforces Marx's assertion that the class does not *in principle* seek to enforce "an egoistic class interest."[52] Nor are ideological spokesmen for the petty bourgeois shopkeepers, for example, themselves "all shopkeepers or enthusiastic champions of shopkeepers." Rather, they share the ideological mentality of shopkeepers and this is, "in general, the relationship between the *political* and literary *representatives* of a class and the class they represent."[53] But they are seeking justice, freedom, and other general benefits for society as a whole—viewing society from a perspective peculiar to those whose place in the economic system causes them to perceive benefits and costs in a particular way. As a modern writer aptly expressed it: "No amount of honest intention to place oneself on the standpoint of the public welfare or of the nation's interests avails. . . . For the point is precisely that these words carry different meanings for different minds."[54] The position of the observer is an integral part of data. The more dedicated people are to justice or to the cause of humanity, the more irreconcilable the clash between classes who give these principles very different specific content. Mere opportunists would be more compromising, especially when their own survival was at stake.

In what sense did *The Communist Manifesto* mean its epi-

66

gram: "The ruling ideas of each age have ever been the ideas of its ruling class"?[55] Two years earlier, in *The German Ideology* (1846), Marx and Engels were less cryptic:

> The ideas of the ruling class are in every epoch the ruling ideas: i.e., the class, which is the ruling material force of society, is at the same time its ruling intellectual force. The class which has the means of material production at its disposal, has control at the same time over the means of mental production, so that thereby, generally speaking, the ideas of those who lack the means of mental production are subject to it.[56]

At some point, however, new classes evolve under the influence of changing technology and the changing social relations which derived from it. Thus the emergence of "revolutionary ideas in a particular period presupposes the existence of a revolutionary class"[57] which paves the way for a new era. In short, the ruling ideas of an age may in general be those of its ruling class, but revolutionary transformations are possible precisely because this is not always continuously the case.

CLASSES AND CLASS STRUGGLE

The definition of a class is by no means a simple matter, especially when classes are to play the historic roles envisioned by Marx. Human beings may be classified by an observer in innumerable possible ways. But how they actually behave depends upon how they see themselves. An observer may classify people into such categories as left-handed carpenters, but the question is: Do left-handed carpenters act any differently toward each other than toward people who are not left-handed or not carpenters? If there is no subjective sense of solidarity and no ideological principle or behavior pattern peculiar to the group as classified, then in terms of explaining historical transformations, the classification is arbitrary and barren.

This point was faced early by Marx and Engels, in *The German Ideology:* "The separate individuals form a class only insofar as they have to carry on a common battle against another class; otherwise they are on hostile terms with each other as competitors."[58] Thus, medieval journeymen did *not* constitute a class, because the subjective bond of a journeyman was to his own master, not to other journeymen, and his ambition was to become a master himself, not to overthrow the guild system which classified people as journeymen and masters.[59] There were "small acts of insubordination within separate guilds"[60] but no class struggle over the guild system. Similarly, the French peasants of the nineteenth century were not a class in Marx's sense, though they could readily be classified as people who "live in similar conditions"—but, as Marx noted, "without entering into manifold relations with one another."[61] Marx's *Eighteenth Brumaire* repeated the reasoning of *The German Ideology:*

> In so far as millions of families live under economic conditions of existence that separate their mode of life, their interests, and their culture from those of the other classes, and put them in hostile opposition to the latter, they form a class. In so far as there is merely a local interconnection among these small holding peasants, and the identity of their interests begets no community, no national bond and no political organization among them, they do not form a class.[62]

Thus, although classes are based ultimately on objective differences among sets of human beings—so that equalization of classes is a contradiction in terms[63]—a subjective cohesion within each set is also essential. It is easy to classify people according to objective criteria, but their subjective cohesion is more difficult to determine—or to create. For example, the *Communist Manifesto* declares that the workers "have no country,"[64] but the crucial question is whether the workers themselves feel this way, or whether nationalism (or race, religion, etc.) is a force that runs deeper than their consciousness of class.

DETERMINISM

The degree of determinism is a crucial issue in Marx's theory of history, as in other forms of philosophic materialism. *The Communist Manifesto* declared "the victory of the proletariat" to be "inevitable,"[65] and *Capital* referred to "tendencies working with iron necessity toward inevitable results."[66] But in later years Marx wrote to a friend: "World history would indeed be very easy to make, if the struggle were taken up only on condition of infallibly favourable chances."[67] In a still later letter, Marx continued to say, as he had in *Capital,* that a system of production "begets its own negation with the inexorability which governs the metamorphoses of nature."[68] Yet in this later letter, he also suggested that determinism has its limits, well short of inevitability. Referring to a reviewer of *Capital,* Marx said:

> He feels himself obliged to metamorphose my historical sketch of the genesis of capitalism in Western Europe into an historico-philosophic theory of the *marche generale* imposed by fate upon every people, whatever the historic circumstances in which it finds itself. . . . But I beg his pardon. (He is both honouring and shaming me too much.)[69]

Marx, like Engels, was different in later years from his youth—less brash, less absolute. The substance of his theories had not changed, but the manner in which he expressed them was modified. He continued to look forward to revolution—to repeatedly see signs of it that repeatedly proved false[70]—but this hopefulness and general confidence were apparently personal rather than a rigorous deduction from a theory.

Even the personal confidence was not always as it was before. Marx wrote to Engels in 1863 that "the comfortable delusions and the almost childish enthusiasm with which we hailed the era of revolution before February 1848 have all gone to hell."[71] Later that year he mentioned to Engels that he was becoming "regretfully aware of our increasing age," and of the accompanying "learned and scientific doubts" in contrast to earlier "bold anticipations" and the youthful "illusion that the result itself will leap into the daylight of history tomorrow or the day after."[72] There is no reason to believe that Marx ever abandoned his hope and belief that revolution would eventually come, but again, not inevitably in the literal sense, or perhaps not even with the apparent confidence that continued to pervade his public statements.

SUMMARY

The Marxian theory of history attempts to explain the transformations of whole societies from one era to another. It sees the source of these changes in changing technologies ("productive relations") which brings changes in the way people are organized for production ("social relations"). These changing relationships among people cause changing ideas and ideologies, in keeping with the materialist doctrine that environments shape thinking. By creating new possibilities of benefits unattainable before, the new technology and changing organization create political conflict between those devoted to existing laws and institutions and those who perceive a need to make drastic changes in them. The more earnestly and public-spiritedly the opposing groups strive for the general good, the more they are on a collision course on specifics, for their different positions in the social organization cause them to perceive the specifics in irreconcilably different ways.

To the actors in the drama, the conflict is one of ideas, principles, or of philosophy. They are *not* deliberately pursuing material self-interest, for where that prevails there is compromise rather than a revolutionary fight to the finish. But to the observer and the analyst, what matters is not the perception of the actors themselves but the underlying economic changes that have led to such conflicting perceptions. The conflict—the problem—has emerged precisely from the prospect of a new solution more socially beneficial than the options available before.

It is almost a matter of definition that classes produce the ideological conflicts which cause historic social transformations. Social groups who acquire no common ideology or no cohesive organization to promote their ideologies are not called "classes" in the Marxian sense, however numerous and objectively similar the people may be. Thus French peasants were not regarded by Marx as a class in his sense, though they might be a majority of the population of France.

Because of interactions among many traditions, institutions, and numerous individual strivings—in short, because causation was dialectical rather than mechanistic—outcomes were not completely determined. The Marxian theory of history did not attempt to predict "every sparrow's fall." Nor did the histories that Marx and Engels actually wrote present any such simplistic tableau as might be inferred from a literal reading of some of Marx's epigrams. What Marx and Engels did expect was that the great lasting social transformations in history would tend to follow the pattern they outlined. More specifically, they hoped and believed that capitalism would undergo such a change.

Chapter 5

THE CAPITALIST ECONOMY

      While the skeletal framework of Marxian philosophy and the Marxian theory of history might be applied to any era or social system, its prime application was of course to the capitalist world of the nineteenth century. For a growing number of leading capitalist nations, the democratic republic was the political form of capitalist society, and Marxism had to deal with this emerging reality. Moreover, Marx and Engels found already in existence a variety of socialist and communist theories, ideas, tendencies, groups and organizations. Marxian polemical writings dealt episodically with all these phenomena—in the process defining the Marxist position by the nature and degree of its opposition and concurrence with those of others, rather than by a systematic elaboration of its own assumptions, analysis, and evidence. Only in *Capital* was the Marxian position given a full-scale, systematic exposition, and even that was conceived polemically, as a "Critique of Political Economy" as it was subtitled.

CAPITAL AND CAPITALISM

Marx's sociological conception of an economic system, as the relationships among people rather than the relationships among things or magnitudes, leads to a unique definition of capital and of capitalism. What are normally conceived of as economic functions—the allocations of resources, production, the distribution of output, etc.—are functions common to the widest variety of economies and societies. Marx sought what specifically differentiated capitalism—a system he saw as originating in the sixteenth century[1]—from preceding and succeeding social systems. Capital, therefore, could not be defined as other economists had defined it, as an implement of production, for in that sense it was common to feudalism, barbarism, and all other forms of society:

> The conditions which govern production must be differentiated in order that the essential points of difference be not lost sight of in view of the general uniformity which is due to the fact that the subject, mankind, and the object, nature, remain the same. The failure to remember this one fact is the source of all the wisdom of modern economists who are trying to prove the eternal nature and harmony of existing social conditions. Thus they say, e.g., that no production is possible without some instrument of production, let that instrument be only the hand; that none is possible without past accumulated labor, even if that labor consists of mere skill which has been accumulated and concentrated in the hand of the savage by repeated exercise. Capital is, among other things, also an instrument of production, also past impersonal labor. Hence capital is a universal, eternal natural phenomenon; which is true if we disregard the specific properties which

73

turn an "instrument of production" and "stored up labor" into capital.[2]

Capital in this sense "would be only a new name for a thing as old as the human race." This kind of reasoning, to which Marx objected, proceeds by abstracting away precisely "the specific aspects" that make capital a feature of "a specific developed *historic* stage of human production."[3]

What, then, specifically defines capital as it exists under capitalism? It is earning power—its "property of producing profit or interest."[4] This means that capital "is a social relation of production,"[5] a claim on goods produced by others, and therefore on the working time of others. A capitalist's power "is the *purchasing* power of his capital, which nothing can withstand."[6] It is this social relation which turns a given physical thing into capital. For capital, "without wage labour, ceases to be capital!"[7] Conversely, the physical substance of capital "can change continually without the capital suffering the slightest alteration."[8] As long as it can command a given amount of goods or a given amount of labor time, it is a given amount of capital, regardless of what physical form it takes.

Capital in Marx's sense represents a set of social relations that is "a product of a long process of development."[9] Thus, "capital is not a thing, but a social relation between persons, established by the instrumentality of things."[10] This "social relation" in the productive process is "an even more important result of the process than its material results."[11] It is, in fact, the defining feature of capitalism.

For capitalism to exist, the workers must have no means of production, no means of subsistence, and "nothing to sell but their labour-power."[12] The means of production— too large to be used or owned by each worker—belong to a separate class, the capitalists, who are thus in a position to force the workers to produce more than enough output for the workers' own use, and to allow the capitalists to appropriate the surplus. While the particular process by which surplus labor is induced, and surplus output appropriated, are peculiar to capitalism, this general pattern of class "exploitation" was seen as common to innumerable kinds of economies and societies scattered throughout history.[13] According to Marx: "The essential difference between the various economic forms of society, between, for instance, a society based on slave labour, and one based on wage labour, lies only in the mode in which this surplus labour is in each case extracted from the actual producer, the labourer."[14]

What is peculiar to capitalism is "exploitation of the nominally free labour of others."[15] In *appearance* there is a free exchange of labor for wages, but in *essence* there is not. While a peasant performing corvée labor knows when he is working for himself and when he is working for his feudal lord,[16] the wage worker under capitalism does not, and in fact regards the social relations in which he works as "self-evident laws of nature."[17] Marx sees his own task in *Capital* as exposing the essence beneath the appearance, so that "the relation between capital and labor is laid bare," even though on the surface the appropriated surplus "seems to be due to hidden qualities inherent in capital itself."[18]

When workers or peasants owned their own individual means of production (including small plots of land in some cases), there was no capitalism.[19] But this represented a low-productivity, stagnant form of society, in Marx's view:

> To perpetuate it would be, as Pecqueur rightly says, "to decree universal mediocrity". At a certain stage of development it brings forth the material agencies for its own dissolution. From that moment new forces and new passions spring up in the bosom of society; but the old social organizations fetter them and keep them down. It must be annihilated; it is annihilated. Its annihilation, the transformation of the individualised and scattered means of pro-

duction into socially concentrated ones, of the pigmy property of the many into the huge property of the few, the expropriation of the great mass of the people from the soil, from the means of subsistence, and from the means of labour, this fearful and painful expropriation of the mass of the people forms the prelude to the history of capital.[20]

Thus capitalism is not synonymous with the private ownership of the means of production, and in fact requires "the dissolution of private property based upon the labour of the owner."[21] While others see capitalism as the epitome of private property, for Marx capitalism was the "negation of individual private property," which is transformed into *collectively* used means of production—huge implements which "from their very nature, are only fit for use in common,"[22] but with *private* appropriation of the surplus. Socialism later negates this arrangement, becoming an Hegelian "negation of the negation"—which does not restore the original situation of "private property for the producer" but rather "possession in common of the land and of the means of production."[23]

THE HISTORIC ROLE OF CAPITALISM

In the pre-capitalist era of individual private property in the means of production, the productive implements were "adapted for the use of one worker, and, therefore of necessity, small, dwarfish, circumscribed." To bring together the means of production in gigantic new forms, "to turn them into the powerful levers of production of the present day—this was precisely the historic role of capitalist production and of its upholder, the bourgeoisie."[24] These words of Engels repeat Marx's conception of "the greatness and temporary necessity of the bourgeois regime."[25]

The *Communist Manifesto* declared: "The bourgeoisie, during its rule of scarce one hundred years, has created more massive and more colossal productive forces than have all preceding generations together."[26] Capitalism was conceived as inherently dynamic, with capitalists "constantly revolutionizing the instruments of production, and thereby the relations of production, and with them the whole relations of society."[27] The need for markets "chases the bourgeoisie over the whole surface of the globe"—in the process becoming cosmopolitan and undermining narrow nationalisms.[28] Moreover, capitalism disrupts precapitalist economies through economic competition: "The cheap prices of its commodities are the heavy artillery with which it batters down all Chinese walls."[29] Less advanced economies are forced to adopt the productive methods of capitalist nations "on pain of extinction." In short, capitalism "creates a world after its own image."[30]

The central Marxian concern for social *development*—for human transformation, rather than simply the quantitative growth of things—is not met by the capitalistic expansion of output. But this burgeoning productivity creates the historic basis, the preconditions, for a new society which can at last make the development of all people its primary concern. As Engels said in a review of *Capital:*

Marx sharply stresses the bad sides of capitalist production, but with equal emphasis clearly proves that this social form was necessary to develop the productive forces of society to a level which will make possible an equal development worthy of human beings for *all* members of society. All earlier forms of society were too poor for this.[31]

The historic role of capitalism is that it creates the economic preconditions of socialism and communism. Marx and Engels were very unlike other socialists and communists, whose timeless criticisms of capitalism were intended to show the general superiority of socialism or communism. These other, timeless, utopian socialists and communists "attired their demands in the form of pious wishes of which one could not say why they had to be fulfilled at that very time and not a thousand years earlier or later."[32] By contrast, the Marxian dialectical conception of evolving possibilities depicted capitalism as creating the expanded set of options that—for the first time in human history— made it possible for all persons to have the leisure to develop their own creative potential. Previously, the general poverty of society meant that only a privileged few could be spared from all-absorbing production to think about more general human concerns and to carry forward art, science, and civilization:

> The separation of society into an exploiting and an exploited class, a ruling and an oppressed class, was the necessary consequence of the deficient and restricted development of production in former times. So long as the total social labor yields only a produce which but slightly exceeds that barely necessary for the existence of all; so long, therefore, as labor engages all or almost all of the time of the great majority of the members of society—so long, of necessity, this society is divided into classes. Side by side with the great majority, exclusively bond slaves to labor, arises a class freed from directly productive labor, which looks after the general affairs of society: the direction of labor, state business, law, science, art, etc.[33]

But although this productive potential was created by capitalism, it could not be utilized for egalitarian and humanitarian purposes under a system which Marx and Engels saw as funnelling its benefits to a few capitalists, while keeping the workers overworked despite labor-saving machinery. This made it *desirable,* from their perspective, to change to a collectivized economy and society. What made it *necessary* was that capitalism was inherently incapable of continuing as it was indefinitely. Its own inner stresses—"internal contradictions" in Hegelian language[34]—would metamorphose it into a new social system.

In keeping with the general Marxian conception of the evolving and expanding possibilities of history and the morality of "historical justification," to say that a system or a class has an historic role is not a timeless approval or a belief in their subjective nobility. Just as capitalists are driven by the logic of profit-seeking to economically revolutionize the world, so the workers are driven by their class position to destroy the whole system of classes. Being at the bottom of the social pyramid, the proletariat cannot rise to dominance without destroying the social and economic privileges that keep other classes above them. Even imperialism has an historic role, according to Marx and Engels—to civilize and advance more primitive societies.[35]

INTERNAL STRESSES

The relationship between capitalists and workers is the defining characteristic of capitalism, and it is from the stresses between these inherent elements that capitalism metamorphoses toward a new social system. According to Marx, the industrial workers—the proletariat—are forced to band together to resist the efforts of capitalists to overwork and underpay them, and out of these scattered economic struggles against individual capitalists arises a political struggle against the capitalist class, the capitalist economic system, and the capitalist state.[36]

Another inherent feature of capitalism is the production of commodities—goods made for sale rather than for use by their producers.[37] But production for others implies production for an unknown and ever fluctuating demand for each commodity, and for commodities in general. The proportionate allocation of resources to each of the commodities is a *necessity* for the economic system, but it is *accidental* whether this happens at any given time and place.

While within the workshop, the iron law of proportionality subjects definite numbers of workmen to definite functions, in the society outside the workshop, chance and caprice have full play in distributing the producers and their means of production among the various branches of industry. . . . The *a priori* system on which the division of labour, within the workshop, is regularly carried out, becomes in the division of labour within the society, an *a posteriori*, nature-imposed necessity, controlling the lawless caprice of the producers and perceptible in the barometrical fluctuations of the market prices.[38]

Like other economists, Marx saw that price fluctuations were the key to the process of allocating productive resources under capitalism, but in this process he saw the dialectical interplay of necessity and accident. For example: "The mutual confluence and intertwining of the reproduction or circulation processes of different capitals is on the one hand necessitated by the division of labour, and on the other hand is accidental."[39] According to Marx, "all equalisations are *accidental,* and although the proportionate use of capitals in the various spheres is equalised by a continuous process, nevertheless the continuity of this process itself equally presupposes the constant disproportion, which it has continuously, often violently, to even out."[40]

These violent phases of the resource allocation process "bring with them the most fearful devastations and, like earthquakes, cause bourgeois society to tremble to its foundations."[41] These are the Marxian economic "crises" of capitalism—depressions or downturns in the business cycle, in the language of other economists. For Marx, they were inherently part of the process of allocating resources through price fluctuations: "Violent fluctuations of prices . . . cause interruptions, great collisions, or even catastrophes in the process of reproduction."[42] The recurring economic crises are among the inherent internal stresses—Hegelian "contradictions"—that ultimately transform capitalism into socialism or communism. The *Communist Manifesto* referred to "the commercial crises, that by their periodic return put on its trial, each time more threateningly, the existence of the entire bourgeois society."[43]

The capitalists themselves unwittingly facilitate the ultimate destruction of capitalism. Each capitalist seeks to increase his profits by lowering production costs through more efficient production. This in turn leads to an increasing scale of production, as the minimum size necessary for achieving the level of efficiency required to survive in competition increases over time.[44] The means of production are increasingly centralized in a few businesses, and the ownership of these businesses increasingly concentrated in a few capitalists. "One capitalist kills many," in Marx's words.[45] Eventually there are so few capitalists that it is politically relatively easy to achieve their "expropriation" by "the mass of the people."[46]

SUMMARY

Capital and capitalism were defined by Marx in terms of the relationships they created among people. Capital as a financial claim—ultimately a claim on the labor of other human beings—was a pervasive new historic feature that marked the era of capitalism. The impersonal aspects of capital, as an accumulation of productive potentialities (whether in materials or skills), were common to the most varied economic systems scattered over thousands of years of human history. In this second sense, it would not be the defining characteristic of capitalism.

Private property did not define capitalism for Marx. Private property existed and was widespread long before the advent of capitalism as conceived by Marx. These earlier systems of private property featured individually owned and individually worked means of production, whether family farms or hand-made industrial production. The historically new social relations that defined capitalism emerged when production facilities were widely consolidated into *collective* means of production, whose surplus was appropriated by private owners who did not work in them. Socialism was seen as the next logical stage, when ownership would also become collective.

In keeping with the Marxian theory of history, capitalism was seen as emerging historically because it offered wider potentialities for mankind than those contained in feudalism and earlier systems. Despite the ideologically inspired opposition of many individuals and groups wedded to pre-capitalist concepts, capitalism had emerged by the revolutionary political and economic activities of the bourgeois class, conceiving of themselves as acting for the benefit of all mankind. Only in a very different sense were they doing so, according to Marx and Engels—only in the sense of preparing the way for a higher form of society.

With the very rapid increase of production brought on by capitalism, all forms of human exploitation lost their historical justification. In contrast to the timeless moral condemnations, by other socialists and communists, of the unremitting toil of the many and the leisure of the few, Marx and Engels regarded such arrangements as absolutely *necessary* throughout most of human history, if the human race was to progress. Only by freeing a privileged few to look beyond the urgent needs of keeping alive could mankind as a whole advance intellectually, economically, politically, or otherwise. In short, individual injustice served a social purpose. But the great economic productivity created by capitalism also offered the means of ending this injustice by making leisure general and making human development available to the masses.

But by creating this solution, capitalism created a problem. Those wedded to the capitalist ethos were certain to resist collectivization of ownership and all the other legal, political, and social changes implied by it. Another revolutionary confrontation, immediately of ideologies but ultimately of classes, was thus in the offing.

Capitalism, however, did more than present new revolutionary opportunities, according to Marx and Engels. Its economic functioning created even more painful social dislocations than earlier social systems. Chief among those were the recurrent economic crises of mass unemployment with production and commerce brought to a standstill.

Chapter 6

MARXIAN ECONOMIC CRISES

Marx criticized traditional economics for implicitly assuming the framework of capitalist society in its analysis[1]—eternalizing capitalist relationships, instead of seeing them as historically transient peculiarities of a given economic system. By contrast, Marxian economic analyses treat the capitalist framework as one of the causes of economic phenomena, including depressions or "crises." This makes his analysis more difficult to interpret, for those who are used to the conventional way of reasoning. For example, Marx and Engels in various places refer to the poverty of the proletariat as a factor restricting demand under capitalism.[2] Yet they were scathing in their denunciations of socialists and other underconsumptionists who saw crises being precipitated by the inability of the masses to "buy back what they had produced."[3] As Engels expressed it in *Anti-Duhring:*

84

MARXIAN ECONOMIC CRISES

But unfortunately the underconsumption of the masses, the restriction of the consumption of the masses to what is necessary for their maintenance and reproduction, is not a new phenomenon. . . . Therefore, while underconsumption has been a constant feature of history for thousands of years, the general shrinkage of the market which breaks out in crises as the result of a surplus of production is a phenomenon only of the last fifty years. . . . The underconsumption of the masses is a necessary condition of all forms of society based on exploitation, consequently also of the capitalist form, but it is the capitalist form which first produces crises. The underconsumption of the masses is therefore also a necessary condition of crises, and plays in them a role which has long been recognised; but it tells us just as little why crises exist today as why they did not exist at earlier periods.[4]

Similar reasoning appeared in Marx's *Capital:*

It is purely a tautology to say that crises are caused by the scarcity of solvent consumers, or of a paying consumption. . . . If any commodities are unsaleable, it means that no solvent purchasers have been found for them. . . . But if one were to attempt to clothe this tautology with a semblance of a profounder justification by saying that the working class receive too small a portion of their own product, and the evil would be remedied by giving them a larger share of it, or raising their wages, we should reply that crises are precisely always preceded by a period in which wages rise generally and the working class actually get a larger share of the annual product intended for consumption. From the point of view of the advocates of "simple"(!) common sense, such a period should rather remove a crisis.[5]

After this contemptuous dismissal of a traditional (and still common) underconsumptionist argument, how could Marx also say that "the last cause of all real crises always remains the poverty and restricted consumption of the masses"?[6] Because the "limit of production is the *capitalist profit* and not at all the *needs of the producers.*"[7] Production "comes to a standstill at a point determined by the production and realisation of profit, not by the satisfaction of social needs."[8] These are statements about the institutional framework of capitalism, rather than statements about the behavior of precipitating economic variables within an implicitly given institutional framework. It is *not,* as one well-known interpretation claims, a matter of there being *some* crises caused by underconsumption and other crises caused by other factors.[9] The poverty of the masses, according to Marx, is the last cause of *all* crises—without being the immediate cause of any.

What must be distinguished are those features of the capitalist framework that are necessary conditions for crises to occur, and those that are precipitating factors bringing on cyclical downturns.

THE CAPITALIST FRAMEWORK

The cyclical swings of a capitalist economy were referred to by Marx as the "peculiar course of modern industry, which occurs in no other period of human history."[10] Inherent tensions—Hegelian "contradictions"—in the nature of commodity production "imply the possibility, and no more than the possibility, of crisis."[11] That is, they are preconditions, not precipitating factors.

Commodities are goods produced for sale, rather than for use by the producer, or for direct expropriation (as under feudalism or slavery) or for barter. Therefore an economy of commodity production implies producing for the unknown demands of others, the use of money, specialization or division of labor, and a necessary allocation of resources achieved through the accidental fluctuations of prices. Marx said:

MARXIAN ECONOMIC CRISES

Since the production of commodities is accompanied by a division of labor, society buys these articles by devoting to their production a portion of its available labor-time. Society buys them by spending a definite quantity of the labor-time over which it disposes. That part of society, to which the division of labor assigns the task of employing its labor in the production of the desired article, must be given an equivalent for it by other social labor incorporated in articles which *it* wants. There is, however, no necessary, but only an accidental, connection between the volume of society's demand for a certain article and the volume represented by the production of this article in the total production, or the quantity of social labor spent on this article, the aliquot part of the total labor-power spent by society in the production of this article.[12]

While the labor of society—"social labor" in Marx's terminology[13]—may be conceived as a homogeneous mass that is rationed out in varying quantities for producing different commodities, the actual performance of this labor takes specific forms (carpentry, tailoring, assembly, etc.) which Marx called "concrete labor."[14] Social labor is the underlying essence, but concrete labor is the visible appearance. Social labor is an abstraction, and was sometimes referred to by Marx as "abstract labor" or "abstract social labor,"[15] in contradistinction to "individual labor" or "individual concrete labor."[16]

Concrete labor differs from social labor not only qualitatively but also quantitatively. That is, in an economy of ever-fluctuating supply and demand, the amount of labor actually expended on a given commodity at a given time may be either more or less than the amount needed to achieve equilibrium among the various sectors of the economy. There may be "too much" carpentry and "too little" tailoring, or vice versa. This is not simply a matter of inefficient allocation but also of prices that cannot not help changing until the balance is restored. The particular labor that is oversupplied is, in effect, discounted, as the price of the overproduced commodity declines. According to Marx, "if this commodity has been produced in excess of the temporary demand for it, so much of the social labor has been wasted, and in that case, this mass of commodities represents a much smaller quantity of labor on the market than is actually incorporated in it."[17] Conversely, the labor-time that is insufficiently supplied is in effect counted as if it were at a premium, in that the commodity it produced rises in price because it is insufficiently supplied relative to the demand.

The amount of labor that would represent an optimal allocation (and at the same time therefore produce a price in equilibrium) was called by Marx the "socially necessary labor." This had two distinct components—one technological and one economic. First, the technological component: "The labour-time socially necessary is that required to produce an article under the normal conditions of production, and with the average degree of skill and intensity prevalent at the time."[18] Then the economic component, where such necessary labor was defined by Marx as "only the labour-time which is required for the satisfaction of the social need (the demand)."[19] For example:

> . . . suppose that every piece of linen in the market contains no more labour-time than is socially necessary. In spite of this, all these pieces taken as a whole, may have had super-fluous labour-time spent on them.[20]

The socially necessary labor was defined by Marx as "value." He repeatedly referred to his *definition* of value,[21] and nowhere to a *theory* of value, despite a voluminous—and undocumented—interpretive literature to the contrary. The classical tradition in economics—notably Adam Smith and David Ricardo—had a theory that commodities tended to exchange in proportion to their labor cost, but according to Marx in the first volume of *Capital,* "average prices do not directly coincide with the values of commodities, as Adam Smith, Ricardo, and others believe."[22] Definitional values equal to empirical prices were a *postulate* serving as the "starting point"[23] of the analysis of the first approximation of Volume I, but was not a *theory* to be proved or disproved.

By the time Marx reached his final approximation on the subject in Volume III, he could say that only in a "vague and meaningless form are we still reminded of the fact that the value of the commodities is determined by the labor contained in them."[24] The definition of value and what Marx called the "law of value" were discussions of resource allocation problems under capitalism, not the determination of individual commodity prices (sometimes called "exchange-values"),[25] which were repeatedly referred to in such terms as mere "appearances"[26] or outward "phenomenal forms"[27] of an underlying "essence" represented by "value."[28]

While others have interpreted Marx's "law of value" as a theory of individual commodity prices, Marx himself flatly contradicted this. Marx presented a picture of "the law of value enforcing itself, not with reference to individual commodities or articles, but with reference to the total products of the particular social spheres of production made independent by division of labour."[29] The law of value was thus essentially a principle of resource allocation, rather than of price determination. The "law of value," according to Marx, serves to "maintain the social equilibrium of production in the turmoil of its accidental fluctuations."[30] As he wrote to Engels, who was at work on *Anti-Duhring:*

And as for Duhring's modest objections to the definition of value, he will be astonished when he sees in Volume II how little the determination of value "directly" counts for in bourgeois society. *No form* of society can indeed prevent the fact that, one way or another, the working time at the disposal of society regulates production. So long, however, as this regulation is accomplished not by the direct and conscious control of society over its working time—which is only possible under common ownership—but by the movement of commodity prices, things remain as you have already quite aptly described them in the *Deutsche-Franzosische-Jahrbucher.* [31]

This was a reference to an essay that Engels had written more than twenty years earlier. This "ingenious critical essay" so struck Marx at the time that he began "continually corresponding and exchanging ideas" with its author[32] —an historic collaboration that would continue the rest of their lives. The essay was also historic in another sense, for in it Engels outlined what was to become the basic Marxian vision of a capitalist economy. According to that essay of Engels:

> The law of competition is that demand and supply always strive to complement each other, and therefore never do so. The two sides are torn apart again and transformed into flat opposition. Supply always follows close on demand without ever quite covering it. It is either too big or too small, never corresponding to demand; because in this unconscious condition of mankind no one knows how big supply or demand is. If demand is greater than supply, the price rises and, as a result, supply is to a certain degree stimulated. As soon as it comes on to the market, prices fall; and if it becomes greater than demand, then the fall in prices is so significant that demand is once again stimulated. So it goes on unendingly—a permanently unhealthy state of affairs—a constant alternation of overstimulation and collapse which precludes all advance—a state of perpetual fluctuation perpetually unresolved. This law with its constant balancing, in which

whatever is lost here is gained there, seems to the economist marvellous. It is his chief glory—he cannot see enough of it, and considers it in all its possible and impossible applications. Yet it is obvious that this law is a purely natural law, and not a law of the mind. It is a law which produces revolution.[33]

Revolution eventually results from these price fluctuations because of workers' bitter reactions to economic depressions, or "trade crises" in Engels' words, which "reappear as regularly as the comets, and of which we have on the average one every five to seven years."[34] The economists' law of supply and demand is in a sense vindicated by these fluctuations of price and output, but not in the smooth and easy way suggested by the economists:

Of course, these trade crises confirm the law, confirm it exhaustively—but in a manner different from that which the economist would have us believe to be the case. What are we to think of a law which can only assert itself through periodic crises? It is just a natural law based on the unconsciousness of the participants. If the producers as such knew how much the consumers required, if they were to organise production, if they were to share it out amongst themselves, then the fluctuations of competition and its tendency to crisis would be impossible. Produce with consciousness as human beings—not as dispersed atoms without consciousness of your species—and you are beyond all these artificial and untenable antitheses. But as long as you continue to produce in the present unconscious, thoughtless manner, at the mercy of chance—for just so long trade crises will remain; and each successive crisis is bound to become more universal and therefore worse than the preceding one; is bound to impoverish a larger body of small capitalists, and to augment in increasing proportion the numbers of that class who live by labour alone, thus visibly enlarging the mass of labour to be employed (the major problem of our economists) and finally causing a social revolution such as has never been dreamt of by the school-wisdom of the economists.[35]

The crucial elements later elaborated by Marx in *Capital* were already present in this 1844 publication by Engels:

1. Crises are inherent in capitalist commodity production because producers cannot accurately predict the demand of the consumers or the supply of other producers.
2. Price fluctuations reflect—and correct—production imbalances or disproportionalities among the various sectors of the economy, but in a way that often leads to crises, rather than to the smooth adjustments suggested by economists.
3. Successive crises become progressively worse because they are ever *widening* in their scope ("more universal"[36]) rather than ever *deepening* in their declines, as often suggested in the interpretive literature.[37] The ever-widening crises are consistent with the Marxian view of the capitalist system as beginning as part of a given economy and then spreading out to become the whole national economy and finally international in its scope.[38]
4. The growing size of an impoverished proletariat eventually leads to social revolution, in conjunction with the crises.

Neither underconsumption nor a permanent "breakdown" plays any role in this picture—nor later in Marx, despite an interpretive literature driven to the expedient of quoting numerous post-Marxian writers and ignoring Marx himself.[39]

Long before Engels and Marx came upon the scene, economists had divided into two main groups—(1) those who explained depressions by inadequate aggregate demand (the "general glut" theorists, led by Sismondi and Malthus[40]) and (2) those who insisted that depressions were caused by internal disproportionalities in the composition of aggregate output—too much of *A* and too little of

MARXIAN ECONOMIC CRISES

B—rather than by its total being excessive relative to aggregate demand. These latter economists were led by J. B. Say, David Ricardo, and James and John Stuart Mill. Ricardo summed up this viewpoint by saving: "Men err in their productions, there is no deficiency of demand."[41] Engels and Marx saw these errors or disproportionalities as inherent in the very nature of capitalist production, thereby explaining why economic crises were peculiar to this system, and not mere accidents. In short, disproportionality was central to the Marxian theory of crises.

The alternative, or underconsumption, interpretation of Marx often concludes that some permanent breakdown of the capitalist economy will eventually occur, due to an inability to achieve sufficient aggregate demand to revive production after a depression or economic crisis.[42] But no such theory exists in Marx, who repeatedly referred to the *transitory* nature of individual crises. They were referred to by Marx in such terms as "general stopages of a transient nature,"[43] a "momentary suspension" of economic activity,[44] or in Engels' words "temporary overproduction."[45] According to Marx: "The crises are always but momentary and forcible solutions of the existing contradictions, violent eruptions which restore the disturbed equilibrium for a while."[46] More fundamentally: "There are no permanent crises."[47]

Attempts to salvage the underconsumptionist breakdown interpretation of Marx have sometimes fastened on Hegelian terms like "contradiction" or "negation" to suggest that Marx meant that capitalism reaches an insoluble impasse or somehow annihilates itself as an economy. But, as noted in the previous paragraph, contradictions were for Marx not insoluble but were in fact solved by crises. Hegelian contradictions are inner tensions, not logical impossibilities. As Hegel said: "Contradiction is the very moving principle of the world: and it is ridiculous to say that contradiction is unthinkable."[48] Marx repeatedly used the

93

term contradiction in ways that clearly did not imply logical impossibility, but Hegelian inner tensions.[49] As for "negation," that too had its own special meaning in Hegel as transformation or metamorphosis, not self-annihilation. According to Hegel, negation "resolves itself not into nullity, into abstract Nothingness, but essentially only into the negation of its *particular* content."[50] A capitalist economy thus "begets . . . its own negation," in Marx's words,[51] when it changes its content to a socialist economy.

Some underconsumption breakdown interpretations resort to the desperate argument that Marx *would have* developed such a theory had he lived to complete *Capital* himself. According to the interpretation of American Marxist Paul Sweezy, whether or not crises "must occur first in the consumption-goods department" is a question on which "Marx's silence" only shows "that he never worked the 'underconsumption' theory out in any detail."[52] But Marx was not "silent" on this at all. He said the direct opposite, that "crises do not show themselves, nor break forth, first in the retail business, which deals with direct consumption, but in the spheres of wholesale business and banking."[53]

More generally, it is completely misleading to depict *Capital* as an *analytically* unfinished work, even though it was, in a literary sense, far from a finished piece of writing when Marx died in 1883. However, Marx wrote to Engels in 1866 that the entire manuscript of *Capital* was "finished," though far from a publishable condition, and that the first volume still needed *"polishing of style."*[54] Indeed, Marx insisted on seeing *Capital* "as a *whole"* before sending the first volume off to the printer.[55] After Marx's death, Engels wrote to Marx's daughter that the third volume (in which "crisis" theory was developed) had been "complete since 1869–1870 and has never been touched since."[56] It took Engels more than a decade to decipher Marx's handwriting and pull together overlapping and repetitious manuscripts into reasonably organized books for Volumes II and III of *Capital,* but the "essential parts" of Volume III had been completed before Marx published Volume I in 1867.[57] In short, the evidence indicates that *Capital* was completed by Marx as a piece of analysis, though not as a piece of literature, in his lifetime, so the speculation as to what his analysis would have contained had he lived is gratuitous.

A still earlier voluminous draft has since been published as Marx's *Grundrisse*—and it too contains no underconsumptionist breakdown theory. It too emphasized disproportionality among the various sectors, rather than aggregate underconsumption. The *Grundrisse* stated that "if the supplied product is unsaleable, it proves that too much has been produced of a supplied commodity and too little of what the supplier demands."[58] Overproduction was balanced by underproduction, in the manner of disproportionality theorists in general. Therefore capital "withdraws" from one sector and "throws itself" into another sector in response to competitive pricing. But Marx pointed out here, as elsewhere, that "this necessity of evening up already *presupposes* the unevenness" that is inherent in capitalism and the precursor of crises.[59] A similar point was made in the 1840s in Marx's pamphlet *Wage Labour and Capital,* where he said: "If the price of a commodity rises considerably because of inadequate supply or disproportionate increase of the demand, the price of some other commodity must necessarily have fallen proportionately," leading to capital migrations toward the more profitable sectors of the economy.[60]

Disproportionality was present—and underconsumption absent—from Marx's economic writings over a period of three decades.

PRECIPITATING FACTORS

Marx depicted the disproportionality theorists as having understood the fundamental nature of capitalism better than those theorists who emphasized a deficiency of aggregate demand.[61] This was somewhat ironic because the disproportionality school of economists were supporters of Say's Law—roughly, the proposition that supply creates its own demand[62]—and proponents of that doctrine often used it to dismiss fears of depressions, which were seen as short-lived happenstances. Marx was a bitter critic of Say's Law, which he called "preposterous,"[63] "a paltry evasion,"[64] "childish babble,"[65] and "pitiful claptrap."[66] J. B. Say himself he denounced as "inane,"[67] "miserable,"[68] "thoughtless,"[69] "dull,"[70] and a "humbug."[71] For Marx, disproportionality did not end with a smooth restoration of equilibrium but precipitated further complications that ended in aggregate overproduction relative to a shrinking monetary demand.

Marx recognized that the classical supporters of Say's Law had admitted "the glut of the market for particular commodities," and had denied only "the *simultaneity* of this phenomenon for all spheres of production, and hence general overproduction."[72] According to classical economics, too much production of *A* implied too little production of *B* but not too much output in the aggregate.[73] This was because total supply equals total demand (Say's Law) and therefore each excess of either supply or demand in the case of a given commodity was necessarily offset by a corresponding deficiency in the case of some other commodity. This equality of supply and demand existed from the outset in the mind of each producer, who supplied commodities only because of—and only to the extent of—his demand for other commodities.[74]

Marx, however, spotted the fatal flaw in this reasoning—that the supplier could only *attempt* to equate his own supply with his own demand by imagining what price he would receive for his own output. If he guessed wrong, his individual supply might not equal his own individual demand —and since all producers were in the same position, aggregate supply *as conceived* need not equal aggregate demand as *realized.* While Marx recognized that "commodities are equated beforehand in imagination, by their prices, to definite quantities of money,"[75] he did not assume that they were necessarily *correctly* equated. He said:

> My supply and demand are thus as different as something conceptual is from something real. Further, the quantity I supply and its value stand in no proportion to each other. The demand for the quantity of use-value I supply is however measured not by the value I wish to realise, but by the quantity which the buyer requires at a definite price.[76]

Here Marx was developing an idea originated decades earlier by the Swiss economist J.C.L. Simonde de Sismondi, who had likewise sought to explain "violent crises,"[77] and who considered "the balance of consumption and production" to be "the fundamental question in political economy."[78] Sismondi said that producers' attempts to balance their own supply with their own demand—quantities "independent of one another"—could only proceed by "divination" because "even the most knowledgeable have only conjectural knowledge."[79] Marx was familiar with the work of Sismondi, who anticipated him in other areas as well,[80] but deliberately neglected to cover Sismondi's economic theories in his massive *Theories of Surplus Value,* [81] the first great history of economic thought.

While Sismondi had indicated much earlier that the attempt to equate supply and demand was likely to fail in a complex capitalist economy, Marx elaborated more rigorously and mathematically (in the second volume of *Capital*) just how complex the relationships were among the various sectors of the capitalist economy and among various flows of purchasing power. These interrelationships became quite complex, even under the assumption of "simple reproduction"[82]—unchanging total output from year to year—and still more so under the more realistic assumption of "accumulation and reproduction on an enlarged scale,"[83] or a growing capitalist economy. Dynamically growing capitalism—the only kind of capitalism Marx thought possible[84]—was one in which there was no "predestined circle of supply and demand"[85] known to the producers beforehand. Moreover, growing output might be absorbed for some time by wholesalers before reaching the stage where the ultimate consumer demand for it was put to the test:

> . . . the entire process of reproduction may be in a flourishing condition, and yet a large part of the commodities may have entered into consumption only apparently, while in reality they may still remain unsold in the hands of dealers, in other words, they may still be actually in the market. Now one stream of commodities follows another, and finally it becomes obvious that the previous stream had been only apparently absorbed by consumption. The commodity-capitals compete with one another for a place on the market. The succeeding ones, in order to be able to sell, do so below price. The former streams have not been utilized, when the payment for them is due. Their owners must declare their insolvency, or they sell at any price in order to fulfill their obligations. This sale has nothing whatever to do with the actual condition of the demand. It is merely a question of a demand for payment, of the pressing necessity of transforming commodities into money. Then a crisis comes. It becomes noticeable, not in the direct decrease of consumptive demand, not in the demand for individual consumption, but in the decrease of exchanges of capital for capital, of the reproductive process of capital.[86]

There were other complicating factors in crises. A growing capitalist economy implied, for Marx, the sporadic formation and liquidation of hoards of money at various places and unpredictable times. These added to the conditions of capitalism which "become so many causes of abnormal movements, implying the possibility of crises, since a balance is an accident under the crude conditions of this production."[87]

The crucial question for Marx, as for Sismondi before him, was not how particular imbalances—overproduction in a particular sector, for example—might arise, but how that led to *general* overproduction, to economic crises. Both Sismondi and Marx recognized that the pricing mechanism tended automatically to restore imbalances through declining prices for overproduced goods, rising prices for underproduced goods, and rising or falling interest rates according to supply and demand in the capital markets. But both also argued that beyond some magnitude of imbalance, this no longer worked—that there were de-stabilizing responses to extreme conditions, responses that took the economy further away from equilibrium rather than back toward it. Sismondi's destabilizing responses[88] were somewhat different from Marx's, but like Marx's they served to delay rather than to prevent eventual equilibrium. According to Sismondi, "a certain equilibrium is reestablished, it is true, in the long run, but it is by a frightful suffering."[89] To Marx, these frightful sufferings provoked a political revolt against the whole capitalist system. It was this political revolt—not an economic "breakdown"—that ended capitalism, in the Marxian vision.

The de-stabilizing force in Marx was the monetary and credit system. Money and credit turned partial overproduction into general overproduction. Marx did not consider them as initiating causes of crises—"both make their appearance long *before* capitalist production, without crises occurring"[90]—but they were mechanisms which could make sectoral disproportionalities become general over-production, relative to a declining demand, provided that the initial imbalances were large enough. According to Marx: "For a crisis (and therefore also overproduction) to be general, it is sufficient for it to grip the principal articles of trade."[91] When particular producers or middlemen—like the wholesalers already mentioned—suddenly find themselves financially over-extended through excessive output or inventory, and unable to pay previously con-tracted debt obligations, their immediate demand for money may be more than the system can supply while main-taining existing output and employment. While monetary crises could occur as independent entities,[92] they were, more generally, phases of larger crises growing out of over-production in particular sectors—disproportionality.

Overproduction in particular sectors thus generates financial panic in those sectors, when money receipts are insufficient to meet existing fixed contractual obligations when they are due. Rather than face bankruptcy, producers sell whatever output is on hand, at whatever price they can get, and use the proceeds to meet financial obligations, rather than to spend for consumer goods or to re-order new supplies. Marx said:

> A man who produced has not the choice whether he will sell or not. He *must* sell. And in crises appears precisely the circumstance that he cannot sell, or only below the price of production, or even that he must sell at a positive loss. What does it avail him or us, therefore, that he has produced in order to sell? What concerns us is precisely to discover what has cut across this good intention of his.[93]

In response to Ricardo's argument that producers sell in order to spend on consumption or on new production—all of which would make their demand equal their supply—

MARXIAN ECONOMIC CRISES

Marx replied: "Ricardo even forgets that a man may sell in order to pay, and that these compulsory sales play a very significant role in crises."[94] Marx added: "During the crisis the man may be very pleased when he has made a sale, without any immediate thought of a purchase."[95] His demand need not equal his supply at that point.

In short, there is an increasing demand to hold money during unsettled economic conditions—a point made by many other economists before and since. But Marx did not "seek to explain crises by these simple *possibilities* of crises"[94]—an approach he criticized in John Stuart Mill.[97] Rather, he sought to show how the disproportionality inherent in capitalist production would episodically reach levels that would precipitate financial panics and contractions of aggregate monetary demand. This was not only because of a failure to re-spend on the part of some capitalist producers, but also because others could not re-spend or even went into credit default.

When there are "debts due to A from B, to B from C, to C from A, and so on,"[98]—in short, "an ever-lengthening chain of payment"[99] or "mutual claims and obligations"[100]—then a monetary crisis develops "from the non-fulfillment of a whole series of payments which depend on the sale of these particular commodities within this particular period of time."[101] A general financial panic ensues. According to Marx, "in periods of crisis when credit collapses completely . . . nothing goes any more but cash money."[102]

With the shrinkage of credit, aggregate money demand becomes insufficient: "At a given moment the supply of all commodities may be greater than the demand for all commodities, because the demand for the general commodity, money, exchange value, is greater than the demand for all particular commodities. . . . "[103] Marx was aware that the insufficiency of demand was an insufficiency only at given prices:

101

> The excess of commodities is always relative, that is, it is an excess at certain prices. The prices at which the commodities are then absorbed are ruinous for the producer or merchant.[104]

The lower prices are ruinous because the whole price structure cannot deflate smoothly: "The fixed charges . . . remain the same, and in part cannot be paid."[105] Even commodities which were not among those which had been overproduced "are now suddenly in *relative* overproduction, because the means to buy them, and therewith the demand for them, have contracted."[106] Thus, "in times of general overproduction, the overproduction in some spheres is always the *result,* the *consequence,* of overproduction in the leading articles of commerce."[107]

What Marx did not explain was why the monetary contraction originating in sectors that were overproducing and incurring losses was not offset by monetary expansion originating in other sectors that were underproducing and making unusually high profits due to the rising prices of their unusually scarce goods. An earlier exponent of a similar theory, Robert Torrens, was more explicit. Torrens' theory that "a glut of a particular commodity may occasion a general stagnation"[108] was based on his assumption that "multiplied failures in agriculture, manufacturers, and trade, would strike a panic into the holders of floating capital, and they would refuse to grant accommodation upon securities, which in more prosperous times they would be disposed to consider unobjectionable."[109] In short, not merely the producers in distress but the economy as a whole would have a rising demand for money—a desire to be more liquid than usual—and these desires could not be realized simultaneously without a declining aggregate money demand for output. This seems consonant with Marx's theory, though less explicitly stated. Marx did say, however:

MARXIAN ECONOMIC CRISES

> During crises—*after* the moment of panic—during the stand-still of industry, money is immobilized in the hands of bankers, billbrokers, etc.; and, just as the stag cries out for fresh water, money cries out for a field of employment where it may be realized as capital.[110]

This not only indicates why there were crises, but also suggested why crises were transient. The purchasing power needed to restore prosperity was never annihilated, but only temporarily withdrawn from circulation pending restoration of sufficient confidence for the normal incentives of profit-seeking to draw it back into circulation again.

PERIODICITY

In Marx, crises were not merely episodic—as might be expected from a purely random process, in which sectoral disproportionalities exceed certain critical limits at unpredictable intervals, by chance. Rather, crises occur in a "periodic cycle,"[111] at relatively regular intervals. Marx and Engels saw these periodical recurrences of crises as having begun in 1825.[112] Over the years they revised their estimates of the length of the period between crises. In *Capital* Marx referred to the "decennial cycle,"[113] but after his death Engels said that "the ten-year cycle seems to have broken down."[114] Earlier, Engels had estimated the cycle as from five to seven years.[115] Marx seemed not to attach any great significance to the exact period of business cycles, as compared to their inevitable recurrence. He seemed to suggest that the economic life of fixed capital was related to the business cycle, presumably because so much capital was invested simultaneously during the recovery phase after a crisis:

> To the same extent that the volume of the value and the duration of the fixed capital develop with the evolution of

the capitalist mode of production, does the life of industry and of industrial capital develop in each particular investment into one of many years, say of ten years on an average. . . . However, it is not a question of any one definite number here. So much at least is evident that this cycle comprising a number of years, through which capital is compelled to pass by its fixed part, furnishes a material basis for the periodical commercial crises in which business goes through successive periods of lassitude, average activity, overspeeding, and crisis. It is true that the periods in which capital is invested are different in time and place. But a crisis is always the starting point of large amount of new investments. Therefore it also constitutes, from the point of view of society, more or less of a new material basis for the next cycle of turn-over.[116]

This aspect of Marx's theory was left in a very sketchy state, perhaps because periodicity was not in itself crucial to his picture of the end of capitalism. After Marx's death, Engels began to suggest that the periodic cycle had been superseded by chronic economic stagnation.[117] But no coherent theory was presented to account for this, any more than there had been for the earlier Marxian assertions of regular periodicity.

SUMMARY

Periods of depression, unemployment, or economic "crises" in Marx's terminology were seen by some schools of economists as resulting from a lack of proportion between the output of some sectors—not by an excess of total output. Marx and Engels repeatedly took this position in writings that spanned the decades from Engels' first economic essay of the early 1840s to the elaborate vision of Marx's *Capital.* The competing school, which saw crises originating in excessive total output—notably Sismondi and Malthus—was explicitly repudiated by Marx, and the ever-popular underconsumption versions ridiculed unmercifully.

Marxian economics did, however, move beyond the classical disproportionality theory by arguing that monetary reactions to severe disproportionality could in fact temporarily reduce aggregate demand below aggregate supply, in defiance of Say's Law.

Attempts to interpret Marx as an underconsumptionist who foresaw a permanent breakdown of the capitalist economy have had to rely on speculation rather than concrete statements by Marx or Engels. Yet these speculations fly in the teeth of massive evidence of disproportionality theory pervading the Marxian vision of capitalism. That vision was in fact first put forward by Engels and its essential elements later elaborated in Marx's *Capital.* The impression on Marx made by Engels' early economic essay is also shown by the fact that it caused the young Marx to seek out Engels, thus leading to their historic collaboration.

The Marx-Engels vision of economic crises encompassed not only individual depressions but also the pattern of their recurrence over the years. Crises were expected to widen in their scope as capitalism itself spread—not deepen in their severity otherwise. A regularity in the period between crises was claimed by Marx and Engels but neither a fixed period nor a developed theory of periodicity was ever determined.

Even the Marxian "law of value" was primarily a discussion of the difficulties of maintaining necessary proportions among the various sectors of a capitalist economy. But Marxian "value" is an elusive concept that requires a careful analysis in its own right.

Chapter 7

MARXIAN VALUE

The historical and intellectual context of Marxism is nowhere more important than in understanding the Marxian concept of value. Nowhere have earlier and later theories been read into Marx with more disastrous effects on accuracy. As already noted in Chapter 6, Marx did not have a *theory* of value, but rather what he himself repeatedly referred to as a "definition" or "concept" of value.[1]

Value represented the units in which social labor was measured, and the "law of value" was the allocational principle by which this social labor was distributed to the various sectors of the economy. For example, in *Capital* Marx said that "the law of value of commodities ultimately determines how much of its disposable working-time society can expend on each particular class of commodities."[2] Those who read into Marx the earlier classical—and especially Ricardian—theory of value were accused by Marx of bad faith in trying "to burden me with all Ricardo's limitations."[3] That he should be expected to prove a concept—as distinguished from a theory—left Marx flabbergasted:

> The nonsense about the necessity of proving the concept of value arises from complete ignorance both of the subject dealt with and of the method of science. Every child knows that a country which ceased to work, I will not say for a year, but for a few weeks, would die. Every child knows too that the mass of products corresponding to the different needs require different and quantitatively determined masses of the total labour of society.[4]

Marx was himself largely to blame for the confusion, having ignored Engels' warnings that the dialectical approach would not be understood by the public—or even by scholars, who were "no longer at all accustomed to this kind of thinking."[5] Engels had given similar warnings about Marx's earlier *Critique of Political Economy*[6]—and they had been similarly ignored. More generally, Marx refused to believe that his writing was difficult to understand,[7] and even entertained the idea of writing a popular explanation of Hegel that would be "accessible to the ordinary human intelligence."[8] Engels more realistically evaluated his own *Anti-Duhring* in this regard: "The semi-Hegelian language of a good many passages of my old book is not only untranslatable but has lost the greater part of its meaning even in German."[9]

The disappointing reception of *Critique of Political Economy*[10] in 1859 led Marx to try to make *Capital* at least "bearably popular"[11] and to seek Engels' help in making the discussion of value "specially popularized for the philistine."[12] Yet the basic stumbling block was not literary but methodological. Marx insisted on presenting *Capital* as an

MARXISM

argument unfolding "dialectically"—in successive approximations—so that statements that would be presented in the first volume, under one set of simplifying assumptions, would be drastically changed in later volumes, under more complex and realistic assumptions. At a number of points in the first volume Marx mentioned concepts that could not be dealt with under the assumptions of that volume or whose apparent contradictions would be resolved in Volume III.[13] Still, this procedure virtually invited misunderstandings of the first approximation. Engels could readily foresee objections to the discussion of "surplus value" in the first volume of *Capital* and wrote to Marx: "I marvel that you have not taken this into consideration already, for it will *quite certainly* be held up to you at once and it is better to dispose of it in advance."[14] But Marx insisted that the fuller discussion "can be set forth only in the third book."[15] He added:

> If I were to *silence* all such objections *in advance,* I should ruin the whole dialectical method of development. On the contrary, this method has the advantage of continually *setting traps* for these fellows which provoke them to untimely demonstrations of their asininity.[16]

Marx expected publication of the succeeding volumes of *Capital* to follow fast upon publication of the first volume,[17] so that his idea of embarrassing the critics of his first approximation may have been understandable. In reality, however, for various reasons—notably failing health —Marx never had the later volumes published—despite living sixteen years after publication of the first volume. By the time Engels laboriously pieced together and deciphered the handwritten manuscripts left by Marx, more than a quarter of a century had elapsed between publication of Volume I and Volume III of *Capital.* By that time, critics and disciples alike had hardened their positions, taken on the basis of a first approximation. Moreover, this was a quarter of a century of decisive change in economics.[18] The classical framework, which Marx was able to take for granted as a familiar intellectual setting for explaining his own analysis, was devastated by the rise of revolutionary new "marginalist" concepts—concepts which were dominant in economics by the time the third volume of *Capital* finally appeared. What Marx wrote in the 1860s was interpreted in the context of a new framework of economics in the 1890s.

The classic "refutation" of *Capital* was made by a leading figure in the new economics, Eugen von Bohm-Bawerk.[19] His refutation repeatedly misunderstood what it was refuting, and unknowingly repeated criticisms that Marx had made of Ricardo in manuscripts still unpublished at that time.[20] Bohm-Bawerk also made the claim, often echoed since then, that in his discussion of value Marx had attempted "a stringent syllogistic conclusion allowing of no exception,"[21] that Marx attempted "a logical proof, a dialectical deduction."[22] As already noted, Marx considered the idea of proving a concept to be ridiculous.[23] Moreover, Engels had asserted, long before Bohm-Bawerk, that one only proves one's ignorance of dialectics by thinking of it as a means by which things can be proved.[24] This was typical of a tragi-comedy of errors that has plagued the interpretation of Marx ever since.

Contrary to some interpretations, Marx did not change his mind about value and price between volumes of *Capital*. He explicitly worked out the analysis to be followed in Volume III in a letter to Engels written several years before publication of Volume I.[25]

Given that Marx chose to present his ideas as he did, there is little choice but to follow him through the labyrinth that he created.

METHOD AND NOMENCLATURE

Of a number of simplifying assumptions made in Volume
I of *Capital,* the most crucial was one that Marx mentioned
casually in a footnote:

> We have in fact assumed that prices = values. We shall,
> however, see in Volume III, that even in the case of average
> prices the assumption cannot be made in this very simple
> manner.[26]

A number of such "time bomb" statements, made in
footnotes in the first volume of *Capital,*[27] raised the distinct
possibility that Marx was unduly preoccupied with "setting
traps" for his critics. In any event, Marx clearly distinguished his definitional "value" from empirically observable prices, or a statistical average of such prices, or even
the long run equilibrium prices toward which such an average would tend to move. Yet price and value were not
wholly unrelated. Price was "exchange value"—the ratio in
which one good exchanged for another[28]—as expressed in
money,[29] and exchange value was in turn the outward man-
ifestation, the phenomenal form, of the underlying essence
that was value.[30] For purposes of Volume I, Marx *postulated*
a one-to-one correspondence between these magnitudes,
without actually assuming that in fact there was such a
correspondence. As he explained in a letter to a friend:

> That this necessity of distributing social labour in definite
> proportions cannot be done away with by the *particular form*
> of social production, but can only change the *form it assumes,*
> is self-evident. No natural laws can be done away with. What
> can change, in changing historical circumstances, is the *form*
> in which these laws operate. And the form in which this
> proportional division of labour operates, in a state of soci-

ety where the interconnection of social labour is manifested in the *private* exchange of the individual products of labour, is precisely the *exchange value* of these products.

The science consists in working out *how* the law of value operates. So that if one wanted at the very beginning to "explain" all the phenomena which apparently contradict that law, one would have to give the science *before* the science. It is precisely Ricardo's mistake that in his first chapter on value he takes as given all possible categories, which have still to be developed, in order to prove their conformity with the law of value.[31]

He contrasted his approach with the conventional one:

The vulgar economist has not the faintest idea that the actual everyday exchange relations need not be directly identical with the magnitudes of value. The point of bourgeois society consists precisely in this, that *a priori* there is no conscious, social regulation of production. The reasonable and the necessary in nature asserts itself only as a blindly working average. And then the vulgar economist thinks he has made a great discovery when, as against the disclosures of the inner connection, he proudly claims that in appearance things look different. In fact, he is boasting that he holds fast to the appearance and takes it for the last word. Why, then, any science at all?[32]

Marx's conception of economics, as already noted in Chapter 5, was that of a study of the social relations among *people* engaged in production, and only derivatively a study of the relations among the instrumental *things* involved in that process, such as money, commodities, or machinery. The Marxian vision of a capitalist economy was one in which independent producers unknowingly "work for one another,"[33] but in a state of Hegelian "alienation" in which they regard the derivative phenomena as the sole or primary reality. A "social relation among men" according to Marx, "assumes, in their eyes, the fantastic form of a relation between things."[34] According to Marx, "their own social action takes the form of the action of objects, which rule the producers instead of being ruled by them."[35] This was called "the fetishism of commodities."[36] Marx said:

> The sum total of the labour of all of these private individuals forms the aggregate labour of society. Since the producers do not come into social contact with each other until they exchange their products, the specific social character of each producer's labour does not show itself except in the act of exchange. In other words, the labour of the individual asserts itself as a part of the labour of society, only by means of the relations which the act of exchange establishes directly between the products, and indirectly, through them, between the producers.[37]

"Value" for Marx shows "a relation between persons expressed as a relation between things."[38] The value—the units of society's labor—is the underlying essence and the relations among commodities—*exchange value*—is only a surface appearance. Exchange value (price) was repeatedly referred to by Marx in such terms as an "appearance,"[39] an outward "form,"[40] a "phenomenal form,"[41] or part of the "surface phenomena."[42] As in other cases, the appearance was not a sheer delusion, but a derivative phenomenon imperfectly reflecting an underlying reality. Value "lies hidden behind" exchange value,[43] and Marx criticized classical economics for not understanding "the hidden relations between value and its form, exchange value,"[44] for confusing "the form of value with value itself,"[45] and for failing to discover specifically how "value becomes exchange-value."[46]

MARXIAN VALUE

The difference between value and exchange-value was not merely a terminological fine point. The two differ quantitatively as well as qualitatively. Two commodities may contain the same amount of social labour and by definition have the same value, and yet exchange in the marketplace at different ratios with other goods.

Values differ from exchange-values for two reasons. First, because exchange-values themselves fluctuate with supply and demand—the allocational mechanism by which the "law of value" governs the distribution of factors of production, so that the average around which they fluctuate is seldom the observed price. Second, even "average prices do not directly coincide with the values of commodities," according to Marx.[47]

Before proceeding more specifically to the economic reasons why values differ even from long run equilibrium prices, it should also be noted that not only value but "surplus value" belong on the plane of underlying essences imperfectly represented by observable appearances.[48] While value is the labor socially necessary to produce a commodity, surplus value is that proportion of society's labor that exceeds what is required to produce the livelihood of the workers themselves.[49] Out of this surplus value comes all the income of the non-working classes—the profit, interest, rent, etc. These latter "determinate forms" of surplus value are each "determined by quite different laws" from each other and from surplus value in general.[50] Marx criticized Adam Smith for confusing profit with surplus value[51] and criticized Ricardo for seeking "to present the laws of profit directly, without intermediate links, as laws of surplus value."[52] By contrast, Engels pointed out that in Marxian economics "many intermediate links are required for the passage from an understanding of surplus value in general to that of its transformation into profit and ground-rent."[53]

In short, Marxian value and surplus value are on an entirely different plane of abstraction from price, profit, rent, interest, and other "surface phenomena." Only as successive approximations establish "intermediate links" are these latter phenomena systematically dealt with in the later parts of *Capital* where, in the third volume, the analysis begins to "approach step by step" concrete economic entities in "that form which they assume on the surface of society, in their mutual interactions in competition, and in the ordinary consciousness of the human agencies in this process."[54] As Marx expressed it to Engels, only in the third volume would he begin to analyze "the *forms of appearance* which serve as the *starting point* in the vulgar conception" of economics.[55]

Although the classical economists, as contrasted with the vulgar economists,[56] had also dealt with the social essence of the capitalist economy, they had in Marx's view done so without systematically separating concepts belonging on different levels of abstraction. According to Marx, "while Ricardo is accused of being too abstract, the opposite accusation would be justified—i.e., lack of power to abstract; inability, when dealing with the values of commodities, to keep out of his mind profit, a thing which confronts him as a result of competition."[57] Ricardo "skips intermediate links and tries to establish *direct* proof of the consistency of economic categories with each other."[58] Classical economics in general was accused of making "a regular hash"[59] of concepts belonging on different levels of abstraction. For himself Marx preferred the Hegelian "method of advancing from the abstract to the concrete,"[60] though he admitted in one of his prefaces to *Capital* that his "method of analysis" might make the opening chapter on value "arduous" for those who were "impatient to come to a conclusion."[61]

MARXIAN VALUE

The First Approximation

The labor that is "socially necessary" to produce a given commodity is not all necessary to provide the livelihood of the workers who make that commodity. What the capitalist purchases from these workers is not their finished product but only their ability to work—their "labor power" in Marxian terminology.[62] Their output must exceed the cost of their livelihood in order for the capitalist to have any incentive to hire them, whether this cost and this output are measured in money or in units of Marxian value. The amount by which their output exceeds the wages they receive for their labor power is the Marxian surplus value.

Viewed from the capitalist's perspective, money has been invested (in machinery, raw materials, etc., as well as workers) in order to produce commodities, in order to receive money again later from their sale. The capitalist circuit from money to commodities to money was abbreviated in the Marxian formula M-C-M. The second M must be larger than the first, for "the circuit M-C-M would be absurd and without meaning if the intention were to exchange by this means two equal sums of money."[63] Marx concluded:

> The exact form of this process is therefore M-C-M', where $M' = M + \Delta M$ = the original sum advanced, plus an increment. This increment or excess over the original value I call "surplus value."[64]

The value of a given commodity includes this surplus value, as well as the amount of value represented by the goods that provide the workers' livelihood. The total value of the commodity is the total *labor* expended on its production, but the value received by the worker is only that of his labor *power.* In short, labor creates more value than it receives for its own subsistence, the difference being surplus value. The capital invested in hiring workers was seen by Marx as being transformed into a "variable magnitude" because of the surplus value added by the workers, and so was named "variable capital."[65] That portion of capital invested in other, non-labor resource inputs was conceived merely to be included among the costs to be reimbursed from the sale of the commodity at their original amount, and so were named "constant capital."[66]

Terminology changes nothing analytically, but this particular terminology was in keeping with a substantive assumption by Marx that labor was in reality what created output—that capitalists, as such, were wholly superfluous, though able to receive an income because the legal institution of property rights made their permission necessary for the socially created means of production to be used. This was *not* a claim that capital equipment as an input into the production process was worthless. On the plane of human relations, what mattered was what particular *people*—classes —contributed personally toward social output, and what they received from it. From Marx's perspective, the physical capital equipment was as much a product of labor—past labor—as the labor currently performed with that equipment to produce a commodity. This conception was by no means unique to Marx, but reflected a way of thinking that derived from the dominant classical economics of his time. This conception was implicit in the first sentence of Adam Smith's introduction to *The Wealth of Nations:* "The annual labour of every nation is the fund which originally supplies it with all the necessaries and conveniences of life which it annually consumes, and which consist always either in the immediate produce of that labor, or in what is purchased with that labor."[67]

What was in Adam Smith a vague conception, inconsistent with much of what followed in *The Wealth of Nations*, became in Marx a crystal clear postulate whose implications were relentlessly pursued to their logical conclusion. It was not the first time that Smith's inconsistencies had historic impact on later generations of economists, who seized upon different parts of his vision to reach opposite conclusions from each other.[68] In this case, Adam Smith provided the basis both for Ricardo's *laissez faire* and for Marx's communism.

Marx's central purpose was not to denounce surplus value as immoral, though he frequently depicted profit in unsavory or even lurid terms.[69] The so-called "Ricardian socialists" had already morally condemned profit, but Marx scorned their approach as "the utopian interpretation of Ricardo's theory."[70] Engels pointed out that Marx "never based his communist demands upon this," which was "simply an application of morality to economics."[71] Marx's central purpose was not a timeless moral condemnation of capitalism (which would have been wholly undialectical) but rather an attempt to construct the elements of a systematic theory that would show the historical tendencies of capitalism—in Marx's words "lay bare the law of motion of modern society."[72]

Marx's elementary building blocks in his theory were the formula M-C-M' and his definitions of constant capital, variable capital, and surplus value. The formula M-C-M' expressed the "boundless greed after riches, this passionate chase after exchange-value"[73] that had no logical stopping place, so that capitalism could never settle back into a comfortable stagnant routine like other systems, but must relentlessly innovate and increase output. An "increase of wealth," for Marx, "is implied in capitalist production."[74] Systems of production for use—whether by the producer or by feudal lords or by non-capitalist slave owners—had more or less natural limits to their demand for output. But output expressed in abstract money terms had no such limits. Technological innovations were relentlessly sought by capitalists, for the temporary increase in profits they bring, even though such extra profits were then competed away as other firms were forced to copy them and lower prices in order to survive.[75] Marx said:

> Modern Industry never looks upon and treats the existing form of a process as final. The technical basis of that industry is therefore revolutionary, while all earlier modes of production were essentially conservative. By means of machinery, chemical processes and other methods, it is continually causing changes not only in the technical basis of production, but also in the functions of the labourer, and in the social combinations of the labour-process. At the same time, it thereby also revolutionizes the division of labour within the society, and incessantly launches masses of capital and of work people from one branch of production to another.[76]

Capitalism was dynamic not only in a productive sense but also, because of that, it tended to displace over time all pre-capitalist production, whether at home or abroad. Capitalism "extends its scope until it becomes the prevailing social condition."[77] Earlier systems, based on production for use, simply cannot stand up to the competition of capitalism:

> In proportion as the capitalist mode of production develops it has a disintegrating effect on all older forms of production, which were mainly adjusted to the individual needs and transformed only the surplus over and above those needs into commodities.[78]

Economies based on M-C-M defeat economies based on C-M-C.

The Marxian value of a commodity can be disaggregated

into its constant capital, variable capital and surplus value. In the Marxian formula, value = c + v + s.[79] The constant capital (c) in this formula is depreciation, not the total investment in machinery, raw materials, and other non-labor inputs. In the first volume of *Capital*, Marx said: "Throughout this Book therefore, by constant capital advanced for the production of value, we always mean, unless the context is repugnant thereto, the value of the means of production actually consumed in the process, and that value alone."[80]

On the basis of his postulate that "surplus-value is purely the result of a variation in the value of v,"[81] Marx made the rate of surplus-value equal to s/v[82] and made this measure "the degree of exploitation of labour-power."[83] For example, if half of a worker's day was sufficient for him to produce an output that would supply (or exchange for) enough goods for his own livelihood, then that laborer "works one-half of the day for himself, the other half for the capitalist."[84] In Marx's terms, the rate of surplus value would be one hundred percent in this case. Marx said that the rate of surplus value was often "confounded with the rate of profit"[85] but was both conceptually and quantitatively different. But such a comparison was inappropriate at this level of abstraction:

> Of course the ratio of surplus-value not only to that portion of the capital from which it immediately springs, and whose change of value it represents, but also to the sum total of the capital advanced is economically of very great importance. We shall, therefore, in the third book, treat of this ratio exhaustively.[86]

The Final Approximation

The arbitrarily postulated equality of value and price made little difference for the principal issues dealt with in the first volume of *Capital*—wages and working conditions,[87] capital growth,[88] and the origins and destiny of capitalism.[89] But the use of value as a proxy for price could no longer continue as the analysis moved on to other issues. The simplifying assumptions of Volume I began to be relaxed as more complicating factors began to be taken into account.

While Volume II begins with its being "taken for granted at this point that commodities are sold at their values,"[90] the complications introduced there begin the process of destroying the equality of price and value. The second volume, for example, refers to "expenses which increase the price of a commodity without adding anything to its value."[91] More fundamentally, Volume II introduced *differences* in the duration of fixed capital[92] and in the turnover time of circulating capital,[93] from one commodity to another. Thus, two commodities may have equal values, based on equal labor and equal depreciation of capital, and yet have different prices because more total capital is invested per commodity in one case, and the rate of profit is determined in part by that total investment, not just by the amount of "wear and tear" incurred in producing current output. But at a sufficiently macroeconomic level that still did not matter. As Marx said: "Should there be any divergence of prices from values, this would not exert any influence on the movements of *social* capital."[94]

In the third volume of *Capital,* Marx confronted head-on the inherent deviations—even in equilibrium—between price and value. These deviations turn on the difference between the rate of surplus value and the rate of profit. The rate of surplus value was s/v, while the rate of profit was defined by Marx as $s/c + v$.[95] If the ratio of c/v varies from one commodity to another—if there are different ratios of capital to labor—then they cannot have both equal rates of surplus value and equal rates of profit. Competition in a capitalist economy tends to equalize rates of profit.[96] Therefore, commodities with different ratios of constant to variable capital cannot exchange in proportion to their values. To take a hypothetical example used by Marx in writing to Engels,[97] if a total capital of 100 units of labor is advanced for the production of each of four commodities (A, B, C, D below), but in different ratios of constant to variable capital, then equal rates of surplus value (50 percent in this example) would yield unequal profits.

TABLE 1

commodity	c	v	s	commodity value (c + v + s)	rate of profit (s/c + v)
A	50	50	25	125	25%
B	70	30	15	115	15%
C	80	20	10	110	10%
D	90	10	5	105	5%

Because surplus value comes from labor, and is therefore proportioned to the wages bill—variable capital (v)—the amount of surplus value will vary from commodity to commodity. The more labor-intensive commodity A will have more surplus value than the more capital-intensive commodity D. Since they all have the same cost of production (c + v) or "cost price" in Marx's terminology,[98] they end up in this example with different rates of profit. In short, it is impossible for these commodities with different capital-labor ratios (c/v) to have both equal rates of surplus value and equal rates of profit. Marx repeatedly pointed out that such an outcome was impossible in a competitive capitalist economy.[99] As he wrote to Engels, before publication of the first volume of *Capital:*

> In these circumstances, with *equal* exploitation of the worker in *different* trades, different capitals of *the same size* will yield very *different* amounts of surplus value in different

121

spheres of production and therefore *very different rates of profit,* since profit is nothing but the proportion of the surplus value to the total capital advanced.[100]

What must in fact happen is that the rates of profit must be equalized by the pressures of competition for investment capital.[101] With the same total surplus value of 55 for the same four commodities, each still having a cost of production of 100, there is an industry-wide profit rate of $55/400$ or 13.75 percent. Each commodity must therefore sell for its cost of production—its "cost-price" in Marxian terminology—plus a profit mark-up of 13.75 percent. This result is shown in Table 2.

TABLE 2

commodity	c	v	s	commodity value	commodity price	rate of profit
A	50	50	25	125	113.75	13.75%
B	70	30	15	115	113.75	13.75%
C	80	20	10	110	113.75	13.75%
D	90	10	5	105	113.75	13.75%
	400		55			

The ratio of c/v was called by Marx the "organic composition of capital."[102] Differences in the organic composition of capital prevent goods from exchanging in proportion to their values, even in equilibrium. As Marx said:

Competition does *not* therefore reduce commodities to their *value,* but to their *cost price,* which is *above, below,* or *equal* to their *value,* according to the organic composition of the respective capitals.[103]

In this particular example, none of the commodities has a price equal to its value. If there had been a commodity with the exact average rate of c/v ($4\frac{1}{12}$:1 in this example), it would have sold at its value, which would have been 113.75. Note, however, that the total number of commodities in the economy, taken as a whole, must have the average ratio of c/v, so that purely macroeconomic conclusions are unchanged by the deviations of individual commodity prices from Marxian values—there being no such source of deviations at the macro level. Moreover, Marx did not consider surplus value to be rendered wholly meaningless. Its total magnitude (55 in this example) determined the total profit and therefore the profit rate, which then determined the price. He said:

> The average profit, and therefore also the production prices, would be purely imaginary and without basis if we did not take the determined value as the foundation. The equalisation of the surplus values in different spheres of production makes no difference to the absolute magnitude of this total surplus value, but only alters its distribution among the different spheres of production. The determination of the surplus value itself however only arises from the determination of value .by labour time. Without this, the average profit is an average of *nothing,* a mere figment of the imagination. And in that case it might just as well be 1,000 per cent as 10 per cent.[104]

Note, however, that the crucial role of surplus value depends on Marx's original arbitrary postulate that labor was the source of wealth, and therefore of all non-labor income —a postulate less likely to be questioned within the classical economics framework in which he wrote than after the marginalist revolution that took place in economics before Volume III was published. In any case, neither evidence nor analysis was given to support it.

Differing capital-labor ratios (c/v) were only one of the reasons cited by Marx for differences between value and price. Prices are also affected by the turnover time of circulating capital—the interval between the capitalist's expenditures on wages and raw materials and the return of those expenditures from the sale of the output.[105] Commodities of equal value may have different prices for this reason as well. Engels attempted to rescue the Marxian analysis with a parenthetical note, changing the profit formula to allow for turnover differences.[106]

Still another reason for a difference between price and value might be the difference between capital depreciation —indicated by c in the Marxian profit formula $(s/c + v)$— and total capital investment, on which profits are in fact calculated in a capitalist economy. However, Marx inexplicably rejected the proposition that profit was calculated—and equalized—on total investment rather than on depreciation, wages and raw material costs.[107] Marx at various places referred to the rate of profit as the ratio of surplus value to "total capital"[108]—but by total capital in this context he specified constant capital plus variable capital (depreciation plus wages)—not the total investment, including the undepreciated remaining capital.

Finally, prices may deviate from values because those sectors of the economy producing the means of production for other sectors need not have the average capital-labor ratio (c/v) and so may be selling their output at prices that deviate from values—these deviations then entering into the prices of all other goods produced by the use of these means of production.[109]

These various deviations of values from equilibrium price in Marxian economics are secondary, however, when compared to the deviations between value and price due to prices almost never being in equilibrium[110] because of the "anarchy" of production under capitalism. Nevertheless, these secondary deviations of prices from Marxian values have provoked a voluminous literature on the "transformation problem"[111]—that is, the logical inconsistency of Marx's transformation of values into prices with the other assumptions of his system. Even if all these inconsistencies could be satisfactorily resolved, however, it would make a minor difference in the Marxian system as a whole. It would not, for example, make surplus value anything other than an arbitrary postulate.

Some have surmised that Marx *would have* worked out the transformation problem more fully and consistently had he lived to complete *Capital.*[112] It is also possible that he did so, but that the material was omitted by Engels, who considered the issue peripheral. An editorial note by Engels in the third volume of *Capital* said:

> The manuscript contains also very detailed calculations of the difference between the rate of surplus-value and the rate of profit (s' − p'); these show very interesting peculiarities and their movement indicates the cases in which the two rates draw apart or approach one another. These movements may be represented by curves. I do not reproduce this material, because it is of less importance for the immediate purposes of this work.[113]

Marx was well aware that capitalists and capitalist competition operated on the basis of observable magnitudes such as profit, while surplus value was an "invisible and unknown essence."[114] Marx said:

> It is immaterial for the capitalist whether he is supposed to advance constant capital in order to make a profit out of his variable capital, or whether he advances variable capital in order to make a profit out of the constant capital; whether he invests money in wages in order to make his machinery and raw materials more valuable, or whether he invests money in machinery and raw materials in order to be able to exploit labor. Although it is only the variable portion of

125

capital which creates surplus-value, it does so only on condition that the other portions, the material requirements of production, are likewise advanced.[115]

Yet, inconsistently, Marx argued as if the workers were motivated by the unseen rate of exploitation, rather than by the tangible reality of wages. Workers were assumed by him to migrate from one employer to another until the rates of exploitation (s/v) were equalized.[116] Why they would not equalize real wages instead was left unexplained. The same implicit assumption—that workers were motivated by exploitation rates, or perhaps that the differences in these rates bore some close relationship to differences in real wages—also underlay the Marxian theory of the increasing misery of the proletariat, as will be seen below. The implications of this assumption reached well beyond economics, for if workers are *not* motivated in this way, then the whole basis for proletarian revolution is undermined.

FIAT PRICING AND LABOR TIME CERTIFICATES

The Marxian value concept and the Marxian "law of value," or resource allocation principle, were applied by Marx and Engels to a competitive capitalist economy. Other socialists, both before and after them, have wanted to have the government or some cooperative association simply *decree* that goods must exchange in proportion to the labor time that went into their production. Some would have each worker be issued a certificate or receipt showing how many hours he had worked, and entitling him to a corresponding amount of goods. Marx and Engels, throughout their careers, were unsparing in their rejection and denunciation of such schemes.

In Marx's *The Poverty of Philosophy* (1847) he attacked a fiat pricing scheme of Proudhon:

MARXIAN VALUE

Let M. Proudhon take it upon himself to formulate and lay down such a law, and we shall relieve him of the necessity of giving proofs. If, on the other hand, he insists on justifying his theory, not as a legislator, but as an economist, he will have to prove that the *time* needed to create a commodity indicates exactly the degree of its *utility* and marks its proportional relation to the demand, and in consequence, to the total amount of wealth.[117]

People like Proudhon "reduce socialism to an elementary misconception" of economics, according to Marx.[118] They wish to eliminate the very process of market competition which tends to produce the equality of price and product cost that they desire. This would destroy the whole allocation process, as Engels explained: "Only through the undervaluation or overvaluation of products is it forcibly brought home to the individual commodity producers what things and what quantity of them society requires or does not require."[119] Without this mechanism, Engels wondered "what guarantee we have that necessary quantity and not more of each product will be produced, that we shall not go hungry in regard to corn and meat while we are choked in beet sugar and drowned in potato spirit, that we shall not lack trousers to cover our nakedness while trouser buttons flood us in millions. . . ."[120]

According to Marx, "the worker's particular labour time cannot be directly exchanged for every other particular labour time."[121] That would be "assuming that the labor-time contained in commodities is *directly* social labor-time,"[122] that "the isolated labor of the individual . . . is direct social labor."[123] In short, "socially necessary labor" is an unseen determination resulting from a social process, not a directly observable magnitude. Marx opposed the passing out of "time-chits" which presupposed the two to be identical.[124] As shown above, Engels opposed the same scheme for the same reasons, but because he did so without arcane jargon, some later interpreters have claimed that he *favored* these schemes, in opposition to Marx.[125]

Marx and Engels were likewise agreed in substance as to the continued existence of surplus labor time under socialism. Engels declared that "it is the characteristic peculiarity of all social confusion that ruminates on 'true value' to imagine that in existing society the worker does not get the full 'value' of his labour, and that socialism is destined to remedy this."[126] But "in no conceivable state of society can the worker receive for consumption the entire value of his product."[127] Similarly, according to Marx, "deductions from the 'undiminished proceeds of labor' are an economic necessity, and . . . they are in no way calculable by equity."[128]

How, then, would allocation and distribution take place under socialism? Marx and Engels provided only the sketchiest suggestions, in keeping with their aversion to utopia-building for the future. There would, however, be some sort of "plan" which would in some unspecified way determine what is "really" needed. According to Marx:

> Only when production will be under the conscious and prearranged control of society, will society establish a direct relation between the quantity of social labor time employed in the production of definite articles and the quantity of the demand of society for them.[129]

It will take a long time to reach this point, but the socialist mode of operation remained unclear. Marx said:

> The life-process of society, which is based on the process of material production, does not strip off its mystical veil until it is treated as production by freely associated men, and is consciously regulated by them in accordance with a

settled plan. This, however, demands for society a certain material groundwork or set of conditions of existence which in their turn are the spontaneous product of a long and painful process of development.[130]

Engels was somewhat clearer than Marx, though no more detailed:

The useful effects of the various articles of consumption, compared with each other and with the quantity of labour required for their production, will in the last analysis determine the plan. People will be able to manage everything very simply without the intervention of the famous "value."[131]

This is in contrast to a well-known interpretation which claims that "Marx believed that, under socialism, the labour theory of value would come into its own."[132] The vast amount of attention devoted to the "transformation problem" might make sense if Marx had expected labor values to become the basis of a socialist economy, but in fact he and Engels repeatedly repudiated any such approach.

"TENDENCIES" OF WAGES AND PROFITS

The term "tendency" had a long and ambiguous history in classical economics,[133] well before Marx wrote *Capital.* In classical economics, tendency sometimes referred to an empirical generalization about the observable course of events, and sometimes referred to a cause which—if unimpeded—*would* produce a given effect.[134] Marx used tendency in this second sense, as an analytical rather than an empirical concept. For example: "To appropriate labour during all 24 hours of the day is, therefore, the inherent tendency of capitalist production."[135] But a "normal working day" emerges empirically from a struggle between "two opposed tendencies"[136]—namely, capitalists and workers pulling in opposite directions. Similarly, there was a "constant tendency of capital" to force the wages of labor to zero,[137] though it was obviously impossible to do so.

Two major tendencies in Marxian economics are more readily understandable when (1) the analytic nature of his tendencies is understood, and (2) both are interpreted in the light of Marx's conception of value. These two tendencies are the falling rate of profit and the increasing exploitation of the proletariat. Both are long-run tendencies, expressed in value terms. Both also depend upon Marx's assumption that growing mechanization of production would cause a rising ratio of capital to labor over time.

The Rate of Profit

Marx's chapter on the tendency of the falling rate of profit in Volume III of *Capital* was followed immediately by a chapter entitled "Counteracting Causes."[138] These counteracting causes leave "merely the character of a tendency"[139]—by which he means "a law whose absolute enforcement is checked, retarded, weakened, by counteracting causes."[140] In short, there is no determinate observable outcome. It had been assumed and reiterated, at least as far back as Adam Smith, that profit rates declined over time, so Marx was not establishing a new proposition but exploring the implications of an existing proposition.

According to Marx, "it is one of the laws of capitalist production" that the ratio of capital to labor—of "constant capital" to "variable capital"—increases over time. He said:

> This is only another way of saying that the same number of laborers, the same quantity of labor-power set in motion by a variable capital of a given value, consume in production an ever increasing quantity of means of production, such as

130

machinery and all sorts of fixed capital, raw and auxiliary materials, and consequently a constant capital of ever increasing value and volume, during the same period of time, owing to the peculiar methods of production developing within the capitalist system.[141]

If there is an increasing ratio of capital to labor over time, then we can now choose to view the numbers in Table 1 as showing a changing organic composition (c/v) of capital over time, rather than simultaneous differences among contemporary producers. If the first time period is A, the second time period B, etc., then the numbers illustrate the Marxian proposition that "the same rate of surplus-value, with the same degree of exploitation, would express itself in a falling rate of profit."[142] This referred to a long-run fall in the profit rate, though Marx also noted that profit rates may fall "temporarily for other reasons."[143]

In Ricardian economics, a falling rate of profit led toward the stationary state, in which the return on investment was just sufficient to induce replacement of capital as it wore out, but not sufficient to induce net additions to capital. Some interpreters have suggested that something similar happened in Marx, that a "breakdown" or permanent stagnation of the capitalist economy is reached via this route.[144] But the only causal link between crises and the falling rate of profit ran the other way: the cheapening of capital as a result of depression was an offsetting factor retarding the long-run decline in profit rates.[145] The economic consequences of secular falls in the rate of profit were much milder in Marx than in Ricardo. Where the profit rate fell, it hastened the concentration of capital as smaller capitalists found themselves unable to survive;[146] it encouraged speculation in a desperate search for higher rates of return,[147] and increased foreign investment for the same reason.[148]

The crucial role of the long-run profit rate, however, is

precisely as a *tendency,* not as a materialized actuality. The tendency calls forth numerous reactions, such as lengthening the working day or speeding up the work pace, which amount to raising the rate of surplus value—the rate of exploitation of labor—which in turn hastens revolution. Whether the profit rate still falls despite these efforts is a secondary question in this context. The tendency provides incentives to increase the exploitation of labor, and that, in Marx's system, means hastening the day of revolution.

"Increasing Misery" of the Proletariat

When the wages of labor are expressed in Marxian value terms, that is more than a matter of innocuous nomenclature. It means that wages are being expressed in terms radically different from those of virtually every other economist except Marx and Ricardo. In both the Marxian and Ricardian systems of economics, the value of wages meant the quantity of labor expended on production of the wage-earner's livelihood. With rising productivity over time, less and less labor time is required to produce a given output, so that the livelihood of workers, capitalists, landlords, etc., may all rise simultaneously with a given number of hours in the working day. But this rise in the *quantity* of output does not mean a rise in the *value* of output, which both Ricardo and Marx measured in units of labor input.

To use an example from Ricardo, if capitalists received half the output initially, and workers and landlords one quarter each, then a doubling of output might cause everyone to receive more. But if the workers and landlords now receive only 22 percent each from this doubled output, then according to Ricardo, "I should say, that wages and rent had fallen and profits risen; though in consequence of the abundance of commodities, the quantity paid to the labourer and land lord would have increased in the proportion of 25 to 44."[149] This fall in the worker's wages—measured in Ricardian value terms—"will not the less be a real fall, because they might furnish him with a greater quantity of cheap commodities than his former wages."[150] In short, in the words of John Stuart Mill, "Mr. Ricardo did not use the word value in the sense of exchangeable value" but rather "in a sense peculiar to himself, to denote cost of production."[151] So did Marx, and the consequence was the same in one sense. As Mill explained:

> Mr. Ricardo, therefore, would not have said that wages had risen, because a labourer could obtain two pecks of flour instead of one, for a day's labour; but if last year he received, for a day's labour, something which required eight hours' labour to produce it, and this year something which requires nine hours, then Mr. Ricardo would say that wages had risen. A rise in wages, with Mr. Ricardo, meant an increase in the cost of production of wages; an increase in the number of hours' labour which go to produce the wages of a day's labour; an increase in the *proportion* of the fruits of labour which the labourer receives for his own share, an increase in the ratio between the wages of his labour and the produce of it.[152]

We need not speculate as to whether Marx accepted the Ricardian conception of wages and the peculiar sense in which wages were said to "rise" or "fall." In his giant history of economics, *Theories of Surplus Value,* Marx explicitly endorsed the Ricardian approach.

> The value of wages has to be reckoned not on the basis of the quantity of necessaries which the worker receives, but on the basis of the quantity of labour which these necessaries cost—actually the proportion of the working day which he appropriates for himself; the proportionate share of the total product, which the worker receives. It is possible that, reckoned in use values (quantities of commodities or

money), his wages may rise as productivity increases, and yet reckoned in value they may fall, and *vice versa*. It is one of Ricardo's greatest merits that he made an examination of relative wages and established them as a definite category. Previously wages had always been looked upon as a simple element, and consequently the worker had been regarded as an animal. In Ricardo, however, he is considered in his social relationship. The position of the classes in relation to each other depends to a greater extent on the proportion which the wage forms than on the absolute amount of the wage.[153]

Despite Marx's attempt to read his own social philosophy into Ricardo, in reality Ricardo treated the absolute standard of living of the workers as socially central. The special meaning of the value of wages in the Ricardian system was simply a corollary of his conception of value. But, as Ricardo said:

Does my view prevent an examination into the real condition of the labourer? It is true that I say the labourers wages are high if he receives a high value for his work, that is to say if he receives the produce of a great deal of labour. To know his real condition we must still enquire what this produce is in quantity. . . . I should first enquire what the labourers money wages were, and should estimate his condition by the abundance of necessaries which those money wages would procure him.[154]

With Marx, however, the concept of rises and falls in the value of wages reflected not only economic definitions but also social philosophy:

A noticeable rise in wages presupposes a rapid growth of productive capital. The rapid growth of productive capital brings about an equally rapid growth of wealth, luxury, social wants, social enjoyments. Thus, although the enjoyments of the worker have risen, the social satisfaction that they give has fallen in comparison with the increased enjoyments of the capitalist, which are inaccessible to the worker, in comparison with the state of development of society in general. Our desires and pleasures spring from society; we measure them, therefore, by society and not by the objects which serve for their satisfaction. Because they are of a social nature, they are of a relative nature.[155]

Marx declared: "Real wages may remain the same, they may even rise, and yet relative wages may fall."[156] This has social as well as economic implications:

If capital is growing rapidly, wages may rise: the profit of capital rises incomparably more rapidly. The material position of the worker has improved, but at the cost of his social position. The social gulf that divides him from the capitalist has widened.[157]

While the Marxian system defined rises or falls in wages in relative terms throughout his career, Marx's *ad hoc* assessments of trends in real wages (measured in quantities of goods)[158] varied somewhat between his earlier and later writings. During the depressed economic conditions of the 1840s, christened by economic historians "the hungry forties," Marx seemed to expect that an absolute decline in real wages would accompany a relative decline in wages measured in "value" terms.[159] In an 1847 article, Marx said:

In the course of development, there is a double fall in wages:
Firstly: relative, in proportion to the development of general wealth.
Secondly: absolute, since the quantity of commodities

135

which the worker receives in exchange becomes less and less.[160]

In 1848, the *Communist Manifesto* flatly declared: "the modern labourer . . . instead of rising with the progress of industry, sinks deeper and deeper below the conditions of existence of his own class."[161] Marx's *The Poverty of Philosophy* (1847) declared: "The natural price of labour is no other than the wage minimum."[162] But nearly four decades later, Engels appended a footnote to this statement, indicating how he and Marx had changed their views on this over time:

> The thesis that the "natural", i.e., normal, price of labour power coincides with the wage minimum, i.e., with the equivalent in value of the means of subsistence absolutely indispensable for the life and procreation of the worker, was first put forward by me. . . . Marx at that time accepted the thesis. Lassalle took it over from both of us.[163]

Lassalle's "iron law of wages" was excoriated, both publicly and privately, by Marx and Engels in their later years. Engels called it "a quite antiquated economic view, namely, that the worker only receives on the average the *minimum* of the labour wage."[164] Marx wrote to Engels in the 1860s that Lassalle "collects in his manure factory the party excrements we dropped twenty years ago."[165] Publicly, in 1875, Marx called Lassalle's theory of fixed wages an "outrageous retrogression" in the light of recent and "more scientific" understanding of the subject.[166] What Marx did not point out was that he was the source both of the views to which Lassalle was "retrogressing" and of the new and "scientific" correction. Engels, however, later specified that it was in *Capital* that the new view was to be found, that "the laws regulating wages are very complicated" and that "they are in no sense iron but on the contrary very elastic."[167]

MARXIAN VALUE

What made wages flexible in *Capital* was the Marxian conception of "subsistence" as whatever consumptions had become part of the worker's expected livelihood. The worker's subsistence included both his "natural wants" (food, shelter, fuel, clothing) and his "so-called necessary wants" which are "the product of historical development."[168] The value of labor-power was that value or labor-cost "required for the conservation and reproduction of his labor-power, regardless of whether the conditions of this conservation and reproduction are scanty or bountiful, favorable or unfavorable."[169] Contrary to Samuelson's interpretation, for example, *Capital* does not show wages falling to subsistence over time;[170] wages tend to be *at* subsistence over time, with the specific contents of that subsistence tending to increase. According to Marx, "it is possible with an increase in productiveness of labour, for the price of labour-power to keep on falling, and yet this fall to be accompanied by a constant growth in the mass of the labourer's means of subsistence."[171]

The subsistence level of goods, as it exists at a given moment, provides a floor below which wages cannot fall or at least remain very long. According to Marx, "the value of labour-power cannot fall, and consequently surplus value cannot rise, without a rise in the productiveness of labour."[172] The fruits of growing productivity need not be equally shared between workers and capitalists, and when in fact the capitalists appropriate more of the growing output (both as profit and as replacement of depreciation on the growing mass of capital), then the "value" of labor-power falls, even though "the lowest possible point consistent with its new value" still represents "an increased mass of necessaries."[173]

During the advance of a capitalist economy, particular groups of workers may suffer not only relative but absolute impoverishment, and passages in *Capital* describing their plight have been seized upon by some interpreters as showing the fate of the entire working class as an absolute decline in real living standards.[174] Marx spared no effort to paint the fate of these unfortunate groups of workers in the most vivid—not to say lurid—colors, but that still did not amount to an analysis of the value of labor-power in the economy as a whole—an analysis that pointed in the opposite direction. Ignoring the context of Marx's statements and collecting quotations at random, without regard to the period of his long career from which they came, interpreters can "prove" remarkable conclusions and inconsistencies—and not only on this subject. What validity this has is another question. As the late Marxist scholar Ronald L. Meek observed, as regards the doctrine of increasing misery of the proletariat, "the significant point here, surely, is not that Marx made such statements as this in 1844, but that he did not repeat them in 1867, when Volume I of *Capital* appeared."[175]

As revolutionaries, Marx and Engels tried in every way to minimize the improvement in the worker's standard of living that had taken place under capitalism in their lifetime, but even so they did not deny it. *Capital,* for example, acknowledged that from 1849 to 1859 a rise of agricultural wages took place in Britain, but called it "practically insignificant."[176] Yet when Marx specified the amount of this rise at a public lecture, it was *"about 40 percent."*[177] Engels in his later years likewise noted that factory workers in England "are undoubtedly better off than before 1848."[178]

The fundamental objection of Marx and Engels was to the whole capitalist-worker relationship, which they saw as exploitation—an exploitation that must increase over time, since growing masses of capital required growing amounts of surplus value for replacement of depreciation, as well as to maintain the profit rate on a growing investment. To miss this was to miss the whole point of capitalism according to Marx, by being distracted by questions of living standards:

> . . . the whole bourgeois conception of wages hitherto, as well as all the criticism hitherto directed against this conception, was thrown overboard once for all and it was made clear that the wage worker has permission to work for his own subsistence, that is, *to live,* only in so far as he works for a certain time gratis for the capitalist (and hence also for the latter's co-consumers of surplus value); that the whole capitalist system of production turns on the increase of this gratis labour by extending the working day or by developing the productivity, that is, increasing the intensity of labour-power, etc.; that, consequently, the system of wage labour is a system of slavery and indeed of a slavery which becomes more severe in proportion as the social productive forces of labour develop, whether the worker receives better or worse payment. . . .

> It is as if, among slaves who have at last got behind the secret of slavery and broken out in rebellion, a slave still in thrall to obsolete notions were to inscribe on the program of the rebellion: "Slavery must be abolished because the feeding of slaves in the system of slavery cannot exceed a certain low maximum!"[179]

There was also a non-economic dimension to Marx's increasing misery of the proletariat. The dialectical conception of man unfolding his potentialities in the process of working—"the creation of man by human labour"[180]—underlies many Marxian discussions of history and of a future communist society.[181] Capitalism, however, produces a division of labor that thwarts such development. It "attacks the individual at the very roots of his life,"[182] converting the worker into "a crippled monstrosity" by developing his manual dexterity in a narrow detail "at the expense of a world of productive capabilities and instincts; just as in the States of La Plata they butcher a whole beast for the sake of his hide or his tallow."[183] This must grow worse over time under capitalism because the methods which increase productivity also "mutilate the labourer into a fragment of a man" and "estrange from him the intellectual potentialities of the labour-process in the same proportion as science is incorporated in it as an independent power."[184] It was supremely important to Marx—"a question of life and death"—that the worker under capitalism, "crippled by life-long repetition of one and the same trivial operation, and thus reduced to a mere fragment of a man" be allowed to become a "fully developed individual . . . to whom the different social functions he performs, are but so many modes of giving free scope to his own natural and acquired powers."[185] This would not happen under capitalism where, "in proportion as capital accumulates, the lot of the labourer, be his payment high or low, must grow worse."[186]

It has been claimed that the increasing misery of the proletariat and the falling rate of profit are mutually incompatible, since the relative shares of property income and of wage income cannot simultaneously decline.[187] But both tendencies are based on an increasing mechanization over time, a rising proportion of "constant capital" to "variable capital," and with it an increased share of gross output going to replace depreciation of a growing stock of physical capital. Marx said: "If a falling rate of profit goes hand in hand with an increase in the mass of profits, as we have shown, then a larger portion of the annual product of labor is appropriated by the capitalist under the name of capital (as a substitute for consumed capital) and a relatively smaller portion under the name of profit."[188] In short, wages may take a smaller share of output, and at the same time *net* profits can be a lower percentage on a growing investment. Again, Marx's theories must be interpreted in his own terms, not in terms of the models which modern economists supply to analyze a "Marxian" economics of their own concoction.

SUMMARY

Marx's conception of "value" continued a pattern of dialectical thinking seen in many other areas of Marxian doctrine. The "law of value" was a principle of resource allocation or the transfer of "socially necessary labor" (value) from one sector of the economy to another—a necessity that was at any given point accidental in a capitalist economy. The conception was dialectical in another sense as well—that value was an underlying "essence" only imperfectly represented by the tangible "appearance" of price or exchange-value. The two concepts belonged on different levels of analysis, and *Capital* proceeded deliberately and laboriously from one level to another through its three large volumes.

Value as defined by Marx cannot equal price, because goods produced by varying combinations of capital and labor cannot exchange in proportion to their respective labor if profit rates are equalized by competition. This point was made by Marx himself, both in developing his own analysis and in criticizing Ricardo's theory of value. It was also the key point in refutations of Marxian value, when misconceived as a theory of prices.

Marx and Engels were especially explicit and vehement in opposing any notion that labor value should become the basis of prices or income distribution under socialism. Even the approximate relationship between price and value under capitalism was the result of a competitive economic process that allocated resources. To assign prices by fiat under socialism was to lose the whole necessary allocational process.

The Marxian concept of "surplus value" expressed and

attempted to quantify the exploitation of man by man. Marx did not attempt to deny that machinery and other invested resources contributed to production. His analysis was in terms of people rather than things. The inanimate equipment used in production was seen within this framework as contributions of past labor. The purpose of the concept of "surplus value" was not, however, simply to call capitalism immoral like earlier socialists, but to trace certain tendencies and their implications.

The tendency of the falling rate of profit called forth an increasing rate of surplus value. Insofar as workers were presumed to view their relative economic position as crucial, as Marx did, this would promote resentment and eventually revolution. The Marxian doctrine of the increasing misery of the proletariat included not only surplus value as such, but also the stultifying effect of routine work as science and technology took over thought and judgment—again, in the interest of increasing surplus value.

Marxian economic analysis was not a separate activity, independent of his other intellectual and revolutionary efforts. Its framework and mode of discussion were given by dialectical thinking, and its conclusions about capitalism were part of a more general analysis of that system's inner tensions and how they would lead to its ending in revolution. Marxian economic theory thus dovetailed with the Marxian theory of history and with Marxian political theory.

Chapter 8
POLITICAL SYSTEMS AND REVOLUTION

For Marx and Engels, the state—*any* state—was an organ of coercion, whether its authority for coercion was derived democratically or otherwise.[1] In a class-based society, the state is an organ for maintaining the prevailing conditions that make possible a given class's dominance. In a capitalist society, the state is simply "a committee for managing the common affairs of the whole bourgeoisie," according to the *Communist Manifesto.*[2] This does not imply a special interest conspiracy theory of the state, for the state in Marxian theory supports the general *conditions* of capitalism[3]—and this may, in fact, require cracking down on particular capitalists. The capitalist state, in Engels' words, "is only the organisation with which bourgeois society provides itself in order to maintain the general external conditions of the capitalist mode of production against encroachments either by the workers or by individual capitalists."[4] Engels cited state action against

143

businesses, adding: "No nation will put up with production conducted by trusts, with so bare-faced an exploitation of the community by a small band of dividend-mongers."[5]

DEMOCRACY AND FREEDOM

Epigrammatic statements that "the state is nothing but a machine for the oppression of one class by another"[6] or that democratic capitalism is merely a matter of "deciding once in three or six years which member of the ruling class was to misrepresent the people in parliament"[7] readily suggest that democracy is an utter fraud. However, in between epigrams, Marx and Engels treated democratic government as a serious and important phenomenon, under both capitalism and socialism—that is, both before and after revolution.

To the French workers in 1870, on the eve of the uprising that produced the Paris Commune, Marx advised against an uprising as a "desperate folly" and urged instead: "Let them calmly and resolutely improve the opportunities of Republican liberty."[8] He closed with the motto: *"Vive la République."* A quarter of a century later, Engels wrote in a similar vein that "the government came to be much more afraid of the legal than of the illegal actions of the workers' party, of the results of election than those of rebellion."[9] In Britain, according to Marx, "the gradually surging revolt of the working class compelled Parliament to shorten compulsorily the hours of labour."[10] In short, democracy was far from a meaningless sham.

Democracy was seen as a necessary, but not a sufficient, condition for freedom. Marx and Engels denounced what they called the confusion of "political emancipation with human emancipation."[11] Freedom for them meant not merely the theoretical right to do something, but with it also the actual means.[12] Thus real freedom requires "quite palpable material conditions."[13] This democracy alone

144

does not provide. Moreover, freedom of institutions was not freedom of individuals, according to Marx and Engels, although often confused with it:

> Indeed, the individual considers as his *own* freedom the movement, no longer curbed or fettered by a common tie or by man, the movement of his alienated life elements, like property, industry, religion, etc.; in reality, this is the perfection of his slavery and his inhumanity.[14]

Purely formal freedom was repeatedly downgraded by Marx. The worker works for the capitalist freely in the sense that he "agrees" to do so, but for Marx this means only that he "is compelled by social conditions"[15] rather than by force. The Marxian view of conventional democratic freedom was further obscured by Marx's use of the phrase "dictatorship of the proletariat," and by modern tendencies to interpret this in the light of such post-Marx phenomena as the Soviet Union and its eastern European and Asian counterparts. But here as elsewhere, reading modern developments back into history is not the way to accurate interpretation.

The *Communist Manifesto* described "the first step in the revolution" as being "to raise the proletariat to the position of ruling class, to win the battle of democracy."[16] In a preliminary draft for the *Manifesto,* Engels declared that a communist revolution "will inaugurate a *democratic constitution* and thereby, directly or indirectly, the political rule of the proletariat."[17] The use of the phrase "dictatorship of the proletariat"—*in Marx's sense*—is little more than a paraphrase of these statements.

> Between capitalists and communist society lies the period of the revolutionary transformation of the one into the other. There corresponds to this also a political transition

145

period in which the state can be nothing but the *revolutionary dictatorship of the proletariat.* [18]

In his correspondence, Marx asserted that "the class struggle necessarily leads to the *dictatorship of the proletariat,*" which in turn represents a "transition" to a classless society.[19] How is this compatible with "winning the battle of democracy," as mentioned in the *Communist Manifesto?* Because "the democratic republic," as Engels explained, is "the specific form of the dictatorship of the proletariat."[20] Just as in a capitalist state "wealth exercises its power indirectly, but all the more surely,"[21] so in a workers' state the numerical superiority of the proletariat turns democracy in form to class dictatorship in substance. Marx's contemporary, John Stuart Mill, agonized over precisely this point.[22] The democratic republic under capitalism becomes the arena in which workers struggle to wrest political control from the capitalists. Once this is accomplished, then under socialism it is the workers' state that exists as long as any state is necessary—i.e., until the "withering away of the state." In his introduction to Marx's book *The Civil War in France,* which describes the Paris Commune, Engels said:

> . . . do you want to know what this dictatorship looks like? Look at the Paris Commune. That was the dictatorship of the proletariat.[23]

What matters in this context is not the actual, historical Paris Commune, but the Paris Commune as seen by Marx. The features he praised in it exemplify the compatibility—indeed, congruence—between a free democratic society and the dictatorship of the proletariat as he conceived it. The Paris Commune, as depicted by Marx in *The Civil War in France,* featured:

146

POLITICAL SYSTEMS AND REVOLUTION

1. UNIVERSAL SUFFRAGE: "The Commune was formed of the municipal councillors, chosen by universal suffrage in the various wards of the town responsible and revocable at short terms."[24] According to Marx, "nothing could be more foreign to the spirit of the Commune than to supersede universal suffrage by hierarchic investiture."[25]

2. AN OPEN SOCIETY: According to Marx, "the Commune did not pretend to infallibility, the invariable attribute of all governments of the old stamp. It published its doings and sayings, it initiated the public into all its shortcomings."[26]

3. FREEDOM OF RELIGION AND SEPARATION OF CHURCH AND STATE: According to Marx, "the pay of the priest, instead of being extorted by the taxgatherer, should only depend upon the spontaneous action of the parishioners' religious instincts."[27]

4. A NON-MILITARISTIC VIEWPOINT: ". . . to broadly mark the new era of history it was conscious of initiating . . . the Commune tore down that colossal symbol of martial glory, the Vendome Column."[28]

According to Marx, the social legislation of the Commune "could but betoken the tendency of a government of the people by the people."[29] Such was the dictatorship of the proletariat, as initially conceived by Marx, in contrast to the meaning it has acquired in the twentieth century.

Putting Marx in his own historical context is necessary to understand his writings on democracy and on coercion. Because Marx's writings were mainly polemical, his differences with contemporaries largely determined the space, the content, and the emphasis of much that he wrote. Marx's chief opponents were contemporary supporters of capitalism, who were also generally supporters of free democratic government. Revolutionaries do not emphasize their points of agreement with the enemy, so it is understandable that Marx usually had little to say about free democratic government. Instead he tended to skirt what has been aptly called an "inconveniently large expanse of common ground."[30]

Within the radical movement of his time, Marx's chief opponents were the anarchists, and against them Marx and Engels had to emphasize the necessity for authority or coercion—that is, for *some* form of government, however democratic. Indeed, Engels argued the need for authority and subordination in industry—an obvious point to non-anarchists but one that had to be made when opposing extreme anarchists who considered voluntarism essential. Engels pointed out that no train could run nor a ship sail the high seas without authority being exercised on board.[31] He said:

> If the autonomists confined themselves to saying that the social organization of the future would restrict authority solely to the limits within which the conditions of production render it inevitable, we could understand each other; but they are blind to all facts that make the thing necessary and they passionately fight the word.[32]

Politically, Engels was defending the "authority of the majority over the minority"[33]—that is, democracy. But statements in defense of authority against anarchy were later used by critics to claim that "an authoritarian principle" was implicit in Marxian philosophy,[34] and by Lenin and other twentieth-century Marxists to defend undemocratic repression.

Proletarian revolution might lead to a more democratic state, but it would not change the essential nature of the state as an organ of repression. Only at a still later stage of development would there emerge sufficient spirit of voluntary cooperation to permit a dwindling role for political power and ultimately its extinction. This hoped-for and eventual end to the state was part of the socialist tradition long before Marx and Engels. Their role was to try to show the preconditions, without which it was a purely utopian dream. Referring to St. Simon's writings of the early nineteenth century, Engels said:

> Yet what is here already very plainly expressed is the idea of the future conversion of political rule over men into an administration of things and a direction of processes of production—that is to say, the "abolition of the state", about which recently there has been so much noise.[35]

Engels' impatience with the notion of *abolishing* the state reflects a different vision, in which it is not an act of will that ends the state, but a set of social conditions that steadily erodes its existence:

> As soon as there is no longer any class of society to be held in subjection; as soon as, along with class domination and the struggle for individual existence based on the former anarchy of production, the collisions and excesses arising from these have also been abolished, there is nothing more to be repressed which would make a special repressive force, a state, necessary. . . . The interference of the state power in social relations becomes superfluous in one sphere after another, and then ceases of itself. The government of persons is replaced by the administration of things and the direction of the processes of production. The state is not "abolished", it *withers away.* [36]

Engels had difficulty with the contemporary socialist slogan of a "free people's state,"[37] which was ultimately a contradiction in terms. For "so long as the proletariat still *uses* the state, it does not use it in the interest of freedom but in order to hold down its adversaries, and as soon as it becomes possible to speak of freedom the state as such ceases to exist."[38] Again, this had nothing to do with whether or not a state was democratic or had civil liberties

149

—however important those issues have become in later discussions of twentieth-century Communism. In Marx's and Engels' time, the issue was whether one was talking about a state or a voluntary association:

> All socialists are agreed that the political state, and with it political authority, will disappear as a result of the coming social revolution, that is, that public functions will lose their political character and be transformed into the simple administrative functions of watching over the true interests of society. But the anti-authoritarians demand that the authoritarian political state be abolished at one stroke, even before the social conditions that gave birth to it have been destroyed. They demand that the first act of the social revolution shall be the abolition of authority. Have these gentlemen ever seen a revolution? A revolution is certainly the most authoritarian thing there is; it is the act whereby one part of the population imposes its will upon the other part by means of rifles, bayonets, and cannon—authoritarian means if such there be at all; and if the victorious party does not want to have fought in vain, it must maintain this rule by means of the terror which its arms inspire in the reactionaries.[39]

Although Marxian discussions of the state were almost all the work of Engels, it must be noted that (1) much of the discussion took place in *Anti-Duhring,* which was read in its entirety to Marx, who also contributed to it, and (2) what was said by Engels in no way contradicted what was said by Marx in the latter's *Critique of the Gotha Programme* or elsewhere. This has not, however, prevented some modern critics from making Engels responsible for a lack of democracy and civil liberties in the Soviet Union[40]—a country which never possessed such things as the Russian Empire under the czars or even before Marx and Engels were born.

In reality, Marx's and Engels' discussions of Russia and the United States provide further evidence of their commitment to the principle of democratic freedom. Marx in 1879 wrote in a letter of the "antitheses" between the two countries that made it "impossible to find any real analogies between the United States and Russia." One difference was that in America "the masses are quicker, and have greater political means in their hands." Marx contrasted the Russians as "barbarians who are fit by nature to be used for anything" to Americans as a "civilized people who apply themselves to everything."[41] Marx was surprised to find *Capital* selling in Russia[42]—the censors permitted it because it seemed unlikely to be comprehensible to the masses[43]—but cautioned against reading any deep significance into its publication there.[44] Russia was not where he looked for his doctrines' first triumph.

REVOLUTION

Engels declared that "the abolition of capital is in itself the social revolution"[45]—that the revolution consisted of a fundamental social transformation, and not the methods used to achieve it. But when Marx and Engels began writing in the 1840s, voting rights for the masses were so rare that a revolution in the sense of a radical transformation and in the sense of an armed uprising were virtually synonymous. With the passage of time and the spread of the franchise, the possibility of a peaceful revolution began to emerge. Near the end of his life, Engels wrote that "the bourgeoisie and the government came to be more afraid of the legal than of the illegal action of the workers' party, of the results of elections than of those of rebellion."[46] Moreover, as political opportunities for revolution had increased, so military opportunities had declined:

> Let us have no illusions about it: a real victory of an insurrection over the military in street fighting, a victory as between two armies, is one of the rarest exceptions.[47]

151

MARXISM

Therefore armed conflict was more likely to be initiated by the capitalist government than by the workers:

> The irony of world history turns everything upside down. We, the "revolutionists", the "over-throwers",—we are thriving far better on legal methods than on illegal methods and overthrow. The parties of Order, as they call themselves, are perishing under the legal conditions created by themselves. . . . And if *we* are not so crazy as to let ourselves be driven to street fighting in order to please them, then in the end there is nothing left for them to do but themselves break through this fatal legality.[48]

Marx wrote in a similar vein nearly half a century earlier, in *The Class Struggles in France:* "The proletariat did not allow itself to be provoked to *revolt,* because it was on the verge of making a *revolution.*"[49]

Violence was never renounced as an instrument of revolution. It was simply not the defining characteristic of revolution. Engels declared that "no party has renounced the right to armed resistance, *in certain circumstances,* without lying."[50] Even when he depicted Marx as a believer in the possibility of a peaceful revolution in democratic nations, that "the inevitable social revolution might be effected by entirely peaceful and legal means," Engels declared that Marx expected violence from the opponents of this peaceful and legal revolution.[51] Even so, Marx expected the proletarian revolution to involve *less* violence than the revolutions that historically gave rise to capitalism:

> The transformation of scattered capitalist property, arising from the division of labour, into capitalist private property is, naturally, a process, incomparably more protracted, violent, and difficult, than the transformation of capitalistic private property, already practically resting on socialised production, into socialised property. In the former case, we

152

had the expropriation of the mass of the people by a few usurpers; in the latter, we have the expropriation of a few usurpers by the mass of the people.[52]

Parliamentary democracy under capitalism was itself a force drawing the masses into the political arena and into political struggle. Marx said:

The parliamentary regime lives by discussion; how shall it forbid discussion? Every interest, every social institution, is here transformed into general ideas, debated as ideas; how shall any interest, any institution, sustain itself above thought and impose itself as an article of faith? The struggle of the orators on the platform evokes the struggle of the scribblers of the press; the debating club in parliament is necessarily supplemented by debating clubs in the salons and the pothouses; the representatives, who constantly appeal to public opinion, give public opinion the right to speak its real mind in petitions. The parliamentary regime leaves everything to the decision of majorities; how shall the great majorities outside parliament not want to decide? When you play the fiddle at the top of the state, what else is to be expected but that those down below dance?[53]

While the *Communist Manifesto* urged all workingmen to unite, and Marx and Engels devoted great amounts of time and energy to promote workers' revolutionary movements, Marx saw a fundamental "difference between a secret political society and a genuine workers' organization."[54] Engels said that the Communist League (for which he and Marx wrote the *Manifesto*) had been "thoroughly democratic, with elective and removable boards." He added: "This alone barred all hankering after conspiracy, which requires dictatorship."[55] This approach contrasted sharply with that of a contemporary revolutionary, Louis Blanqui, and his followers. Engels described Blanquism as "the phantasy of

153

overturning an entire society through the action of a small conspiracy"—an idea that he thought possible only in "exceptional cases," like Russia.[56] His description of the Blanquists reads, in fact, like a preview of the Bolsheviks:

> Brought up in the school of conspiracy, and held together by the strict discipline which went with it, they started out from the viewpoint that a relatively small number of resolute, well-organized men would be able, at a given favourable moment, not only to seize the helm of state, but also by a display of great, ruthless energy, to maintain power until they succeeded in sweeping the mass of the people into the revolution and ranging them round the small band of leaders. This involved, above all, the strictest, dictatorial centralization of all power in the hands of the new revolutionary government.[57]

What Engels did not foresee was that such a revolution would be called Marxist, and that it would be read back into history as an expression of Marxian theory. Marxism envisioned a mass workers' movement, taking decades to develop and to acquire the political and economic sophistication necessary to become an effective dominant class. In Marx's words:

> . . . we say to the workers: "You have got to go through fifteen, twenty, fifty years of civil wars and national wars not merely in order to change your conditions but in order to change yourselves and become qualified for political power".[58]

Their own mistakes and the painful consequences of these mistakes were the means by which the proletariat was to acquire the necessary wisdom and transform itself into a class prepared to play an historic role.[59] Workers were neither paragons from the outset[60] nor a group to be educated from the top down by "leaders." According to Marx, the proletariat was to be driven to revolution by the logic of events and despite many hesitations.[61] Engels opposed the contrary approach of the putschists:

> The time of surprise attacks, of revolutions carried through by small conscious minorities at the head of unconscious masses, is past. Where it is a question of a complete transformation of the social organization, the masses themselves must also be in it, must themselves already have grasped what is at stake, what they are going in for with body and soul.[62]

The nature of the revolutionary movement was crucial for the kind of post-revolutionary society that would emerge. A revolution that was essentially the work of a small group of *putschists*—a "vanguard" of the proletariat—implied centralization of power and little prospect of freedom or democracy. But while Marx and Engels envisioned a mass workers' movement making a revolution—"a democratic revolution" in Engels' words—they were not prepared to abandon the idea of revolution where it could not be accomplished democratically. Writing to a German revolutionary in 1884, Engels said that "it cannot be expected that at the moment of crisis we shall already have the majority of the electorate and therefore of the nation behind us."[63] Indeed, "our sole adversary on the day of crisis and on the day after the crisis will be the *whole collective reaction which will group itself around pure democracy.*"[64]

While Engels was discussing specifically German conditions, it is questionable how punctilious he or Marx would have been about a revolution which they so long anticipated and from which they expected so much. Marx not only justified the taking of hostages by the Paris Commune,[65] but was also prepared in general to countenance and even encourage post-revolutionary terrorism:

> Far from opposing so-called excesses, instances of popular revenge against hated individuals or public buildings that are associated only with hateful recollections, such instances must not only be tolerated but the leadership of them taken in hand.[66]

Engels was not so bloodthirsty. In writing to Marx about post-revolutionary reigns of terror in general, he said:

> We think of this as the reign of people who inspire terror; on the contrary, it is the reign of people who are themselves terrified. Terror consists mostly of useless cruelties perpetrated by frightened people in order to reassure themselves.[67]

SOCIALISM AND COMMUNISM

The proletarian revolution—always conceived as international in scope,[68] in order to survive against foreign allies of the defeated classes—was to usher in the next phase of history, described by Marx and Engels as either socialism or communism. Both terms had been in existence before Marx or Engels appeared on the scene, and their specific meanings varied with the passing years.

In the later years of their lives, Marx and Engels used the terms "socialism" and "communism" interchangeably to refer to the post-revolutionary proletarian society in which the means of production would be collectively owned. But in the 1840s it would have been out of the question to have called the *Communist Manifesto* a *Socialist Manifesto,* according to Engels.[69] Yet by 1880 he could title an outline of Marxian theory *Socialism: Utopian and Scientific.* Socialism— the more general term[70]—included in the 1840s many whose views were fundamentally incompatible with Marx-ism—especially as regards the role of classes and class struggle.[71] Decades later, Engels regarded continental European socialism (as distinguished from the Fabian socialism of England) as "almost exclusively the theory heralded in the Manifesto."[72] Whether or not this was true, what is significant here was that Marxian socialism and Marxian communism were by then synonymous.

Early *social*-ism was a more or less vague opposition to *individual*-ism, as exemplified in classical economics and Benthamite utilitarianism. It did not necessarily imply collective ownership of the means of production, and it did not revolve around the concept of a class struggle or revolution. Communism, at that juncture, was a more radical doctrine, implying common ownership and, increasingly, working-class revolution. This was the tradition in which Marx and Engels placed themselves when they titled their work *The Communist Manifesto.* As the older version of socialism died out, and these Marxian themes became more general among socialists, the distinction between communism and socialism eroded away. Engels in 1887 could speak of "socialists of the school of Marx,"[73] whereas in the mid-1840s he and Marx declared communism to be the "contrary" of socialism.[74]

In a later generation, after the Bolshevik revolution of 1917, the terms communism and socialism once again designated very different doctrines, but this later differentiation by Lenin did not reflect the terminology of Marx and Engels. Lenin's "socialism" referred to the first stage of a Marxian society; communism to the later stage.[75] But when Marx and Engels distinguished the two terms in their early writings, socialism was a pre-Marxian doctrine.

Most modern socialist doctrines have taken on such a Marxian flavor, to one degree or another, that it is difficult today to understand what pre-Marxian socialism was like.

MARXISM

Pre-Marxian Socialism

Pre-Marxian socialism was based on a timeless moral critique of capitalism and a classless solution to its problems. Robert Owen, for example, wrote with the idea of making his principles "evident to all classes of the community,"[76] and advocated "a national system for the formation of character."[77] He called upon "the British government and the British Nation" to adopt his reforms,[78] by which the "landholder and capitalist would be benefitted . . . in the same degree with the labourer."[79] Owen rejected "the endless errors and mischiefs of class, sect, party, and of national antipathies,"[80] and wanted a social transformation "effected in peace and quietness, with the goodwill and hearty concurrence of all parties, and of every people."[81]

His message was not addressed to "the common people" but to "those whose minds have had all the benefit of the knowledge which society at present affords."[82] These were the educated individuals, and therefore from the wealthier and more influential classes, including members of Parliament, industrialists, nobility and royalty, both British and foreign.

Owen drew up in detail his plans for a better society,[83] following a practice made famous by Sir Thomas More's *Utopia,* and thus earning himself a place among those whom Marx and Engels designated as Utopian socialists. By contrast, Marx declared that "the construction of the future and its completion for all time is not our task."[84] His goal was not a static ideal, drawn from timeless moral principles, but a dynamic process leading from present tendencies to future developments. Communism, according to Marx, was "the necessary form and dynamic principle of the immediate future but not as such the goal of human development."[85] Engels was appalled by a contemporary socialist who conceived of socialist society "as a stable affair fixed once and for all."[86] According to Marx, the communist society of the future would continue to evolve, but *"social evolutions* will cease to be *political revolutions."*[87]

The dominance of the earlier, pre-Marxian socialism and communism is perhaps best illustrated by Engels' own signs of being under its influence in his first individually written book, *The Condition of the Working Class in 1844:*

> . . . Communism is a question of humanity and not of the workers alone. Besides, it does not occur to any Communist to wish to avenge himself upon individuals, or to believe that, in general, the single bourgeois can act otherwise, under existing circumstances, than he does act.[88]

Later, Engels said of this book:

> . . . great stress is laid on the dictum that Communism is not a mere party doctrine of the working-class, but a theory compassing the emancipation of society at large, including the capitalist class, from its present narrow conditions. This is true enough in the abstract, but absolutely useless, and sometimes worse, in practice. So long as the wealthy classes not only do not feel the want of any emancipation, but strenuously oppose the self-emancipation of the working-class, so long the social revolution will have to be prepared and fought out by the working-class alone.[89]

The original Utopian socialists—Owen, Fourier, St. Simon—were historically justified in the Marxian view because capitalism was in their time "very incompletely developed" and the proletariat "quite incapable of independent action."[90] Thus it was understandable that the Utopian socialists did not step forth as spokesmen for a class but for "the whole of suffering humanity,"[91] that they did not attempt "to emancipate a particular class to begin with, but all humanity at once"—and in the timeless name of "reason and eternal justice."[92] The Utopian approach dealt not with historic tendencies but with individual and accidental feats of the mind. As Engels characterized the Utopian vision:

> If pure reason and justice have not hitherto ruled the world, this has been the case only because men have not rightly understood them. What was wanted was the individual man of genius, who has now arisen and who understands the truth. That he has now arisen, that the truth has now been clearly understood, is not an inevitable event, following of necessity in the chain of historical development, but a mere happy accident. He might just as well have been born five hundred years earlier, and might then have spared humanity five hundred years of error, strife, and suffering.[93]

By contrast, the Marxian theory of history was seen as itself a product of historical development, that "the time was ripe for it and that indeed it *had* to be discovered."[94] Once history was seen in the framework of dialectical materialism, "socialism was no longer an accidental discovery of this or that ingenious brain," but a conclusion derived as the necessary outcome of the class struggle as already manifested. The task of socialism "was no longer to manufacture a system of society as perfect as possible, but to examine the historico-economic succession of events from which these classes and their antagonism had of necessity sprung, and to discover in the economic conditions thus created the means of ending the conflict."[95]

Marxian "Scientific" Socialism
Marxian socialism differed from other elements of the socialist tradition in specific tenets as well as in its general

framework. Some vague socialist notions, such as a "fair" distribution of income, were rejected outright.[96] So was the idea that the worker should receive the "full product" of his labor. Marx pointed out deductions inherent in the need for the maintenance of equipment, society, and social services, even in the absence of capitalism.[97] Marx likewise had little sympathy for the socialist idea of redistributing the total wealth of society, for this "would certainly not assure a high degree of comfort to the individual participants."[98] The notion that society should fix prices according to labor costs was another socialist tradition that Marx and Engels opposed throughout their careers.[99]

As already noted, the traditional idea of the disappearance of the state was discussed by Marx and Engels in terms of its preconditions. So too was the pre-Marxian communist slogan concerning income distribution: "From each according to his abilities, to each according to his needs." Marx questioned the viability of such a principle in a communist society "just as it *emerges* from capitalist society" and is "still stamped with the birthmarks of the old society" in its moral, economic, and intellectual framework.[100] During "the first phase of communist society," people must be paid according to their labor contributions.[101] Only after people themselves change and see work as a major *desideratum* in itself can the old traditional communist doctrine become a reality. Only then, according to Marx, "can the narrow horizon of bourgeois right be crossed in its entirety and society inscribe on its banners: 'From each according to his ability, to each according to his needs!' "[102]

The extreme reluctance of Marx and Engels to follow in the footsteps of the Utopian socialists left the specific features of Marxian communism largely undefined, except for some indications of what would *not* be present. Marx refused to prepare "recipes" for "the cookshops of the future."[103] One consequence of this was that whatever socialist or communist state might historically emerge could plausibly call itself "Marxian," even if it deviated widely from the letter or spirit of Marxism.

SUMMARY

The Marxian view of the state as an inherently coercive institution applied to democratic as well as authoritarian states, and to socialist as well as capitalist states. Democracy was considered important as a necessary, but not a sufficient, condition for freedom. Yet even the democratic state was expected eventually to wither away in the post-revolutionary era.

To say that a state was a capitalist state was to say that it maintained the general conditions necessary for a capitalist society—not that its political leaders did the bidding of individual capitalists. They might well take punitive action against individual capitalists, whenever their actions threatened capitalism as a system, or outraged public opinion. The capitalist class was the ruling class, according to the Marxian view, in that its imperatives were also the imperatives of those with political power. In much the same way, Marx and Engels envisioned a workers' state as responsive to the general necessities of maintaining socialism or communism, and so constituting a "dictatorship of the proletariat." Yet the sense in which they applied the term did not preclude democracy and freedom, nor did their projected dictatorship resemble twentieth-century dictatorships.

Revolution, for Marx and Engels, meant the historic transformation of one kind of society into another. With the growth of voting during their lives, it became increasingly possible in a number of countries to conceive of revolutionary change through the ballot box, though the particular means to be used was a pragmatic question. While peaceful change was preferred, violence was never renounced.

POLITICAL SYSTEMS AND REVOLUTION

The nature of a revolutionary movement was seen by Marx and Engels as crucial for the kind of post-revolutionary society that could be expected to emerge. A mass movement of workers meant that a democratic regime was feasible after the overthrow of bourgeois rule. A small conspiracy of professional revolutionaries implied a dictatorial post-revolutionary regime.

The principles espoused by Marx and Engels may be compared with the principles and practices of modern states ruling in their name. These principles may also be compared with what Marx and Engels actually did in the political struggles of their own time.

Chapter 9

MARX
THE
MAN

After a century of myths and counter-myths, of deification and satanizing, it is hard to realize that behind all the portraits and caricatures to be seen on printed pages and on banners, there really was a flesh-and-blood human being named Karl Marx. He was born in the little German town of Trier in the Rhineland in 1818, in a three-story townhouse in a fashionable part of town. A baron lived nearby,[1] and his four-year-old daughter was destined to become Karl Marx's wife. The people who signed as witnesses on Karl Marx's birth certificate were prominent citizens. The Marxes, like their neighbors and friends, had servants, property, education, and local prominence. Unlike most of their neighbors and friends, however, both Heinrich Marx and his wife Henrietta were descended from a long line of rabbis. Indeed, the town's chief rabbi was his brother, but they were brothers estranged from each other, since Heinrich Marx had abandoned the faith of his fathers.[2] Karl Marx was baptized a

164

Lutheran, and throughout his life he spoke of Jews in the third person—and seldom complimentarily.

Marx was the third child born in his family, the second to survive, and the oldest boy. Younger brothers and sisters were born annually for the next four years, and then two more at two-year intervals.[3] The father was a prosperous lawyer, who also owned vineyards, as well as houses whose rents supplemented his income. He was a man of wide culture and political liberalism. His son idolized him, and in later years spoke of him often to his own children, though they had never seen him—his death having occurred decades before. Marx's mother was Dutch and spoke German with a heavy Dutch accent. She was a devoted housewife, not a woman of learning, and though her son loved her in childhood, they were soon estranged in his early adulthood. When she died, many years later, Marx expressed not the slightest sorrow.[4]

YOUTH

Karl Marx grew up a brilliant, spoiled child, who bullied his younger sisters and taunted his schoolmates with sarcastic witticisms—in addition to entertaining both with imaginative stories. He had a swarthy complexion that in later years earned him the nickname "The Moor"—a name used far more often in his inner circle (including his children) than was his real name. His neighbor, Baron von Westphalen, took a great interest in Marx as a youth, and the learned baron would often take long walks with him discussing Homer, Shakespeare, Voltaire, or other great writers in any of a number of languages that the baron spoke.[5]

As a young man, Karl Marx attended the University of Bonn for one year. There he was an enthusiastic student, but also an enthusiastic drinker, and took part in rowdiness and at least one duel.[6] His father transferred him to the University of Berlin, a larger and more serious institution. But the self-indulgent, bohemian and spendthrift habits that Marx had exhibited at Bonn continued at Berlin, where he was sued several times for non-payment of debts.[7] His father's letters show growing recriminations directed not only at his son's prodigious capacity to waste money—a talent he never lost throughout his life—but also at a more disturbing personal characteristic, egomania.[8] One of Marx's many poems of this period says:

> Then I will wander godlike and victorious
> Through the ruins of the world
> And, giving my words an active force,
> I will feel equal to the creator.[9]

The themes of destruction, corruption, and savagery run through Marx's poems of this era,[10] two of which were published in a small literary magazine of the time under the title "Savage Songs."[11] There was nothing political about these writings. Marx had not yet turned his attention in that direction. He was simply, as one biographer said, "a man with a peculiar faculty for relishing disaster."[12] A contemporary description of Marx as a student depicts the same demonic personality—again, not yet in a political context:

> But who advances here full of impetuosity?
> It is a dark form from Trier, an unleashed monster,
> With self-assured step he hammers the ground with his heels
> And raises his arms in all fury to heaven
> As though he wished to seize the celestial vault and lower it to
>   earth.
> In rage he continually deals with his redoubtable fist,
> As if a thousand devils were gripping his hair.[13]

In short, Marx's angry apocalyptic visions existed before he discovered capitalism as the focus of such visions.

MARX THE MAN

Marx entered the University of Berlin a few years after the death of its most famous professor—G.W.F. Hegel, whose posthumous influence was even greater than during his lifetime.[14] Marx began to associate with a group called the Young Hegelians, who were preoccupied with philosophy in general and religion in particular—or rather, with atheism, for they were radical critics of Christianity. Marx's formal studies languished; he took only two courses in his last three years at the University of Berlin.[15] Marx became a "bohemian student, who merely regarded the university as his camping ground"[16] and he was largely self-taught.[17] The death of his father in 1838, and his long engagement to Jenny von Westphalen eventually made it necessary that he prepare to bring his studies to a close. Although he had studied at the University of Berlin, he applied for a doctorate at the University of Jena—an easier institution, noted as a diploma mill.[18] His doctoral dissertation was on two ancient materialist philosophers, Democritus and Epicurus.

EARLY CAREER

Searching aimlessly for a career, Marx drifted into journalism and became editor of the *Rheinische Zeitung,* a liberal newspaper, reflecting Marx's own political views at that time, as well as that of the Rhineland middle class in general. Under the Prussian repression of that era, liberalism was an embattled and endangered creed, and Marx made the newspaper more controversial and more widely read than before.

His running of the paper was characterized by a contemporary as "a dictatorship of Marx"[19]—as so many groups with which he was affiliated would be throughout his lifetime. Another contemporary described him as "domineering, impetuous, passionate, full of boundless self-confidence."[20] Marx engaged in a running battle of wits with the government's censors,[21] and—ironically—tried to restrain some of the more radical of the newspaper's writers.[22] Among these was another young man from an affluent background named Moses Hess, a communist who eventually converted still another such offspring of wealth to communism—Friedrich Engels.[23] Marx, however, purged Hess from the newspaper for his "smuggling into the newspaper of communist and socialist dogmas disguised as theatrical criticism."[24] Only after Marx finally resigned as editor, to spare the paper from being banned, did he begin the studies that would eventually lead him to communism.

During the same period in the early 1840s Marx had a decisive break with his family. Now that his father was dead, and the estate had to suffice for eight people to live on, Frau Marx was not inclined to continue indefinitely sending money to her eldest son, now fully grown and holding a doctoral degree. Marx had continued his already long-standing practice of running up bills that he could not pay, and was outraged that his mother cut off his remaining small allowance. As he put it in a letter to a friend: "Although they are quite rich, my family has placed difficulties in my way which have temporarily placed me in an embarrassing situation."[25] Such temporary embarrassments were to become a permanent feature of Marx's life over the next four decades. Nevertheless, he eventually persuaded the aristocratic von Westphalens to let him marry their daughter—now 29 years old—who had waited faithfully for him for seven years.

It was not a marriage whose prospects were viewed with favor by either family. There was a church wedding in 1843, but most of her family and all of his family stayed away. However, the bride's mother paid for the honeymoon and in addition turned over to the couple a small legacy which she had received. This legacy was held in the form of coins in a strong box—which Marx and his bride then left open in their hotel rooms, inviting any visitors to take whatever they might need. It was empty before they returned to her home,[26] where they lived with her mother for several months.

In October 1843, Marx and his wife—now pregnant—moved to Paris, where he was hired to contribute to a publishing venture—a bilingual journal for German and French readers. Only one issue ever appeared. Marx and the editor quarreled and broke up, leaving Marx without funds in a foreign land. A collection was hastily taken up by friends in Cologne, and the couple was rescued—as they would be again and again throughout their lives. Here in Paris Marx began the studies that led him to communism. He also began to meet other radical figures of the time—including the radical poet Heinrich Heine, Russian anarchist Mikhail Bakunin, and the French radical writer Pierre Joseph Proudhon. Heine, though at first a great friend of the Marxes, was eventually alienated by Karl Marx's arrogance and dogmatism.[27] In later years, Heine described the Paris radicals—including Marx—as a "crowd of godless, self-appointed gods."[28] Among these radicals was a young German whom Marx had met briefly before—Friedrich Engels.

COLLABORATION WITH ENGELS

Engels, two years younger than Marx, came from an even wealthier family, which owned half-interest in a factory in Germany and half-interest in another factory in England.[29] His father had never been as indulgent as Marx's father, and Engels never attended a university, but he was well read and by middle age could read and write nearly two dozen languages.[30] Engels was sent away at seventeen to get on-the-job training in the family business in Bremen. Here he was "not overworked"—he was, after all, an owner's son—and was known to have beer, cigars, poems, and correspondence with him, and to take a leisurely lunch and a nap afterwards in a hammock.[31] He also found time to study Hegel. Engels eventually became a member of the Young Hegelians, and in 1842 had his first brief meeting with the editor of the *Rheinische Zeitung,* Karl Marx. Their first meeting was cool, for Marx viewed Engels at that point as just another member of the radical group whose literary contributions to the paper were causing him trouble with the censors.

From 1842 to 1844, Engels lived in Manchester, England, working in the family business there and observing the conditions of the working people in this industrial town —observations that led to his first book, *The Conditions of the Working Class in England in 1844.* When he passed through Paris on his way back to the Rhineland in 1844, he again met Marx—and this time, many days of discussion found them "in complete agreement on questions of theory"[32]— as they continued to be for the remaining decades of their lives. At this juncture, Engels was not only further advanced than Marx on the road to communism, but was also much better versed in economics. Although their first joint publication—*The Holy Family*—appeared a year later, there was at that point no suggestion of a continuing collaboration between them. The foreword to *The Holy Family* promised future writings from the pair—"each for himself, of course."[33] But in reality later events brought them together again in England, in a permanent alliance in which their ideas and words were so intermingled that it would be rash to say conclusively, a hundred years later, what was Marx's and what was Engels'. Even Marx's daughter, after his death, mistakenly published a collection of her father's newspaper articles that later turned out all to have been written by Engels.[34]

The most famous of their explicitly collaborative writings was of course *The Communist Manifesto.* Its genesis typified the pattern of Marxian political intrigue. A radical

170

organization in London called the League of the Just was in process of reorganization to become the Communist League, and it involved several people in the drawing up of its credo. One of these submitted his draft to Engels who confessed to Marx that *"just between ourselves* I played a hellish trick on Mosi"[35]—substituting the Marxian program for the draft entrusted to him. Engels realized the enormity of his betrayal, for he cautioned Marx to utter secrecy, "otherwise we shall be deposed and there will be a murderous scandal."[36] Thus Marx and Engels made themselves the voices of communism. Engels wrote up a document in question-and-answer format, but then decided that he did not like it. He turned his work over to Marx to re-do in some other format, and suggested the title, *The Communist Manifesto.* Slowly the document evolved, written mostly in the style of Marx, though reproducing some ideas from Engels' earlier draft. It was published in February 1848 as *The Manifesto of the Communist Party,* with no authors listed, as though it were the work of some major organization, rather than of a relative handful of radical refugees.

The members of the Communist League were overwhelmingly intellectuals and professionals, with a very few skilled craftsmen. Their average age was under thirty.[37] It had the same kind of social composition that would in later years characterize the so-called International Working Mens Association, and many other radical groups in which the youthful offspring of privilege called themselves the proletariat. When Engels was elected as delegate to the Communist League in 1847, in order to conceal what was in fact an unopposed election, in Engels' own words, "a working man was proposed for appearances sake, but those who proposed him voted for me."[38]

Ironically, the year 1848 was a year of revolutions, but revolutions which differed from that described in *The Com-*

munist Manifesto. The bourgeoisie and the proletariat were in revolutionary alliance against the autocratic European governments on the continent. During the upheavals that swept across Europe, Marx and Engels returned to Germany—Marx to edit a newspaper, the *Neue Rheinische Zeitung,* in his familiar dictatorial style.[39] Engels worked at first as his chief assistant, until he had to flee an order for his arrest for inciting to violence. Engels made his way through France to Switzerland, enjoying along the way "the sweetest grapes and loveliest of girls."[40] This continued Engels' long-lasting pattern of womanizing,[41] which included the wife of a fellow communist whose seduction he revealed to another communist "when in my cups."[42] He was particularly fond of French women, reporting to Marx in 1846 "some delicious encounters with *grisettes*"[43] and later observing:

> If I had an income of 5,000 fr. I would do nothing but work and amuse myself with women until I went to pieces. If there were no Frenchwomen, life wouldn't be worth living.[44]

In 1849, Engels returned to Germany, where the revolution was being suppressed, and took part in armed fighting against the government forces. An expulsion order was issued against Marx, who had to liquidate the newspaper with ruinous financial losses.[45] By the latter half of 1849 Marx and Engels had separately made their ways to England, where they were destined to spend the rest of their lives.

EXILES

The dream of returning to the continent in triumph, after revolutions there, continued to fascinate Marx and Engels. One scholar has counted more than forty anticipations of impending revolution in their letters and writings over the next thirty years—none of which materialized.[46] But as early as 1850, Marx and Engels had to begin making some preparations for a livelihood in England. Marx was then thirty-two, Engels thirty, and neither of them had ever been self-supporting. They had lived off allowances and gifts from their families (including Marx's wife's family), off small inheritances from relatives, the sale of belongings, borrowings, credit defaults, emergency collections among friends and colleagues, and a few scattered and meager earnings from their writings. Now most of these sources had dried up.

Both Marx and Engels were estranged from their families, who were as disappointed at their prolonged dependency as they were repelled by their doctrines. Still, as late as 1849, Marx's much-despised mother advanced him enough money from his future inheritance to enable him to live comfortably for years—though in fact it was all gone within one year, much of it spent to buy arms for abortive uprisings and to finance Marx's newspaper.[47] Engels' pious father, described by the younger Engels as "bigoted and despotic,"[48] nevertheless supported him financially.[49] At age thirty, Engels accepted his father's offer to work in the family business in Manchester.[50] This became the source of Engels' livelihood—and much of Marx's. The young Engels called it "forced labor"—a painfully ironic term in view of what that phrase was to come to mean in twentieth-century Communist societies. Engels complained, for example, that "I've now got to be at the office no later than 10 in the morning."[51]

The firm, in which Engels' father had half-interest, employed about 800 workers. Though Engels began on a modest level in the management, his position and his pay rose over the years until he was able to retire at age fifty with substantial funds for himself and at the same time provide a very generous annuity that relieved Marx of financial worry for the rest of his life. But before reaching that point, the financial position of Marx and his growing family was often dire and occasionally desperate.

In 1850 the Marx family moved into the slums of London, where they spent most of the next twenty years. During this time, it was often difficult for Marx to come up with the money to pay the rent, buy groceries or pay his bills. The family often dodged creditors, were evicted for nonpayment of rent, on some occasions had to live on bread and potatoes, frequently pawned their meager belongings, and had three children die amid the squalor—including one for whom there was no money for a burial until a gift was received for that purpose. Yet, despite the very real and very painful poverty in which Marx often found himself, his known sources of income were sufficient for a lower middle class family standard of living at that time, and was about three times the income of an unskilled worker.[52] A contemporary German exile with a similar income to Marx's boasted of eating "luscious beef-steak" regularly.[53]

Marx's only regular earnings were as a foreign correspondent for the *New York Tribune,* but Engels supplemented this even in the early years before his own finances were solid; and other gifts and inheritances added materially to Marx's resources. The problem was Marx's chronic inability to manage money, and especially his and his wife's tendency to splurge when large sums came in. Moreover, Marx spent at least £100 on a futile lawsuit against an obscure slanderer named Vogt—enough to support a family for months in those times[54]—and wasted still more money and time on a long-forgotten book of rebuttal called *Herr Vogt,* for which he was sued in court to collect the unpaid costs of publication.[55] In 1864, Marx received a number of inheritances that added up to ten times what he had been living on annually[56]—and yet he was still debt-ridden in 1868 when Engels came to his rescue by paying off Marx's debts and then giving him an annuity.

MARX THE MAN

Ironically, Marx's most important research and writing were done during these years of travail and heartbreak, and he produced little during the last dozen or so years of his life when he led a prosperous bourgeois existence. During the 1850s he buried himself in the reading room of the British Museum during the day, studying economics. Until late at night and into the wee hours of the morning he scribbled the voluminous manuscripts that represented several abortive attempts to write the book that eventually emerged as *Capital.* Engels wrote little during this period, when he was working as a capitalist in Manchester and underwriting Marx's efforts in the communist cause of overthrowing capitalism.

Physical ills dogged Marx increasingly with the passing years. His irregular sleeping habits, alcohol consumption, and lack of personal cleanliness or exercise may well have contributed to these, as his improvidence made his family prey to hunger, disease, and the deaths of three children in infancy and early childhood. But he blamed these tragedies —like most of his troubles—on other people. The death of his infant son he blamed on "bourgeois misery," which he apparently considered also the cause of the boils that covered his body, for he promised to make the bourgeoisie pay for them via his revolutionary writings.[57] Marx repeatedly denounced creditors who insisted on collecting what he owed them.[58] He even lost his temper at his wife for her bouts of tears in the midst of mounting tragedies.[59]

Even during the long years of poverty, the Marx household had a maid, Helene Demuth, better known by her nickname of Lenchen. She had been a servant of the elder Baroness von Westphalen, who in 1845 sent her as a present to her daughter, who was unprepared to take care of children or a household. Though the Marxes were seldom in a position to pay her, "dear, faithful Lenchen" remained in their service to their dying days—and then went to work for Engels. In her youth she passed up suitors and other opportunities for jobs to stay and serve the Marxes. In 1851, during the most desperate period of the Marx family, when Marx's wife was pregnant, Lenchen soon became pregnant too. Only a few friends knew of the child's birth, he was sent away to be raised by a working class family, and there was no father's name on the birth certificate. Marx's wife was told that Engels—a bachelor—was the father, but long after the death of Marx and his wife, it came out that in fact the father was Karl Marx. Engels confirmed it on his death bed to Marx's tearful daughter.[60] In his life he had taken the blame for Marx, in order to save his friend's marriage, but in death Engels was apparently not prepared to take the blame forever.

The child himself, Freddy Demuth, grew up with no relationship with Marx, and never visited his mother as long as the Marxes were alive. Only after their death, when Helene Demuth became Engels' housekeeper, did the boy begin visiting his mother—entering and leaving by the back door. He was saoficed first to Marx's convenience, then to Marx's image. His mother apparently loved him; when she died, she left everything to him.[61]

Marx's human relationships in general were self-centered, if not exploitative. When his wife gave birth to a child who died immediately, Marx briefly mentioned his own reactions in a letter to Engels, so totally ignoring the effect on his wife that Engels' reply reminded him that "you don't say how *she* is."[62] In 1851, at the age of thirty-three, Marx "wrote to my mother, threatening to draw bills on her and, in the event on nonpayment, going to Prussia and letting myself be locked up."[63] When his mother refused to be blackmailed this way, Marx complained of her "insolent" reply.[64] After his mother later died in 1863, Marx's letter to Engels was a model of brevity, wasting no sentiment on "the old woman" and focusing entirely on getting his inheritance immediately.[65] Nor was this the only occasion when death in the family was seen in purely economic terms. Earlier, in 1852, he referred to some "good news" —the illness of "my wife's indestructible uncle"—and added: "If that dog dies now I'll be out of trouble" financially.[66]

Because Marx wanted German socialist Ferdinand Lassalle to "find me some literary business in Germany" to supplement "my diminished income and increased expenditure,"[67] he cultivated him with flattery to his face and contempt behind his back. Marx referred to Lassalle's book on Hegel as an "exhibition of enormous erudition" when writing to Lassalle and as a "silly concoction" when writing to Engels.[68] Marx added that Lassalle was a "Jewish nigger,"[69] based on Marx's analysis of his appearance:

> It is now perfectly clear to me that, as testified also by his cranial formation and hair growth, he is descended from the negroes who joined Moses's exodus from egypt (unless his paternal mother or grandmother was crossed with a nigger). Well, this combination of Jewish and Germanic stock with the negroid basic substance is bound to yield a strange product. The fellow's importunity is also nigger-like.[70]

Engels likewise seized upon Lassalle's ancestry, called him "a true Jew"[71] and "From firth to latht the thtupid Yid."[72]

Crude and repulsive as Marx's and Engels' racial remarks to each other often were, there is no need to make them still worse by putting them in the same category as twentieth-century racism that has justified genocide.[73] Marx's much criticized essay, "On the Jewish Question,"[74] for example, contains clear statements of his distaste for what he considered to be Jewish cultural or social traits, but in the end it was a defense of Jews' right to full political equality, written as a reply to a contemporary who had claimed that Jews should be required to give up their religion before receiving equal civil status. Marx hoped that the characteristics he disliked in Jews would fade away with the disappearance of capitalism, thus leading to "abolishing the essence of Jewry"[75]—but hardly in the sense of Hitler and the Nazis. Similarly, despite his anti-Negro stereotypes, during the American Civil War he conducted propaganda for the North and for the emancipation of slaves.[76] Perhaps more indicative, he agreed to the marriage of his eldest daughter to a man known to have some Negro ancestry, after discouraging other suitors.[77] Likewise, Engels in 1851 expressed to a friend his hope that "the present persecution of Jews in Germany will spread no further."[78] Marx and Engels were, in short, inconsistent and privately crude, but hardly racial fanatics.

THE FIRST INTERNATIONAL

Along with *The Communist Manifesto* and *Capital,* the other milestone in Marx's career was his leadership of the First International—The International Working Mens Association. Marx's legendary fame today makes it difficult to realize that he was an obscure figure with no substantial following in the early 1860s, that his writings were largely ignored,[79] and that even a man as knowledgeable as John Stuart Mill could live for twenty years in the same city, writing on the same topics, in utter ignorance that someone named Karl Marx even existed.[80] The International Working Mens Association rescued him from that obscurity. As in the earlier case of the Communist League, Marx appeared on the scene just as an existing organization was in process of reorganizing, and seized the opportunity to maneuver his way to control. Initially, Marx was only one of a number of people on a committee charged with drafting a statement of purpose for the International in 1864. He had taken no active part in the organization before,[81] was only belatedly brought into the discussions and was mentioned last on the list of participants.[82] Yet Marx was able to get the group bogged down in interminable discussions, as a prelude to his *coup*. As he described it in a letter to Engels:

> In order to gain time I proposed that before we "edited" the preamble we should "discuss" the rules. This was done. It was an hour after midnight before the first of the 40 rules were agreed to. Cremer said *(and this was what I was aiming for)*: We have nothing to show the committee, which meets on October 25. We must postpone the meeting to November 1. But the sub-committee can get together on October 27 and attempt to reach a definite conclusion. This was agreed to, and the "documents" were "sent back" for my opinion.[83]

From here on, it was Marx's show. On a "pretext" (Marx's own word), "I altered the whole preamble, threw out the *declaration des principes* and finally replaced the 40 rules with ten."[84] He then maneuvered some Marxists into key positions in the new organization,[85] and by 1867 was writing to Engels of "this powerful machinery *in our hands*" and of his own influence "from behind the scenes."[86] The membership of the International was, however, never predominantly Marxist, and conflicting currents were always at work. Engels only *hoped* that the *next* International would become communist and "openly proclaim our principles."[87] Eventually, the commanding figure of the Russian revolutionary anarchist Mikhail Bakunin rose to challenge Marx for control of the International. Their struggle for control ultimately destroyed the organization. Marx managed to get Bakunin expelled and had the headquarters of the International transferred to the United States, where it would be safe from other European revolutionary challenges—even though he knew that would also mean its demise as well. It was a rule-or-ruin tactic that would appear again and again in later communist infiltrations of non-communist organizations.

TWILIGHT YEARS

In the decade that remained of his life after the destruction of the International, Marx published little. His financial worries were largely behind him, but illnesses plagued him and his wife. The completion of *Capital* was delayed not only by illness, but also by Marx's side excursions into other subjects—notably the history of Russia, which required him to learn the Russian language. Even Engels did not know that Marx had let the manuscripts of Volumes II and III of *Capital* sit untouched for years while he dallied with other matters.[88] When Engels discovered this after Marx's death, he said that "if I had been aware of this, I would not have let him rest day or night until everything had been finished and printed."[89] Engels had been vainly urging Marx since 1845 to finish his projected book on economics.[90] As it was, much of the last two decades of Engels' life were taken up trying to decipher and assemble the manuscripts for the remaining two volumes of *Capital.* Realizing the monumental task that this involved, and his own advancing age, Engels initiated the young Karl Kautsky into the mysteries of Marx's handwriting, enabling Kautsky eventually to assemble the remaining manuscripts into *Theories of Surplus Value,* a separate three-volume work originally intended by Marx as the final volume of *Capital.* Thus a work begun in the middle of the nineteenth century was not completely published until the end of the first decade of the twentieth century.

Marx once observed that all his earnings from *Capital* would not pay for the cigars he smoked while writing it. It took four years to sell one thousand copies.[91] And though translations began to appear with the passing years, Marx remained in his lifetime a little known figure outside the ranks of revolutionaries. His greatest notoriety came as a defender of the bloody activities of the Paris Commune of 1871. His book on the subject, *The Civil War in France,* sold far more copies than *The Communist Manifesto.*[92] Marx relished this public notoriety, though it also included death threats.

The Marx family, even after being relieved from dire poverty, had many rocky roads to travel. Marx's wife, a beauty in her youth, found herself with a pock-marked face as result of illness—in her words, "looking more like a kind of rhinoceros which has escaped from a zoo than a member of the Caucasian race."[93] She remained a nervous wreck and irritable with her children as a result of decades of strain, for which her pampered upbringing had not prepared her. While her mother's servant, Helene Demuth, had been a godsend to a young wife unable to take care of children, money, or a household, Lenchen's handling of these responsibilities may also have retarded or prevented Jenny Marx from maturing. Her immaturity was still evident long after she ceased to be young. At age fifty, she realized a lifetime ambition by giving a ball, complete with uniformed servants and hired musicians.[94] Even as a middle-aged woman and the wife of a revolutionary, she had visiting cards printed up identifying herself as "Baroness von Westphalen."[95] Nor were these the only vanities in which she and Marx indulged. They continued to give their daughters piano lessons, music and dancing lessons, even when this sometimes meant not paying the rent.[96]

Keeping up appearances was a major item in the Marxes' budget throughout their lives. During his worst years of financial desperation, Marx strove mightily and with pained embarrassment to prevent visitors from discovering his poverty (though Engels pointed out how futile and pointless this was[97])—even when this required his wife to "take everything that was not actually screwed down to the pawn shop"[98] to pay for entertaining them. During one of his worst financial crises Marx contemplated "the most extreme reduction of expenditure," which might include requiring him to "move into purely proletarian accomodation," and "get rid of the maids."[99]

The three Marx daughters all became involved with men unable to support them—two through marriage and one in a common-law relationship. All received money at one time or other from Engels—the eldest to pay overdue rent,[100] the middle daughter repeatedly for a variety of reasons,[101] and the youngest in a large inheritance which she did not live long to enjoy.[102]

Marx's relationship with his children and grandchildren, however, show his most happy and human side. He was a gentle and indulgent father, who amused his children with his own original fairy tales and picnicked and played with them with great relish.[103] The death of those who perished in childhood severely affected him for years afterwards.[104] Marx wrote in a letter:

> Bacon says that really important men have so many contacts with nature and the world, and have so much to interest them, that they easily get over their loss. I am not one of these important men. My child's death has shattered my heart and brain, and I feel the loss as keenly as on the first day.[105]

ASSESSMENTS

Marx with his children was a very different man from the Marx described by his adult contemporaries. When his father questioned whether his heart was as good as his head,[106] he raised a question that many others would continue to raise about Marx throughout his life. A fellow revolutionary said of Marx: "If his heart had matched his intellect, and if he possessed as much love as hate, I would have gone through fire for him," but *a most dangerous personal ambition has eaten away all the good in him"* (emphasis in the original).[107] Still another radical contemporary, Proudhon, wrote to Marx, "for God's sake, after we have abolished all the dogmatisms *a priori,* let us not of all things attempt in our turn to instill another kind of dogma into the people." He said:

> Let us have decent and sincere polemics. Let us give the world an example of learned and farsighted tolerance. But simply because we are at the head of the movement, let us not make ourselves the leader of a new intolerance, let us not posé as the apostle of a new religion—even though this religion be the religion of logic, the religion of reason.[108]

Carl Schurz, while still a youthful revolutionary in Germany (before his later fame as a liberal in the United States), met Marx and formed an opinion of him that accords with the impressions of many others:

> I have never seen a man whose bearing was so provoking and intolerable. To no opinion, which differed from his, he accorded the honor of even a condescending consideration. Everyone who contradicted him he treated with abject contempt; every argument that he did not like he answered either with biting scorn at the unfathomable ignorance that had prompted it, or with opprobrious aspersions upon the motives of him who had advanced it.[109]

Marx liked to glare at anyone who challenged his conclusions and say "I will annihilate you!" The radicals and revolutionaries whom Marx successively alienated over a period of forty years reads like a *Who's Who* of the nineteenth-century political left. Even the patient and long-suffering Engels came close to a break with Marx, whose curt and clumsy remarks on the death of Engels' common-law wife in 1863 wounded his friend. Engels wrote:

> All my friends, including philistine acquaintances, have shown me more sympathy and friendship on this occasion, which inevitably affected me quite closely, than I had a right to expect. You found the moment suitable for a demonstration of the superiority of your cool manner of thinking. So be it![110]

Marx's apology brought forgiveness[111] and the historic partnership continued.

The younger Marx of the 1840s presented a more humane vision in his writings, and has become something of a refuge for modern radicals disillusioned with the more blatantly severe later Marx, who seemed to presage Lenin and Stalin. Lighthearted humor also brightened some of these earlier writings[112] in a way seldom seen again in the later works of Marx and Engels. Yet it would be a mistake to ignore the authoritarian and terroristic elements that were as present in these earlier writings as in the later ones —and in Engels as well as Marx. Engels' first draft for *The Communist Manifesto* included compulsory labor,[113] a deliberate undermining of the family by ending the dependence "of the wife upon the husband and of the children upon the parents,"[114] and the erection of "common dwellings for communities of citizens" to replace family homes. Marx's *Neue Rheinische Zeitung* declared on its last day of publication: *"When our turn comes, we shall not disguise our terrorism."*[115]

A current vogue, aptly characterized as "Engels-baiting,"[116] makes it especially important to assess Engels' role in Marxism. Engels was much more than Marx's friend and benefactor. He was one of the very few people with whom

MARX THE MAN

Marx had intellectual interchange, and by far the most important. For most of his life, Marx, as an obscure autodidact, was utterly cut off from participation in the world of universities, learned journals, scholarly conferences, and other institutionalized intellectual exchange. Nor did he have any intellectual interaction, by correspondence or in person, with the leading minds of his time—Mill, Darwin, Tolstoy, Menger, or Dostoevski, for example. Marx's relationship with contemporary radical intellectuals was one of tutelage or hostility. His correspondence consisted overwhelmingly of gossip, intrigue, and passing remarks on current events and contemporary personalities. Only with Engels were serious intellectual matters discussed with even occasional regularity.

Engels' early economic writing provided the basic conception that Marx systematized and elaborated in the massive volumes of *Capital.* Finally, Engels' piecing together and editing of the many manuscripts for the posthumous volumes of Marx's magnum opus was a monumental work of dedication and self-sacrifice, stretching over more than a decade.

Engels was not only a far clearer writer than Marx, but often more subtly and accurately conveyed Marx's theories —especially of history—for he did not so readily indulge in Marx's penchant for epigrams at the expense of accuracy. Engels' letters on the Marxian theory of history are a major contribution to understanding what Marx actually did in his historical writings, as distinguished from how Marx tried to encapsulate his practice in clichés that continue to obscure more than they reveal.

There is no way to know what Engels would have accomplished in the decades he devoted, first to earning a living for both himself and Marx, and then to completing Marx's unfinished work. But what he actually accomplished was both impressive and indicative. His *Socialism: Utopian and*

MARXISM

Scientific remains the best summary of the system of thought that bears the name of Marx. How much of Marxism originated in fact with Engels is a question that may never be answered. Engels was clearly a precursor of Marxian crisis theory in economics, as Marx himself indicated.[117] Engels' letters to Marx also presage the content and title of Marx's *Eighteenth Brumaire.*[118] But the collaborative writings of Marx and Engels and their unrecorded conversations over a period of forty years preclude any definitive disentangling of their respective contributions to Marxism.

In 1883, at the graveside of Marx, Engels painted an idealized picture that provided the stuff of which legends are made. He began: "On the 14th day of March, at a quarter to three in the afternoon, the greatest living thinker ceased to think." According to Engels, "Marx discovered the law of development of human history," and also "the special law of motion governing the present-day capitalist mode of production."[119] Innumerable slanders Marx "brushed aside as though it were cobweb," and "though he may have had many opponents he had hardly one personal enemy."[120] This was at best a highly sanitized picture of a man who personalized every quarrel and whose letters to Engels were full of spiteful gossip and petty intrigues. Finally, Engels' funeral oration ended with these words: "His name will endure through the ages, and so also will his work!"[121] Marx's name has indeed become infinitely better known than when he died in relative obscurity in London a hundred years ago. How much of what has happened in the twentieth century is "his work"—and in what sense—is a much larger and more complex question. For Marx the man, he perhaps wrote his own best epitaph when he said: "Nothing that is human is foreign to me."[122] Others made him an abstraction and an icon.

Chapter 10

THE
LEGACY
OF MARX

 K arl Marx left many very different legacies, to many individuals, groups, fields, and institutions. His intellectual legacy, especially some of his insights concerning history, are now part of the general intellectual equipment of Western man. Marx's political theories have inspired both social democrats and Communists. His approach to analyzing the dynamics of economic and social systems has reappeared in thinkers as disparate as Thorstein Veblen[1] and Joseph A. Schumpeter,[2] and the reaction against Marx's assumptions about the role of ideas is apparent in Max Weber.[3] As a distinguished philosopher has said: "Marx's contributions, in whatever modified form, have entered the consciousness of our time, affected the idiom of our language and understanding, and left an ineradicable imprint on the world of scholarship."[4]

Some of Marx's thinking, especially as regards economic and social factors in history, is in fact now so much a part of our general intellectual tradition that it makes interpretation of the original Marxian theory of history more difficult. The normal tendency to view any theory in contrast to what we already believe is here misleading, for much of what we already believe contains insights contributed by Marx. For example, Marx's emphasis on the economic factor in history—in his peculiar, sociological conception of "economics"—often seems an overemphasis or a monistic explanation, simply because we already give it considerable weight *vis-à-vis* ideas or great men, or other factors.

Marx's legacy is not merely an intellectual legacy, however. It is also a legacy of behavior not only in content but in style. Much as Marx may have explicitly advocated the idea of a democratic workers' government, his own personal style was dictatorial, manipulative, and intolerant. Those who complain that the Soviet Union has betrayed Marx have in mind the intellectual theories rather than the actual behavior of Marx the man. Whether Marx would have gone as far as Lenin or Stalin or Pol Pot is one of the great unanswerable questions of history. But Marx's own behavior already pointed in that direction, however much his words proclaimed a proletarian democracy. Moreover, even in the intellectual realm, the long Marxian tradition of speaking boldly in the name of the workers—not only without their consent but in defiance of their contrary views and actions—made Marxism an instrument of elite domination, with a clear conscience, long before Lenin or Stalin.

While Marxian theories do not require condemnation of all holding different views—and indeed Marx's writings contain numerous expressions of respect for Ricardo,[5] Hegel,[6] and others now thought of as conservative—nevertheless, Marx's personal style with living contemporaries was one in which vituperation and contempt were standard features. It is the style that continues in modern Marxist rhetoric. While social democrats might well claim to be truer to Marxian theories, the Communists have been truer to Marxian practice.

Marx's legacy cannot be fully appreciated until it is critically examined for internal consistency and its empirical validity tested in the harsh glare of facts. Interpretation, though a major undertaking, is not enough.

Even in Marx's own time, Marxism began to acquire so many different meanings that Marx himself declared: "I am not a Marxist." With the rise of Communist nations in the twentieth century, the divisions and proliferations of varied versions of Marxism have become even greater. Leninism, Trotskyism, and Maoism are only some of the major divisions among Communists who claim to be lineal descendants of Marx. In addition, there have been social democrats who considered themselves to be purer Marxists than the Communists—notably the German Social Democrats in the era of Karl Kautsky, who challenged Lenin's credentials as a Marxist. Other socialists have also incorporated Marx's doctrines in their goals and policies, often in forms openly revised in the light of modern conditions.

Rather than attempt a fruitless pursuit of all the schools and sects of contemporary Marxism, the discussion here will be limited to (1) the Marxism of Marx and Engels, and (2) the mainstream of twentieth-century Communism, which takes Lenin as the central legitimate inheritor and developer of their tradition.

THE MARXISM OF MARX

Exploitation

The Marxian conception of "exploitation" is the central and enduring message of Marxism. As Edmund Wilson said:

> . . . once we have read Das Kapital, the conventional works on economics never seem the same to us again; we can

always see through their arguments and figures the realities of the crude human relations which it is their purpose or effect to mask.[7]

Marx and Engels themselves likewise saw "surplus value"—the distillation of exploitation—as the major conceptual contribution of Marxism.[8] Yet this crucial concept in the Marxian theoretical framework was insinuated rather than explicitly established, either logically or empirically. As introduced in the first volume of *Capital,* surplus value was defined simply as an "increment or excess over the original value" invested in production.[9] From this definition, Marx glided quickly to the conclusion that labor was the factor responsible for this increment of value or of output. It was an assumption deeply imbedded in classical economics—implicit in literally the first sentence of Adam Smith's *The Wealth of Nations.* [10] Still it was an assumption, and one devastated by the new conceptions and analysis introduced by neo-classical economics while *Capital* was in its decades-long process of being prepared for publication.

As a theoretical system, Marxian economics begins the story of production in the middle—with firms, capital, and management already in existence *somehow,* and needing only the addition of labor to get production started. From that point on, output is a function of labor input, given all the other factors *somehow* already assembled, coordinated, and directed toward a particular economic purpose. Output per unit of labor is then referred to as labor's output, as was traditional in classical economics long before Marx. But longevity is not logic. Where there are multiple inputs, the division of output by one particular input is wholly arbitrary. More generally, making one entity the numerator and another the denominator in a fraction does nothing to establish a causal relationship between them (though one may exist), much less a special or exclusive causal relationship. Yet this procedure is often successful as insinuation

THE LEGACY OF MARX

—in many contexts[11]—especially when it transforms a plausible relationship into a scientific-looking quotient, suggesting precision or certainty.

Vulnerable as Marx's exploitation theory was, part of the marginalist economists' criticism of it missed the mark, for the marginalists argued in terms of the respective contributions and rewards of factor inputs, rather than of people as such. Land may be productive without landlords being productive. Landlords may be growing richer in their sleep, as John Stuart Mill claimed, earning an income solely because of the institutional artifacts of property ownership. Marx made essentially the same argument regarding the capitalist. The contribution of capital equipment to economic progress was not really at issue, for a Marxian revolution was not intended to abolish capital equipment but rather to abolish capital *ownership* by private individuals. The importance of capital equipment was implicitly recognized when Marx made its public ownership a key feature of his projected new society.

Identifying capital's contribution to the economy with capital owners' contributions is clearly invalid in an argument over the desirability of a system of private ownership of capital. However necessary and justified capitalists' revenue may be *within* the system of capitalism, that is hardly relevant when the issue is whether that whole system should continue or be superseded by a different system. A king may play a vital role in a system of monarchy, but that is irrelevant when debating the relative merits of monarchies versus republics.

Marx argued that capital was not in fact a contribution of capitalists but of labor—past labor. It was a collective product,[12] even if individually owned under the capitalist system. According to Marx, there is "not one single atom of its value that does not owe its existence to unpaid labour."[13] When the capitalist advances part of this capital to the worker in exchange for his labor power, he is using "only the old dodge of every conqueror who buys commodities from the conquered with the money he has robbed them of."[14] In other words, "the labourer himself creates the fund out of which the capitalist pays him."[15]

Marx's analysis concerned the contributions and rewards of people—classes—not impersonal inputs. Yet even within this context, he did not succeed, either logically or empirically, in establishing that present capital is simply the result of past labor. All that he did was to push back into the past the key question of the source of capital. That way leads to infinite regress, not evidence or proof. Nor is the question of the origin of capital a purely historical question. It is an analytic question concerning the ongoing sources of capital.

Once output is seen as a function of numerous inputs, and the inputs as supplied by more than one class of people, the notion that surplus value arises from labor becomes plainly arbitrary and unsupported. Factually, it is even worse off. The empirical implication of a special or exclusive productivity of labor would be that countries that work longer and harder would have higher outputs and higher standards of living. But the reality is more nearly the direct opposite—that countries whose inputs are less labor and more entrepreneurship tend to have vastly higher standards of living, including shorter hours for their workers.

Nor is this simply a matter of having more physical capital to work with. Large transfers of physical capital to Third World countries, through nationalization and foreign aid, have often been only a prelude to the deterioration of that capital. Conversely, the apparently miraculous rise of the German and Japanese economies from the rubble after World War II demonstrated that physical capital is only a product of mental capital—organizational and scientific skills, discipline, experience, and habits of mutual cooperation. Despite the offhand assumption of Engels (and later,

Lenin) that managing a business was only a trivial skill,[16] countries where that skill is rare are almost universally sunk in poverty, even in the midst of rich natural resources, while countries where such skills are more abundant are typically prosperous, even when lacking most natural resources—Japan being the classic example. Similarly, racial and ethnic groups possessing such skills have at various times in history been reduced to destitution by hostile political decisions, only to rise rapidly to prosperity again at some other time or place—for example, the Jews in Europe and Chinese minorities scattered throughout Southeast Asia.[17]

For all Marx's intricate and ingenious elaborations of the implications of "surplus value," the original postulate on which it is all based was only the common and crude impression that goods are "really" produced by those who physically handle production in a routine established by others. The early history of the Soviet Union provided the most dramatic empirical refutation of the Marxian assumption that management of economic enterprises is something to be taken for granted as occurring *somehow.* When economic incentives were drastically reduced or abolished in the heady egalitarian period following the Bolshevik revolution, the Soviet economy ground to a halt. Widespread hunger and a halt to vital services forced Lenin to resort to his "New Economic Policy" that restored the hated capitalistic practices. The later nationalizing of all industry under Stalin and his successors did not restore egalitarianism. Quite the contrary. There were highly unequal rewards to management, including today whole systems of special privilege stores to which ordinary Soviet workers have no access. Moreover, the managers of Soviet industry have been disproportionately the descendants of the managerial class of earlier Soviet and czarist times.[18]

Many observers have seen these developments as mere

betrayals of Marxist ideals, missing the more fundamental point that a crucial false assumption must be corrected in practice if people are to survive. Its continuing sacredness in theory can only produce hypocrisy. The betrayal may be real, but in Marxian terminology, "no accident." A similar process is occurring in China, to which many Western Marxists transferred their hopes after disillusionment with the Soviet Union. This too is seen as simply a betrayal of Mao by Deng, rather than a nation's painful learning from experience that a key assumption of Marxian economics is false.

Managerial ability and entrepreneurial innovation are not the only forms of human capital. Workers' skills and experience are also major elements of a country's capital stock. The invisibility of this capital makes it difficult to determine how much of a capitalist nation's capital stock is in fact owned by the workers. However, the presence and importance of workers' human capital are manifested in various ways. Countries whose workers lack industrial skills and experience may have massive unemployment or underemployment, and yet be unable to fill jobs created by new industries—which industries even resort to expensive transportation of workers from distant lands, paying them premium salaries to compensate for the cultural change. Nor is this human capital merely a matter of skills, narrowly defined. Most job skills can be taught in a matter of months, or at most a few years, but national industrial backwardness can continue for generations or centuries on end. For what is not so easily taught are cultural *habits* and orientations toward work and toward life—punctuality, perserverance, attentiveness to detail, cooperation among workers and with supervisors. Enormous disparities may exist in these regards, not only among nations but also among groups within a given nation.[19] The income advantages of experienced over inexperienced workers in a given country can exceed income differences among racial groups in that country,[20] even though the latter differences receive more ideological attention.

In this context, Marx's ringing use of the term "capitalism" was something of a verbal *coup*. It implied a system for the benefit of a small class of people with a unique monopoly of capital assets. But capitalists as thus defined receive only a small fraction of the total income received by labor; yet no one thinks of calling the economic system "laborism," even though that is where three-quarters or more of the income goes. The more fundamental fallacy, however, is in narrowly conceiving capital to mean physical equipment rather than the human capital which may be vastly more valuable and far more widely dispersed, so that much of that vast majority of national income that is statistically counted as a return to "labor" is in fact a return to human capital that is widely owned.

Logically, Marxian economics did not need to assume that management or other non-labor inputs were of minor importance, even though historically this assumption was made and had serious practical consequences. It is the private ownership of capital that defines capitalism, and the capitalist investor rather than the manager who was deemed superfluous and a hindrance to production. *Capital* attempted to establish that capital owners had often acquired their wealth, historically, through force and fraud rather than through personal contributions to the economy's production.[21] An enumeration of lurid examples does not of course establish general causation. But more fundamentally, even if *all* capital were assumed to have had unproductive *retrospective* implications this would still leave untouched the *prospective* policy issue as to whether private or public ownership would be more efficient for an economy and its people.

Whatever the past may have been, the policy question at

any given juncture is what *future* results can be expected from current incentives and constraints, compared to other alternatives. The socialist tradition has long assumed that collectivized production "in the public interest" would in fact serve the masses of people more effectively than private production motivated by a desire for private gain. But the Marxian part of the socialist tradition can less easily make this assumption, for Marxism emphasizes in many contexts that individual *intention* is not the crucial factor in causation.[22] *Capital* reminds us that the road to hell is paved with good intentions,[23] that everything that has been done wrong "has been done wrong for the very best of reasons,"[24] and Engels pointed out that "what each individual wills is obstructed by everyone else, and what emerges is something that no one willed."[25] In short, Marxian analysis is based on systemic interactions, not individual intentions, so the fact that socialists may have nobler intentions than capitalists provides neither a logical nor an empirical reason to expect better results under socialism.

Reasoning systemically, Marx was one of the few socialists to understand that economic competition, motivated by "greed," was what drove prices *down* under capitalism, as capitalists ceaselessly searched for more profits by seeking cheaper ways of producing than those possessed by their fellow capitalist rivals.[26] Mutual competition ensured that capitalists were in no position simply to tack higher profits onto production costs. Therefore, as production costs were driven down throughout an industry, prices tended to be driven down as well, to the benefit of the consuming public. But Marx never faced the issue whether socialist managers and central planners would be equally zealous in weeding out inefficiency and seeking new technologies—whose economic benefits they could not personally reap.

Marx understood that capitalists who introduced cost-saving innovations were motivated by the extra profits they could reap temporarily, until their rivals copied them, after which the production cost savings would accrue to the consumers, due to competition among the producers. But without even this temporary incentive of personal gain, would socialist planners be willing to put forth the same exertions and take on the same risks of disastrous failure that are inseparable from pioneering innovation? Historically, this has not been the case in the Soviet economy, where even the nation's political leaders have publicly complained of the enterprise managers' tendency to stick to "safe" established practices[27] and—in Brezhnev's words— to shy away from innovation "as the devil shies away from incense."[28]

Marx pointed out that the original innovators under capitalism were often ruined financially, and only later would other capitalists finally develop an innovation into a paying proposition.[29] While this may have been meant as a commentary on the individual injustice of rewards and contributions under capitalism, it also showed what desperate gambles innovators were prepared to take, in hopes of a large profit. A collectivized economy that stifles such profits in the interests of individual justice may create an even greater injustice to the consuming public by inhibiting economic innovation.

Price-Allocation and Crises

The neo-classical revolution in economics dealt a death blow to attempts to depict the value of output as a sum derived by adding up the values of the inputs. On the contrary, only a pre-existing value of output to the consumer could make a given expenditure of productive inputs economically viable. Only insofar as consumers' subjective valuations of a product cover the objective costs incurred by producers can the producers continue to make the prod-

197

uct, or to stay in business. There was no "given" assemblage of firms or capital to which labor could be added to get output. Estimating consumer demand and bearing the risks inseparable from these estimates were among the vital non-labor functions to be performed—and rewarded, if such functions were to continue.

Marx implicitly admitted much of this with his concept of "socially necessary labor." No matter how much had been expended (in labor or money) on the production of a given commodity, its value was limited to the amount "socially necessary" to supply the quantity actually demanded at the lowest cost possible under existing technology. In short, value was limited by the consumer, regardless of producer costs.

But however much Marx admitted these realities in an implicit or *ad hoc* sort of way, his explicit formal analysis of value and surplus value was an analysis of *surviving* capitalist firms—firms that had *correctly* estimated consumer demand. But to analyze only survivors is to risk misconceiving the very process from which they emerged. By starting his analysis in the middle, with surviving firms in place, waiting to hire workers, Marx ignored the key implication of failing firms (a majority of all firms in the long run)—that risk is inherent in anticipating consumer demand, and that profit derives from successfully assuming that risk, rather than from merely hiring people to perform the mechanical aspects of producing goods. Failing firms also hire workers —but their very failure shows that that is no guarantee of receiving surplus value.

Despite his insights into the role of ignorance—and hence, risk—in the functioning of *any* division-of-labor economy, Marx repeatedly ignored the importance of knowledge and risk in explaining the phenomena of a capitalist economy. For example, financial speculation was seen in the crudest terms as mere unsavory gambling,[30] with no analysis of its vital role as a social process for conveying the risks inherent in economic activities to those best able or most willing to bear risks. Thus, farmers may grow food for a price guaranteed long before harvest, while commodity speculators carry the risks—each group doing what it knows best.

Although Marx went further than the classical economists before him in showing the crucial role of knowledge and ignorance in the economy, he failed to include knowledge costs or risks in the cost of production that determined value and surplus value. Moreover, Marx seemed to assume that a future communist society could somehow readily overcome these risks inherent in production for an unknown consumer demand. Central planning might enable many producers to become aware of what other producers were doing, but a dynamic economy would present the same difficulties to central planners as to capitalists in guessing how consumers would apportion their growing income or otherwise change their demand. More important, Marx and Engels failed to consider how the very apparatus of central planning would present an ever-present temptation to the holders of political power to turn the whole economy to their own purposes—including military might—rather than let it serve consumers.

What Marx knew or stated in *ad hoc* ways must be clearly distinguished from what he built into his systematic analysis. It might be possible to assemble a substantial collection of random quotes from his passing remarks, showing that Marx knew about skills, risks, etc., but such an exercise would have no significance for Marxian *analysis* as a *system*. Marx's arbitrary assumptions, such as the special productivity of labor, were built into the very framework and definitions of Marxian economics, in effect making the isolated things that he knew *ad hoc* "off limits" to his analysis. As Marx himself observed in a different context: "The label of a system differs from that of other articles, among other things, by the fact that it cheats not only the buyer, but often also the seller."[31] The Marxian system negated the implications of much of Marx's own knowledge of risks and human capital.

Marx's theory of prices and resource allocation meshed with his theory of aggregate economic movements in general and "crises" in particular. Moreover, they meshed not only as economics but also as political philosophy. While the Marxian theory of exploitation performed the key moral function of de-legitimizing profit and capitalism, Marx's theory of economic crises served the key causal function of showing why capitalism could not survive, and why a socialist economy would be a more efficient and more stable economy. How well the Marxian theory performed these functions is another matter.

As seen in Chapter 6, the "ever-deepening" crises of the interpretive literature were in reality ever-*widening* crises in Marx and Engels. That is, the crises endemic to capitalism covered an ever-widening scope as the capitalist economy became a larger part of the national economy and of the international economy. This process is, however, inherently limited, with correspondingly limited potential for revolution. Once capitalism is 90 percent of a given nation's economy, there is little additional trauma to which the economy can be subjected from this source. Moreover, growing experience with recessions and depressions may well evolve both public and private methods of minimizing their impact. The crucial question, however, is why there must be economic crises at all, and how a socialist economy might be expected to have a better performance in this regard.

The disproportionality of production among the various sectors, which Marx saw as inescapable under capitalism, is in fact inescapable under any economic system in which the efficiencies made possible by specialization and division of labor separate the consumer from the producer. A capitalist economy tends to *transmit* these inherent disproportionalities—rapidly and accurately—through price fluctuations. But prices do not *create* what they transmit. Prices are the messengers bringing bad news.

Conversely, while a planned economy can better conceal the problem, it does not solve it. Things can always be found for idle hands to do in a controlled situation. In the extreme, an army can order its soldiers to dig trenches and then fill them in again. That is why armies never have unemployment; nor do Communist states. The crucial difference is between work whose benefits to the consumers exceed their costs to the producers and work whose value is less than its costs. The second kind of work cannot persist in a capitalist economy, where the inherent waste is conveyed forcibly in falling profits (or mounting losses) and growing unemployment. To conceal this with the hidden subsidies made possible by "planning" does not change the underlying reality—the human inability to continuously apply all resources to their most valued uses in an economy with changing tastes, output, and production innovations. Price-coordinated economies convey this reality as effectively as they convey the other economic knowledge that makes for efficiency and a rising standard of living.[32] Indeed, unemployed workers in such economies often live better than workers fully employed in "planned" systems.

Ironically, one of the great historic boosts given to Marxism was the Great Depression of the 1930s, which was widely seen in the Western world as a gigantic failure of capitalism, and by many intellectuals as a special vindication of Marx. It was, however, an economic crisis both deepened and prolonged by disastrous government policies, including monetary mismanagement[33] and disrupted international markets.[34] Marx himself referred to "crack brain meddling by the authorities" that can "aggravate an existing crisis."[35] But although the severity and duration of the Great Depression might have been seen as a demonstration of the difficulty of centrally managing a complex economy—whether capitalist or socialist—most opinion-shapers in the West chose instead to see it as either a general failure of capitalism or as a more specific plot by capitalists to gain from other people's troubles. In reality, profits fell even faster than wages and employment, and American corporations as a whole operated in the red two years in a row. But during this period, when many people's lives were shattered by hopeless unemployment and massive bankruptcies, villain-hunting and sweeping "isms" flourished—including Nazism in Germany and Communism in other countries.

"Increasing Misery" of the Proletariat

The historic impact of apparently minor intellectual flaws is nowhere better illustrated than in Marx's analysis of the role of the proletariat. As Marx himself pointed out, a class cannot be defined solely by objective criteria, but must also include subjective cohesion and shared goals. Moreover, a *revolutionary* proletariat must in fact perceive and be moved by those things that are said to be causes of revolution. The esoteric Ricardian-Marxian conception of wage shares is hardly a weighty matter even to other economists, much less a life-and-death issue to the working class. Similarly, Marxian "alienation" is a philosophically esoteric concept projected by intellectuals onto the working class, rather than a passion felt from within that class with such intensity as to drive the proletariat to the barricades.

Nor are these cases of ideas "too advanced" for the masses to grasp. On the contrary. They are arbitrary definitions rather than substantive propositions with either logical or empirical foundations. Labor's share of national income has not declined over time under capitalism—nor was there any real reason to expect it to—especially when the growing capital component in output is understood to include human capital possessed by the workers. Moreover, in some Western nations, the workers also possess a substantial amount of physical capital, owned by their pension funds. It is estimated that workers in the United States, for example, own a higher proportion of the means of production than do workers in Communist Yugoslavia.[36]

The subjective aspect of "increasing misery" among the working class revolves around the concept of "alienation" —essentially thwarted human development. But this very concept implies that third-party observers can tell untold millions of their fellow human beings how they should "really" evolve, feel, and act. If they could, it would be a mandate for totalitarianism. Indeed, the *assumption* that they can has become an intellectual basis and a moral shield for totalitarianism. Humane and intelligent people excuse lies, repression, slave labor and mass extermination, when they are done in the name of "ultimately" promoting the "real" interest and development of the working class—as conceived by others. Nor is this attitude a twentieth-century phenomenon only. Marx and Engels began their careers in the 1840s by postulating that what ordinary people actually preferred reflected only the latter's mistaken view of the world—their "alienation." For example, the kind of freedom sought by the common man was, as Marx and Engels saw it, "the perfection of his slavery and his inhumanity." A hundred years later, it has become all too painfully clear that it was Marx and Engels whose ideas led to the perfection of slavery and inhumanity, from the Gulag archipelago to the extermination camps of Cambodia.

The contemporary influence of the elusive and pretentious concept of "alienation" reaches well beyond the ranks of Marxists. A wide range of Western intellectuals promote the idea of widespread despair among the masses, the young, or particular social groups—an idea counter to innumerable polls of these people themselves.[37] Moreover, wherever the masses can "vote with their feet," it is almost invariably to move toward capitalist nations where intellectuals say that they are alienated. Nor is this merely a matter of seeking material prosperity—which would hardly explain the desperate gambles people have taken with their own lives, and the lives of their children, trying to crash through the Berlin Wall or setting sail on the open seas in Southeast Asia in hundreds of thousands of leaky and fragile boats.

The Marxian notion that workers are alienated under capitalism included an "estrangement" of workers from the intellectual and scientific aspects of organizing production. In some of the more exuberant projections of Marx and Engels, they imply that specialization itself can be done away with in a future society, and each individual become a kind of Renaissance Man in the production process. This would mean a sweeping duplication of human capital at enormous cost—losing one of the great advantages of civilization over primitive society.[38] Nowhere do Marx and Engels face up to the trade-off between efficiency and personal expression. If worker "participation" and lower production costs invariably go together, nothing is more certain than its spread throughout a system of frenetically competitive profit-seeking (or bankruptcy avoidance).

If "participation" is sometimes efficient and sometimes not, then there is a trade-off to be made between economic and non-economic benefits. Those workers who are more anxious to be a bigger part of the decision-making process could easily convince capitalists to let them—not by words, but by money. To the extent that such workers are prepared to incrementally trade off pay for greater participation, capitalists have every incentive to let them participate, even if this means less efficiency. Conversely, those workers who want their maximum standard of living can trade off part of their autonomy and participation in decision making. The "alienation" approach implies that workers *ought* to make the kind of trade-off that observers would prefer to see. But what observers would like to see—at no cost to themselves—need not coincide with optimality for the actual participants.

Philosophy and History

Marx's dialectical conception of historical development unfolding like the metamorphoses of nature exuded an air of predestination rather than choice. Whatever his intentions, that has been its effect and part of its attraction. Even within their own lifetimes, Marx and Engels saw in their disciples a tendency to use Marxian dialectics as a *substitute* for empirical investigation, rather than as a conceptual aid to empirical analysis.[39]

The Marxian approach to history as analogous to organic metamorphosis makes it easier to take for granted the social benefits of whatever economic, political, and social system exists, and to think only of how it might be improved. But unlike metamorphoses, which move in only one direction, human societies may retrogress disastrously—for generations, for centuries, or in a nuclear era, forever. The dark ages following the fall of the Roman Empire is only one of the more obvious examples.

The possibility of retrogression is not merely a philosophical point, but also a practical matter that can be momentous in its implications. It was a thousand years after the fall of Rome before the average standard of living in Europe rose again to the level of Roman times.[40] Ignoring the dangers of retrogression can mean sliding into the belief that "nothing could be worse" than the existing society being criticized. Such an idea seemed to underlie German Communists' willingness to bring down the ill-fated Weimar republic—setting the stage for Hitler. Many learned in Nazi concentration camps just how much worse things could be. Others before them who had helped bring down the czar likewise learned at the hands of Stalin's secret police just what brutality and de-humanization they had spawned. The mistaken analogy of metamorphosis was not just a theoretical flaw.

Revolutionary zeal for "progress" can mean ignoring the inherent limitations of a given set of circumstances—or of man himself. Marx and Engels repeatedly denounced contemporary "utopian" socialists for ignoring historical circumstances and pre-conditions. Nor were these mere *ad hoc* statements. Inherent constraints are built into the very framework of the Marxian theory of history. But Marxism also envisioned the future evolution of technology and of social systems as eventually opening the prospect of the practical disappearance of these constraints—man's entering the realm of "freedom," in Marxian terms.[41] Thus, no matter how realistic Marxism might be about the limitations and trade-offs of the capitalist and pre-capitalist past, for the communist future it opened the prospect of constructing a society without regard to inherent constraints.

The fact that Marx and Engels refused to draw up details of such a society in advance constituted virtually a blank check for their successors. The starvation and other basic deprivations that struck millions of people in the early post-revolutionary era in Russia, China, and elsewhere were part of the price of this Marxian self-assured optimism. That freedom was conceived in Marxian terms as "freedom to" rather than "freedom from" provided the moral and political impetus to impose these traumatic experiments on masses of human guinea pigs, trampling their "freedom from" authorities in hopes of promoting their "freedom to" achieve various anticipated social and economic benefits. But the much-despised bourgeois "freedom from" authorities owed its evolution precisely to an awareness of the need to protect people from their "betters" or their saviors.

THE LEGACY OF MARX

A related notion that grew out of Marxian dialectics was the concept of historical justification. This too was not just a matter of esoteric words or abstract philosophy. Whatever Marx intended, the actual effect of the doctrine of historical justification was to provide wide latitude for the most sweeping violations of every moral principle and every sense of decency and humanity. Solzhenitsyn's *The Gulag Archipelago* details the practical implications of this philosophical abstraction. Marx's own justifications of the terrorism of the Paris Commune were only a faint foretaste of the butchery under Lenin and Stalin in Russia, Pol Pot in Cambodia, and other Communist despots elsewhere. The emergency conditions used by Marx to justify the atrocities of the Commune were destined to be invoked again and again by his later disciples—not only during the heat of revolution but also long after the new order was solidly entrenched.

Marx's materialist notion of the derivative nature of ideas had a number of important connotations, if not logical implications. Like the eighteenth-century materialists before him, Marx used his assumptions about the roles of matter and mind to support the proposition that people were products of the social environment. But, logically, materialism could just as easily have been used to claim that people's behavior was a product of their genes. While the environmental interpretation of materialism provided a more humane view of the poor, it also provided a temptation toward totalitarian control of the social environment, including ruthless and brutal efforts to "re-educate" those who failed to conform to the preconceived mold. This Marx himself warned against in his "Theses on Feuerbach."[42] But again the inner logic or tendencies of a system of thought must be distinguished from the *ad hoc* statements or even genuine intentions of its creator.

Even within the intellectual realm, the materialist con-

207

ception of history has serious deficiencies. By taking Europe as the model and illustration of his theory of history, Marx missed the implications of the enormous cultural differences between European and non-European civilizations—differences not explainable by any obvious technological differences, for Europe's technological or organizational advantages over China, for example, emerged only within the past few centuries. Taking a global view of history, it might more readily be argued that cultural differences—ultimately, differences in people's thinking—explain much of the difference in material advancement, rather than vice versa. Much of the history of post-World War II efforts at development in the Third World reflect the environmentalist approach that regards the material or economic paraphernalia as primary and changes in attitude as derivative. But often the same material apparatus that produced economic prosperity in its country of origin proved inefficient, or even fell into disuse, rust or decay in the hands of people with different cultural patterns. The repeated disappointments and tragedies that followed the carrying out of environmentalist beliefs[43] again illustrate that philosophic presuppositions have serious human consequences, and that dramatic plausibilities are not enough—not even when welded into an elaborate intellectual system.

Philosophic materialism, in its social environmental version, also provides ways of dismissing ideas according to their supposed origins—"bourgeois," for example—instead of confronting them in either factual or logical terms. Grandly dismissing opposing views as "outmoded" or consigning them to "the dust bin of history" eliminates the need to think about them or to meet their challenge to one's existing presuppositions. Such practices have spread well beyond Marxists. Much of the intellectual legacy of Marx is an *anti*-intellectual legacy. It has been said that you cannot refute a sneer.[44] Marxism has taught many—inside and outside its ranks—to sneer at capitalism, at inconvenient facts or contrary interpretations, and thus ultimately to sneer at the intellectual process itself. This has been one of the sources of its enduring strength as a political doctrine, and as a means of acquiring and using political power in unbridled ways.

LENINISM

Although the Social Democratic tradition in Germany produced a number of theoreticians of Marxian philosophy, and other outstanding Marxist intellectuals have arisen in other countries, the commanding figure of twentieth-century Marxism is V. I. Lenin—partly for his theoretical additions to Marxism, but perhaps more so for putting his own conception of Marxism into practice in the world's largest nation and first Communist state.

As a theoretician, Lenin faced the formidable task of explaining (1) why the increasing misery of the proletariat and the ever-worsening crises of capitalism were nowhere apparent, more than two generations after they had become articles of the Marxist faith, and (2) why the revolution that he engineered in Russia bore so little relationship to the kind of revolution predicted by Marx, and occurred in a setting very different from the capitalist industrial economy and bourgeois democratic republic envisioned in Marx's theory. That the "dictatorship of the proletariat" looked very much like a dictatorship *over* the proletariat, and that the Soviet economy had collapsed into chaos and starvation when revolutionary ideas were first applied on a nationwide basis, added practical urgency to the theoretical controversies.

In the aftermath of the Bolshevik revolution, Lenin had to fight off not only the military intervention of Western nations in Russia and internal civil war, but also an ideological onslaught from Western Marxists, neo-Marxists and anti-Marxists, while the Russian economy was failing to produce and distribute the food, the fuel, and the other ordinary requirements of survival. Moreover, even before coming to power, Lenin's long years of experience as a revolutionary in czarist Russia and in exile had led him to make crucial changes in Marxism—changes which nevertheless had to be presented as continuity in the great tradition to which he was appealing as a rallying point for political support. In short, Lenin faced Herculean tasks requiring—among other things—a master propagandist.

Proletarian Dictatorship

The crucial role of the proletariat in the Marxian theory of revolution determined the nature of post-revolutionary society. A revolution created by an elite corps implied an authoritarian post-revolutionary regime—for sheer survival, since the masses would have neither the experience nor the theoretical insight to cope with anything as momentous as a change in the whole institutional structure of society. By contrast, Marx and Engels had envisioned a long mass struggle for power, extending over decades, during which the proletariat would acquire the experience and clarity needed to become a politically effective force in a democratic society. But long before coming to power, Lenin repudiated this conception of the proletariat's role.

"The history of all countries shows that the working class, exclusively by its own effort, is able to develop only trade union consciousness," according to Lenin in 1902.[45] He disagreed with those who "imagine that the pure working-class movement can work out, and will work out, an independent ideology for itself, if only the workers 'wrest their fate from the hands of the leaders.' " He said: "But this is a profound mistake."[46] According to Lenin: "Class political consciousness can be brought to the workers *only from without.* "[47]

Lenin's doctrine on this point may have been more realistic than Marx's, but what is crucial is that it was profoundly different from Marx's doctrine—both in itself and in its implications for a communist society. It was not the masses but the professional revolutionary who was central to Lenin. He exalted "the miracles that the energy, not only of circles but even of individual persons is able to perform in the revolutionary cause."[48]

The revolutionary struggle in Russia took place under conditions very different from the democratic republic in which Marx and Engels expected the conflict between the proletariat and the bourgeoisie to reach its climax. Under repressive czarist absolutism, a Communist movement had to be clandestine and hence internally undemocratic, for all revolutionaries could not be known to each other nor their records available to be scrutinized by all, including the inevitable spies in their midst. Lenin said:

> Everyone will probably agree that "broad democratic principles" presuppose the two following conditions: first, full publicity, and second, election to all offices. It would be absurd to speak about democracy without publicity, that is, publicity that is not limited to the membership of the organization. We call the German Socialist Party a democratic organization because all it does is done publicly; even its party congresses are held in public. But no one would call democratic an organization that is hidden from every one but its members by a veil of secrecy. What is the use, then, of advancing *"broad democratic principles"* when the fundamental condition for these principles *cannot be fulfilled* by a secret organization?[49]

Lenin asked: "Is it possible for all the revolutionaries to elect one of their number to any particular office, when, in the very interests of the work, he *must* conceal his identity from nine out of ten of those 'all'?"[50] In these circumstances, democracy could be—and was—dismissed by Lenin as "a *useless and harmful toy.*"[51] But once this conception of democracy became fixed during the revolutionary struggle for power, it was hardly likely to be abandoned after power was achieved. Once dictatorial power was centralized by necessity in the hands of revolutionary leaders, they had every incentive to hold on to it long after the revolution—and to continue to dismiss democracy as a "useless and harmful toy." This pattern, once seen as an unfortunate aberration of Lenin or Stalin, has in fact become common as Communist movements have come to power in various parts of the world—sometimes promising democratic elections, but never in fact holding them. Lenin, as a master propagandist, created many of the outward appearances of democracy—a constitution, elections, legislative bodies—but all so structured as to ensure that no effective opposition would ever be possible.

When Lenin warned the masses against "the catchwords and sophisms by which each class and each stratum *camouflages* its selfish strivings,"[52] he neglected to point out that this applied to revolutionary leaders as well. His claim that "this proletarian state will begin to wither away immediately after its victory"[53] was a classic example, increasingly mocked by the passing decades and generations of dictatorship. His calling it "democratic *in a new way*"[54] did little more than add insult to injury.

Engels' statement that the democratic republic was the "specific form" of the dictatorship of the proletariat was changed by Lenin to mean that the democratic republic was the "nearest approach" to the dictatorship of the proletariat[55]—all the while claiming to be following Engels, to be establishing "what Marx really taught."[56] Once in power, Lenin defined dictatorship very clearly as "rule based upon force and unrestricted by any laws."[57] Revolution was likewise changed by Lenin to mean—exclusively—a *violent* rise to power.[58] Here, at least, he conceded that he departed from Marx's view that the spread of the franchise made social revolution possible without violence—a view "no longer valid," according to Lenin, in the era of imperialist war.[59]

Imperialism

Lenin's theory of imperialism rescued Marxian economics from two of its most embarrassing predictions—the increasing misery of the proletariat and the ever more severe economic crises that were supposed to destroy capitalism. It was possible for Marx and Engels to keep looking, throughout their lives, for evidence that such trends existed and were approaching their culmination. But by the time Lenin rose to prominence, the failure of these key Marxian predictions was too obvious to deny.

Some Marxists—notably Eduard Bernstein and his followers among the German Social Democrats—revised Marxian theory. Lenin, however, took the position that capitalism itself had been revised. Lenin spoke of a "new capitalism,"[60] different from that of Marx's time—a capitalism which, since the beginning of the twentieth century was "transformed into imperialism."[61] The new capitalists do not merely exploit their own proletariat but "plunder the whole world" and out of their "enormous *super-profits*" are able to bribe the leaders and upper strata of the working class into acceptance of capitalism. Thus there are in imperialist nations "millions of toilers who live in more or less bourgeois conditions of life."[62]

Despite "the prodigious increase of capital, which overflows the brim,"[63] capitalism escapes catastrophic crises at home by "exporting capital abroad to the backward countries."[64] This "necessity for exporting capital," according to Lenin, arises because "capital cannot find 'profitable' investment" at home.[65] But this is no permanent solution for capitalism. Once "the world is completely divided up" by imperialist nations, only *redivision* is possible[66] and redivision means war among the imperialists, hastening the end of capitalism. Thus imperialism is at the same time the highest stage of capitalism and the era of "the parasitism and decay of capitalism."[67]

Lenin's classic work *Imperialism* contained much statistical data—but it was used to illustrate, rather than to *test,* his theory. *Imperialism* documented extensively what was never at issue—that foreign investments were growing,[68] that railroad track mileage was increasing around the world,[69] that bank deposits were growing,[70] etc. What was not tested was the central proposition that "backward countries" played a major role in absorbing foreign investment capital. Lenin tried to insinuate this instead.

After adding together the total foreign investments of Britain, France, and Germany, and presenting the total with a long string of zeroes, Lenin asked: "*Where* does it go?" This crucial question he never answered. He claimed to give "an approximate answer."[71] But the flaw in his answer, even as an approximation, was that the categories of the investment recipients were *whole continents* and even multiple continents added together. Lenin put the recipients of foreign investments into three vast categories: "Europe," "America" (i.e., the entire Western Hemisphere), and—as one category—"Asia, Africa, and Australia." The enormous range of industrial and nonindustrial countries in each of these categories made it impossible for his data to show whether foreign investments were flowing from industrial economies to nonindustrial economies, or vice versa.

Statistical data on a country-by-country basis show very nearly the opposite of what Lenin claimed. Industrial nations tend to send their foreign investments to other industrial nations, rather than to industrially undeveloped nations. The United States, for example, has more invested in Canada than in Asia and Africa put together—and it has more invested in Europe than in Canada.[72] In Marxian jargon, it was "no accident" that Lenin chose such loose categories. Even his own table in *Imperialism* showed that France and Germany each had more than twice as much invested in "Europe" as in all of "Asia, Africa, and Australia" put together.[73]

The logic of Lenin's economic argument was that "surplus capital" that would otherwise produce crises in industrial nations was prevented from doing so by being sent to non-industrial nations. But if instead it is largely re-shuffled among industrial nations, this does not serve as a safety valve for capitalist nations as a whole. Nor can the rise of workers' incomes in industrial capitalist nations then be depicted as the fruits of exploitation in non-industrial countries. Indeed, it is by no means clear that there is any net flow of capital to the non-industrial world, given the propensity of the more affluent classes in less developed countries to put their money in Swiss bank accounts, American corporations, and other investments in the industrial nations.

Human Capital

In common with Marx and other believers in "exploitation" as the explanation of profits and income disparities, Lenin paid little attention to the role of human capital, except to dismiss or discredit its significance—*before* he came to power. But after being in power for a few years, and discovering the catastrophic effects of neglecting this factor, his later writings reflected a new respect for skills, administrative abilities, and other forms of human capital. He did not, however, take this new insight all the way back to his fundamental vision of "exploitation" as the explanation of income disparaties among classes and nations.

On the eve of revolution, Lenin declared that measures for controlling and directing the society were "generally known and easy to put into effect."[74] He said:

> Capitalist culture has *created* large-scale production, factories, railways, the postal service, telephones, etc. and *on this basis* the great majority of the functions of the old "state power" have become so simplified and can be reduced to such exceedingly simple operations of registration, filing and checking that they can be easily performed by every literate person, can quite easily be performed for ordinary "workmen's wages". . . .[75]

Lenin admitted that a revolutionary government could not immediately "dispense with subordination, control and foremen and bookkeepers,"[76] but argued that such people need receive "salaries no higher than a workman's wage" while "under the control of the armed proletariat."[77] In short, power was all that was really needed to coordinate social processes. Lenin saw "accounting and control" as the key variables that capitalism had already "reduced to the extraordinarily simple operations—which any literate person can perform—of supervising and recording, knowledge of the four rules of arithmetic, and issuing appropriate receipts."[78] He rejected Kautsky's claim that bureaucracy would remain under socialism, for these very simple functions required no permanent class of functionaries, but only easily replaceable individuals with no economic privilege or official grandeur.[79]

Once in power, however, Lenin discovered how much more complicated it all was. Within a few years he was writing of a "fuel crisis" that "threatens to disrupt all Soviet work,"[80] of "ruin, starvation, and devastation" in the land,[81] of "famine" and even admitted that peasant uprisings had become "a common occurrence" under his regime.[82] Factories were closed for lack of raw material, and peasants were destroying their own grain and livestock rather than see them requisitioned by the Communists.[83] Workers demonstrated against Lenin in Petrograd—and their leaders were shot by the Soviet police.[84] Thousands of sailors, who had been staunch supporters of Lenin before, revolted in Kronstadt—and were massacred by the Red Army.[85]

At this desperate juncture, Lenin announced his New Economic Policy, allowing peasants and small capitalists to sell in the marketplace. He also drastically revised his view of the importance of skills. Lenin declared before the Communist Party Congress in 1920 that "we need people who are versed in the art of administration," and admitted that "there is nowhere we can turn to for such people except the old class."[86] As the New Economic Policy unfolded, Lenin came down hard on the side of capitalist management prerogatives, including "authority independently to fix wages" in order to make each business "pay its own way" to produce "increasing profits," with attention to "carefully selecting the most talented and capable administrative personnel."[87] He warned that "all direct interference by the trade unions in the management of factories must be regarded as positively harmful and impermissible."[88] Indeed, he declared the role of trade unions to be "to act as mediators" between workers and management,[89] and their success to be judged by "the degree to which they succeed in averting mass disputes."[90] In his 1920 address to the Communist Party Congress, Lenin declared: "Opinions on corporate management are all too frequently imbued with a spirit of sheer ignorance, an anti-expert spirit."[91] He did not say who had promoted such a spirit, but his own ideas on this subject had now turned completely around.

AN ASSESSMENT

Marx and Engels argued that an individual or an era must be judged not by what they intend or conceive, but by what they actually accomplish.[92] Marxism itself cannot be exempt from this standard. What Marx accomplished was to produce such a comprehensive, dramatic, and fascinating vision that it could withstand innumerable empirical contradictions, logical refutations, and moral revulsions at its effects. The Marxian vision took the overwhelming complexity of the real world and made the parts fall into place, in a way that was intellectually exhilarating and conferred such sense of moral superiority that opponents could be simply labelled and dismissed as moral lepers or blind reactionaries. Marxism was —and remains—a mighty instrument for the acquisition and maintenance of political power. Once such an instrument has come into existence, those who wield the enormous power it makes possible have every incentive to use it and preserve it for their own purposes, regardless of what purposes may have motivated Marx or Engels.

But however instrumental Marxism becomes in the hands of latter-day power-wielders, its intellectual structure and foundation do not become irrelevant. On the contrary. Precisely as it is applied in the real world, intellectual flaws and blemishes too slight to be noticed amid the heady rhetoric become manifest in terms as concrete as hunger, terror, and death. Lenin was unique in having to confront the failure of his assumptions and having to improvise an alternative while literally millions died around him—some from starvation and others slaughtered by his secret police and the Red Army, both of whom drowned in blood the revolt of the very masses in whose name he ruled.

While in one sense this represented the unfolding of

erroneous assumptions implicit in Marxism, in a larger sense it represented the hubris of imagining that a whole society could be constructed from the ground up on the vision of one man, rather than evolving from the experiences of millions, spread over the generations or the centuries. It was not simply that Marx happened to be unequal to the task, but that anyone was foredoomed to be unequal to such a task.

Despite choosing a world stage on which to operate, Marx's vision was a very insular one. Much of Marx's conception of the capitalist and of the capitalist economy reflected the insularity of the urban intellectual. Marx repeatedly depicted and disdained the capitalist entrepreneur as an uncultured *parvenu*[93]—someone lacking in bookish accomplishments, as if these were the universal litmus tests of contributions to society. Marx's own life was the most overwhelming evidence that bookish accomplishments and economic effectiveness had no necessary correlation. Similar narrowness and snobbery were evident toward what the *Communist Manifesto* called "the idiocy of rural life"[94]—a foretaste of Marxists' inability to take farmers seriously, or to manage agriculture effectively.

The Marxist constituency has remained as narrow as the conception behind it. The *Communist Manifesto,* written by two bright and articulate young men without responsibility even for their own livelihoods—much less for the social consequences of their vision—has had a special appeal for successive generations of the same kinds of people. The offspring of privilege have dominated the leadership of Marxist movements from the days of Marx and Engels through Lenin, Mao, Castro, Ho Chi Minh, and their lesser counterparts around the world and down through history. The sheer reiteration of the "working class" theme in Marxism has drowned out this plain fact. But the crucial point is not privilege, as such, but the insulation from responsibility that that provides, particularly during youth.

Intellectuals enjoy a similar insulation from the consequences of being wrong, in a way that no businessman, military leader, engineer or even athletic coach can. Intellectuals and the young have remained historically the groups most susceptible to Marxism—even though the young have often abandoned it as they grew older and more experienced, being replaced by ever renewed sources of more youths following in their wake.

The disjuncture between vision and experience was nowhere better illustrated than in the traumatic post-revolutionary experience of Lenin, as he applied the Marxist vision and watched a whole nation sink into economic chaos and starvation by the millions. The Leninist-Stalinist modifications—or "betrayals"—of Marxism have mitigated the severity of the Soviet Union's economic problems, but at the cost of turning a humanitarian creed into a ruthless mode of power consolidation. Both denunciations and apologetics for this often miss the point that a vision that departs from reality must be either abandoned or changed.

Despite the massive intellectual feat that Marx's *Capital* represents, the Marxian contribution to economics can be readily summarized as virtually zero. Professional economics as it exists today reflects no indication that Karl Marx ever existed. This neither denies nor denigrates *Capital* as an intellectual achievement, and perhaps in its way the culmination of classical economics. But the development of modern economics has simply ignored Marx. Even economists who are Marxists typically utilize a set of analytical tools to which Marx contributed nothing, and have recourse to Marx only for ideological, political, or historical purposes.

In professional economics, *Capital* was a detour into a blind alley, however historic it may be as the centerpiece of a worldwide political movement. What is said and done in its name is said and done largely by people who have never read through it, much less followed its labyrinthine reasoning from its arbitrary postulates to its empirically false conclusions. Instead, the massive volumes of *Capital* have become a quasi-magic touchstone—a source of assurance that somewhere and somehow a genius "proved" capitalism to be wrong and doomed, even if the specifics of this proof are unknown to those who take their certitude from it.

In agriculture especially, Marxists' grand dismissals of what they did not understand had far-reaching practical consequences, including desperate food shortages in modern Communist nations, dependence on grain imports from the West, Stalin's wholesale slaughter of the kulaks, and innumerable agricultural reforms—the most effective of which proved to be allowing some portion of agriculture to operate through a market system. In the Soviet Union, the market sector occupies only about 3 percent of the farm land, but produces about 30 percent of Soviet agricultural output.[95]

The supreme irony of Marxism was that a fundamentally humane and egalitarian creed was so dominated by a bookish perspective that it became blind to facts and deaf to humanity and freedom. Yet the moral vision and the intellectual aura of Marxism continued to disarm critics, quiet doubters, and put opponents on the moral defensive. It has provided both intellectual and moral insulation for those who wield power in its name. Some of the most distinguished names in Western civilization—George Bernard Shaw, Jean-Paul Sartre, Sidney and Beatrice Webb, among others—have become apologists for brutal dictatorships ruling in the name of Marx and committing atrocities that they would never countenance under any other label. People who could never be corrupted by money or power may nevertheless be blinded by a vision. In this context, there are grim implications to Engels' claim that Marx's name and work "will endure through the ages."

NOTES

PREFACE

1. Karl Marx, "The Leading Article of No. 179 of *Kölnische Zeitung,*" K. Marx and F. Engels, *On Religion* (Moscow: Foreign Languages Publishing House, 1955), p. 31.

CHAPTER 1
ECONOMICS AND PHILOSOPHY

1. Georg Wilhelm Friedrich Hegel, *The Philosophy of History,* translated by J. Sibree (New York: Dover Publications, Inc., 1956), pp. 410–411.
2. Karl Marx, *Capital: A Critique of Political Economy,* Volume I (Charles H. Kerr & Company, 1919), p. 823.
3. *Ibid.,* p. 25.
4. *Ibid.,* p. 24. See also *Ibid.,* p. 22.
5. Joseph A. Schumpeter, *History of Economic Analysis* (New York: Oxford University Press, 1959), p. 392.
6. A landmark in this peculiar approach was Paul A. Samuelson, "Wages and Interest: A Modern Dissection of Marxian

Economic Models," *American Economic Review,* December 1957, pp. 884–992. Other distinguished economists have managed to tie Samuelson's record for zero citations from Marx in a scholarly critique of Marxism. For example, Martin Bronfenbrenner, *"Das Kapital* for the Modern Man," *Science and Society,* Fall 1965, pp. 419–438; William Fellner, *Modern Economic Analysis* (New York: McGraw-Hill, Inc., 1960), pp. 121–141. Others who came close to these performances in ignoring Marx while discussing "Marxism" include Fred M. Gottheil, "Increasing Misery of the Proletariat," *Canadian Journal of Economics and Political Science,* February 1962, pp. 103–113.

7. For example, Shlomo Avineri, *The Social and Political Thought of Karl Marx* (Cambridge: Cambridge University Press, 1968), pp. 6, 65, 66, 69–70, 72, 86, 93, 143, 144, 153, 178n–179n, 229, 235; Joseph A. Schumpeter, *Capitalism, Socialism, and Democracy* (New York: Harper & Row Brothers Publishers, 1950), pp. 11, 39n; David McLellan, *Engels* (Glasgow: Fontana/Collins, 1977), pp. 69, 70–71, 73; John Weeks, *Capital and Exploitation* (Princeton: Princeton University Press, 1981), pp. 8, 26, 28, 36, 41, 53, 57, 61, 62, 93, 94

8. Saul K. Padover, *Karl Marx* (New American Library, 1980), p. 190.

9. Robert Payne, *Marx* (Simon and Schuster, 1968), p. 269. See also Frederick Engels, *Herr Eugen Dühring's Revolution in Science [Anti-Dühring]* (International Publishers, 1939), p. 13; Karl Marx, *Capital,* Volume II, pp. 7–8.

CHAPTER 2
THE DIALECTICAL APPROACH

1. "The semi-Hegelian language of a good many passages in my old book is not only untranslatable but has lost the greater part of its meaning even in German." Karl Marx and Frederick Engels, *Letters to Americans,* translated by Leonard E. Mins (New York: International Publishers, 1953), p. 151. See also J. A. Schumpeter, *History of Economic Analysis* (New York: Oxford University Press, 1959), p. 438n; Allen Wood, *Karl Marx* (London: Routledge and Kegan Paul, 1981), pp.

3–15, 189–206; Herbert Marcuse, *Reason and Revolution: Heyel and The Rise of Social Theory,* 2nd edition (New York: The Humanities Press, 1954), *passim.*

2. Karl Marx, *Capital,* Volume I (Chicago: Charles H. Kerr & Co., 1919), pp. 24–25; Karl Marx, *Critique of Political Economy* (Chicago: Charles H. Kerr & Co., 1904), pp. 292–294; Karl Marx and Frederick Engels, *Selected Correspondence,* translated by Dona Torr (New York: International Publishers, 1942), p. 496.

3. Karl Marx, *Capital,* Volume I (Charles H. Kerr & Company, 1919), p. 25.

4. Friedrich Engels, "Ludwig Feuerbach and the End of Classical German Philosophy," Karl Marx and Friedrich Engels, *Basic Writings on Politics and Philosophy,* edited by Lewis S. Feuer (Anchor Books, 1959), p. 219; Frederick Engels, *Herr Eugen Dühring's Revolution in Science [Anti-Dühring]* (International Publishers, 1939), p. 117; Karl Marx and Frederick Engels, *Selected Correspondence,* translated by Dona Torr (International Publishers, 1942), p. 485n; Karl Marx, "Wage Labour and Capital," Karl Marx and Frederick Engels, *Selected Works,* Volume I (Foreign Languages Publishing House, 1955), p. 83; Karl Marx, *Grundrisse,* translated by Martin Nicolaus (Vintage Books, 1973), pp. 548–549; Frederick Engels, *Engels on Capital,* translated & edited by Leonard E. Mins (International Publishers Co., Inc., 1937), p. 60; Karl Marx, *Capital,* Volume I, pp. 71, 77, 124, 128, 132, 139, 146, 162, 837; Karl Marx, Capital, Volume II, pp. 36, 51, 59, 112, 120, 130, 131.

5. For example, Karl Marx, *Capital,* Volume I, p. 588; *Ibid.,* Volume III, p. 56. See also Karl Marx, *Letters to Dr. Kugelmann* (New York: International Publishers, 1934), p. 74.

6. Karl Marx, *A Contribution to the Critique of Political Economy* (International Library Publishing Co., 1904), p. 292.

7. *Ibid.,* pp. 292–293.

8. Karl Marx and Frederick Engels, *Selected Correspondence,* p. 247.

9. *Ibid.,* p. 247; Karl Marx, *Capital,* Volume III, p. 951.

NOTES

10. Karl Marx, *A Contribution to the Critique of Political Economy,* pp. 293–294.
11. Karl Marx, "Wages, Price and Profit," Karl Marx and Frederick Engels, *Selected Works,* Volume I, p. 424.
12. Karl Marx, *Capital,* Volume I, p. 12.
13. Karl Marx, *Capital,* Volume I, pp. 238, 244n, 425n, 443n, 574, 618–619. See also Leonard E. Mins, ed., *Engels on Capital* (New York: International Publishers, 1937), pp. 126–127.
14. Karl Marx, *A Contribution to the Critique of Political Economy,* p. 9.
15. Karl Marx, *Capital,* Volume III, p. 38.
16. Karl Marx, *Theories of Surplus Value* (International Publishers, 1952), p. 202.
17. *Ibid.,* p. 231.
18. Karl Marx and Frederick Engels, *Selected Correspondence,* p. 246.
19. Karl Marx, *Capital,* Volume I, p. 93n.
20. Karl Marx and Frederick Engels, *Selected Correspondence,* p. 245.
21. *Ibid.,* p. 220.
22. Friedrich Engels, *Engels on Capital,* p. 125.
23. *Ibid.,* p. 127.
24. Karl Marx and Frederick Engels, *Selected Correspondence,* p. 247.
25. Frederick Engels, *Herr Eugen Dühring's Revolution in Science [Anti-Dühring],* p. 13.
26. Frederick Engels, "The Peasant Question in France and Germany," Karl Marx and Frederick Engels, *Selected Works,* Volume II, p. 426.
27. Karl Marx, *Capital,* Volume I, p. 652.
28. *Ibid.,* p. 649.
29. *Ibid.,* p. 15.
30. Friedrich Engels, "Ludwig Feuerbach and the End of Classical German Philosophy," Karl Marx and Friedrich Engels, *Basic Writings on Politics and Philosophy,* p. 226.
31. *Ibid.,* p. 227.

32. *Ibid.,* p. 199.
33. Friedrich Engels, "Socialism: Utopian and Scientific," Karl Marx and Friedrich Engels, *Basic Writings on Politics and Philosophy,* ed. Lewis S. Feuer (Garden City, N.Y.: Anchor Books, 1959), pp. 90, 107–108; *idem,* "Leading Feuerbach and the End of Classical German Philosophy," *ibid.,* pp. 199, 227; *idem,* "The Origin of the Family, Private Property and the State," Karl Marx and Friedrich Engels, *Selected Works,* Volume II (Moscow: Foreign Languages Publishing House, 1955), p. 199n; Karl Marx and Friedrich Engels, *The German Ideology,* edited by R. Pascal (New York: International Publishers, 1947), p. 97; Karl Marx, *Economic and Philosophic Manuscripts of 1844* (Moscow: Foreign Languages Publishing House, 1961), pp. 178–179; Karl Marx, *Theories of Surplus Value-Selections,* translated by G. A. Bonner and Emile Burns (New York: International Publishers, 1952), p. 202.
34. Frederick Engels, Herr Eugen Dühring's *Revolution in Science* [*Anti-Duhring*] (New York: International Publishers, 1939), p. 200; Friedrich Engels, "The Origin of the Family, Private Property and the State," Marx and Engels, *Selected Works,* Volume II, p. 199n.
35. Karl Marx, *Theories of Surplus Value,* pp. 202–203.
36. Karl Marx, *Economic and Philosophic Manuscripts of 1844,* pp. 178–179.
37. Karl Marx and Friedrich Engels, "Manifesto of the Communist Party," Marx and Engels, *Basic Writings,* p. 39; Friedrich Engels, "Socialism: Utopian and Scientific," *ibid.,* pp. 70–81.
38. Karl Marx and Friedrich Engels, "Manifesto of the Communist Party," *ibid.,* pp. 29–36, 39. *Idem, The German Ideology,* pp. 79–193.
39. Frederick Engels, *Herr Eugen Dühring's Revolution in Science* [*Anti-Dühring*], p. 280.
40. *Ibid.,* p. 285.
41. *Ibid.,* p. 290.
42. *Ibid.,* p. 283.
43. Karl Marx and Friedrich Engels, "Manifesto of the Commu-

nist Party," Karl Marx and Friedrich Engels, *Basic Writings on Politics and Philosophy,* p. 39.

44. Karl Marx and Friedrich Engels, *The German Ideology* (International Publishers, 1947), p. 156.
45. *Ibid.,* p. 87.
46. Karl Marx, *Capital,* Volume I, p. 22.
47. According to Hegel, "contradiction" was "the very moving principle of the world," rather than something which was "unthinkable." G.W.F. Hegel, *The Logic of Hegel,* translated by W. Wallace (Oxford: The Clarendon Press, 1892), p. 223. See also J. A. Schumpeter, *History of Economic Analysis,* p. 438n; Allen W. Wood, *Karl Marx* (London: Routledge and Kegan Paul, 1981), pp. 202–206. For Marx as well, "contradiction" was not impossibility, for he referred to "the way in which real contradictions are reconciled" (*Capital,* Volume I, p. 116) and to "contradictions which are constantly overcome." Karl Marx, *Grundrisse,* translated by Martin Nicolaus (New York: Vintage Books, 1973), p. 410. The word "contradiction" was also used in his chapter titles to refer to his own doctrines—clearly not a confession of illogic or impossibility but of the internal conflicting forces they analyzed (*Capital,* Volume I, Chapter V; *ibid.,* Volume III, Chapter XV).
48. Karl Marx, *Theories of Surplus Value,* p. 186.
49. Karl Marx, *Economic and Philosophic Manuscripts of 1844,* pp. 113–114.
50. Karl Marx, *Capital,* Volume I, p. 649.
51. Karl Marx and Friedrich Engels, "Manifesto of the Communist Party," Karl Marx and Friedrich Engels, *Basic Writings on Politics and Philosophy,* p. 29.
52. Frederick Engels, *Herr Eugen Dühring's Revolution in Science* [*Anti-Dühring*], p. 309.
53. *Ibid.,* p. 286; Karl Marx, "Critique of the Gotha Program," Marx and Engels, *Basic Writings,* p. 119.
54. Karl Marx, "Wage Labour and Capital," Karl Marx and Frederick Engels, *Selected Works,* Volume I, p. 83.
55. Karl Marx, *Capital,* Volume I, p. 534.

56. Karl Marx, "Theses on Feuerbach," Karl Marx and Friedrich Engels, *Basic Writings on Politics and Philosophy*, p. 244.
57. Karl Marx, *Writings of the Young Marx on Philosophy and Society*, edited and translated by Loyd D. Easton and Kurt H. Guddat (Doubleday and Company, Inc., 1967), p. 246.
58. *Ibid.*, pp. 267–268.
59. Karl Marx, *Economic and Philosophic Manuscripts of 1844* (Foreign Languages Publishing House, 1961), p. 69.
60. Karl Marx and Friedrich Engels, *The German Ideology*, p. 22.
61. *Ibid.*, pp. 22–23.
62. Sidney Hook claimed that Marx later "repudiated" the concept but provided no evidence. Sidney Hook, *From Hegel to Marx* (Ann Arbor: University of Michigan Press, 1978), pp. 4, 5. *Cf.* Shlomo Avineri, *The Social & Political Thought of Karl Marx* (Cambridge University Press, 1968), p. 105n.
63. Karl Marx, *Capital*, Volume I, p. 339.
64. *Ibid.*, p. 86.
65. *Ibid.*, p. 471.
66. *Ibid.*, p. 625.
67. *Ibid.*, p. 555.
68. *Ibid.*, pp. 680–681.
69. Karl Marx, *Grundrisse*, pp. 146, 147, 157, 160, 161, 453, 470, 674.
70. Frederick Engels, *Herr Eugen Dühring's Revolution in Science [Anti-Dühring]*, p. 19.
71. *Ibid.*
72. Karl Marx, *Capital*, Volume I, p. 117.
73. *Ibid.*, p. 116.
74. Frederick Engels, *Herr Eugen Dühring's Revolution in Science [Anti-Dühring]*, p. 101.
75. Frederick Engels, *Dialectics of Nature* (Progress Publishers, 1964), p. 216.
76. Karl Marx, "Wage Labour and Capital," Karl Marx and Frederick Engels, *Selected Works*, Volume I, p. 87.
77. Karl Marx, *Writings of the Young Marx on Philosophy and Society*, pp. 265–266.

NOTES

78. Karl Marx, *Capital,* Volume I, pp. 86–87, 114–115, 120–121, 589; *ibid.,* Volume III, pp. 220–221.
79. Frederick Engels, *Dialectics of Nature,* p. 223.
80. Friedrich Engels, "Ludwig Feuerbach and the End of Classical German Philosophy," Karl Marx and Friedrich Engels, *Basic Writings on Politics and Philosophy,* p. 230.
81. *Ibid.,* p. 226.
82. Frederick Engels, *Dialectics of Nature,* p. 311.
83. *Ibid.,* p. 222.
84. Karl Marx and Frederick Engels, *Selected Correspondence,* p. 484.
85. Georg Wilhelm Friedrich Hegel, *The Philosophy of History,* translated by J. Sibree (Dover Publications, Inc., 1956), pp. 9–19.
86. Karl Marx, *Capital,* Volume I, p. 25. See also K. Marx and F. Engels, *The Holy Family* (Foreign Languages Publishing House, 1956), p. 115.
87. Karl Marx, *Letters to Dr. Kugelmann* (International Publishers, 1934), p. 112.
88. Karl Marx, *Capital,* Volume I, p. 24.
89. *Ibid.,* p. 22.
90. *Ibid.,* p. 24.
91. *Ibid.,* p. 25.
92. Karl Marx and Frederick Engels, *Selected Correspondence,* p. 105.
93. For example, *ibid.,* Volume I, pp. 24–25.
94. Karl Marx, *Economic and Philosophic Manuscripts of 1844,* p. 115.
95. Frederick Engels, *Herr Eugen Dühring's Revolution in Science* [*Anti-Dühring*], p. 136.
96. Karl Marx, *Capital,* Volume I, p. 837.
97. Frederick Engels, *Herr Eugen Dühring's Revolution in Science* [*Anti-Dühring*], pp. 138, 144.
98. *Ibid.,* p. 145.
99. *Ibid.,* p. 147.
100. Karl Marx and Frederick Engels, *Selected Correspondence,* p. 473.

101. See Gustav E. Mueller, "The Hegel Legend of 'Thesis-Antithesis-Synthesis,' " *Journal of the History of Ideas,* June 1958, pp. 411–414.

CHAPTER 3
PHILOSOPHIC MATERIALISM

1. Epicurus, "Letter to Pythocles," *The Stoic and Epicurean Philosophers,* edited by Whitney J. Oates (The Modern Library, 1957), p. 19.
2. Epicurus, "Principal Doctrines," *ibid.,* p. 36.
3. Epicurus, "Letter to Pythocles," *ibid.,* p. 19.
4. Epicurus, "Letter to Herodotus," *ibid.,* p. 14.
5. Epicurus, "Letter to Menoeceus," *ibid.,* p. 30.
6. *Ibid.,* p. 31.
7. *Ibid.,* p. 30.
8. *Ibid.,* p. 32.
9. Epicurus, "Principal Doctrines," *ibid.,* p. 35.
10. *Ibid.,* p. 36.
11. Epicurus, "Fragments," *ibid.,* p. 43.
12. *Ibid.,* p. 49.
13. *Ibid.,* pp. 42–43.
14. *Ibid.,* p. 49.
15. Lucretius, "On the Nature of Things, Book III," *ibid.,* p. 115.
16. Lucretius, "On the Nature of Things, Book I," *ibid.,* p. 70.
17. Lucretius, "On the Nature of Things, Book V," *ibid.,* p. 164; Lucretius, "On the Nature of Things, Book VI," *ibid.,* p. 193.
18. Lucretius, "On the Nature of Things, Book I," *ibid.,* p. 70.
19. Lucretius, "On the Nature of Things, Book III," *ibid.,* p. 130.
20. Lucretius, "On the Nature of Things, Book II," *ibid.,* p. 112.
21. Lucretius, "On the Nature of Things, Book I," *ibid.,* pp. 86–87.
22. Lucretius, "On the Nature of Things, Book II," *ibid.,* p. 108.
23. Lucretius, "On the Nature of Things, Book III," *ibid.,* p. 116.
24. *Ibid.,* p. 118.
25. *Ibid.,* p. 124.

NOTES

26. *Ibid.,* p. 131.
27. Lucretius, "On the Nature of Things, Book II," *ibid.,* p. 95.
28. *Ibid.,* p. 96.
29. Epicurus, "Letter to Menoeceus," *ibid.,* p. 33.
30. Epicurus, "Fragments," *ibid.,* p. 42.
31. Karl Marx and Friedrich Engels, *The Holy Family* (Moscow: Foreign Languages Publishing House, 1956), pp. 175, 178–179.
32. Baron D'Holbach, *The System of Nature* (J. P. Mendum, 1889), p. 99.
33. *Ibid.,* p. 95.
34. *Ibid.,* p. ix.
35. *Ibid.,* p. x.
36. *Ibid.,* p. 72.
37. *Ibid.,* p. 92.
38. For example, *ibid.,* pp. 40, 42, 97, 112, 116, 148.
39. *Ibid.,* p. 73.
40. *Ibid.,* p. 94.
41. *Ibid.,* p. 97.
42. *Ibid.,* p. 98.
43. Karl Marx "Theses on Feuerbach," Karl Marx and Friedrich Engels, *Basic Writings on Politics and Philosophy,* edited by Lewis S. Feuer (Anchor Books, 1959), p. 244.
44. K. Marx and F. Engels, *The Holy Family* (Foreign Languages Publishing House, 1956), pp. 178–179.
45. Sidney Hook, *From Hegel to Marx* (Ann Arbor: University of Michigan Press, 1978), p. 240.
46. *Ibid.,* p. 246.
47. Sidney Hook, *From Hegel to Marx: Studies in the Intellectual Development of Karl Marx* (Ann Arbor: University of Michigan Press, 1978), pp. 248–251. Karl Marx, *Capital,* Volume I, pp. 81–96.
48. Karl Marx, *Capital,* Volume I (Charles H. Kerr & Company, 1919), p. 82.
49. *Ibid.,* p. 83.
50. K. Marx and F. Engels, *On Religion* (Foreign Languages Publishing House, 1955), p. 42.
51. *Ibid.,* pp. 41–42.

52. *Ibid.*, p. 42.
53. *Ibid.*, p. 50.
54. Karl Marx, "Theses on Feuerbach," Karl Marx and Friedrich Engels, *Basic Writings on Politics and Philosophy,* p. 245.
55. K. Marx and F. Engels, *The Holy Family,* pp. 168, 169.
56. *Ibid.*, p. 177. See also p. 176.
57. *Ibid.*, p. 176.
58. K. Marx and F. Engels, *On Religion,* p. 21.
59. *Ibid.*, p. 28.
60. Karl Marx, "Critique of the Gotha Program," Karl Marx and Friedrich Engels, *Basic Writings on Politics and Philosophy,* p. 130.
61. *Ibid.*
62. K. Marx and F. Engels, *The Holy Family,* pp. 219–248, *passim.*
63. *Ibid.*, p. 219.
64. *Ibid.*, p. 220.
65. *Ibid.*, p. 127.
66. Karl Marx and Friedrich Engels, *The German Ideology* (International Publishers, 1947), p. 74.
67. K. Marx and F. Engels, *The Holy Family,* p. 157.
68. *Ibid.*, p. 227.
69. Karl Marx, *Capital,* Volume I, p. 297.
70. *Ibid.*, p. 330.
71. *Ibid.*, p. 836.
72. *Ibid.*, p. 15.
73. Karl Marx, "Critique of the Gotha Program," Karl Marx and Friedrich Engels, *Basic Writings on Politics and Philosophy,* p. 131. See also Karl Marx & Frederick Engels, *Letters to Americans,* translated by Leonard E. Mins (International Publishers, 1953), pp. 202–203.
74. Karl Marx and Friedrich Engels, "Letters and Essays on Political Sociology," Karl Marx and Friedrich Engels, *Basic Writings on Politics and Philosophy,* p. 487.
75. *Ibid.*, p. 488.
76. *Ibid.*, p. 489.
77. Karl Marx and Frederick Engels, *Selected Correspondence,* translated by Dona Torr (International Publishers, 1942), p. 373.
78. Robert Payne, *Marx* (Simon and Schuster, 1968), p. 540.
79. *Ibid.*, p. 499.

NOTES

80. Friedrich Engels, "End of Classical German Philosophy," Karl Marx and Friedrich Engels, *Basic Writings on Politics and Philosophy,* p. 215.
81. *Ibid.,* p. 206.
82. *Ibid.,* p. 210.
83. *Ibid.,* p. 208.
84. Frederich Engels, "On Historical Materialism," Karl Marx and Friedrich Engels, *Basic Writings on Politics and Philosophy,* p. 51.
85. Karl Marx, "Theses on Feuerbach," Karl Marx and Friedrich Engels, *Basic Writings on Politics and Philosophy,* p. 243.
86. ". . . the order of human progression in all respects will mainly depend on the order of progression in the intellectual convictions of mankind, that is, on the law of the successive transformations of human opinions." John Stuart Mill, *A System of Logic* (Longmans, Green and Co., Ltd., 1959), p. 605. See also pp. 604, 610.
87. Karl Marx, *A Contribution to the Critique of Political Economy* (International Library Publishing Co., 1904), p. 11.

CHAPTER 4
THE MARXIAN THEORY OF HISTORY

1. Karl Marx, *A Contribution to the Critique of Political Economy* (International Library Publishing Co., 1904), p. 11.
2. Karl Marx, *The Poverty of Philosophy* (International Publishers, 1963), p. 109.
3. *Ibid.,* p. 133.
4. *Ibid.,* p. 188.
5. Karl Marx, "Wage Labour and Capital," Karl Marx and Frederick Engels, *Selected Works,* Volume I (Foreign Languages Publishing House, 1955), p. 87.
6. Karl Marx and Friedrich Engels, *The German Ideology* (International Publishers, 1947), p. 29.
7. Karl Marx and Frederick Engels, *Selected Correspondence,* translated by Dona Torr (International Publishers, 1942), p. 512.
8. *Ibid.,* p. 477.
9. Indeed, the economic effect often seems very much sub-

merged—perhaps because, as Engels suggested, the history of brief periods (such as covered in these books) takes economic conditions as more or less constant. Frederick Engels, "The Class Struggles in France 1848 to 1850," Karl Marx and Frederick Engels, *Selected Works,* Volume I, p. 119.

10. Karl Marx, *The Poverty of Philosophy,* p. 109.

11. Karl Marx, *Capital,* Volume I (Charles H. Kerr & Company, 1919), p. 94n.

12. See, for example, Shlomo Avineri, *The Social & Political Thought of Karl Marx* (Cambridge University Press, 1968), pp. 6, 65, 66, 69–70, 93, 143, 144.

13. Karl Marx, *A Contribution to the Critique of Political Economy,* p. 12.

14. Frederick Engels, *Herr Eugen Dühring's Revolution in Science* [*Anti-Dühring*] (International Publishers, 1939), p. 292.

15. Karl Marx, *A Contribution to the Critique of Political Economy,* p. 12.

16. Karl Marx, *The Poverty of Philosophy,* p. 181.

17. *Ibid.,* p. 182.

18. Friedrich Engels, "Ludwig Feuerbach and the End of Classical German Philosophy," Karl Marx and Friedrich Engels, *Basic Writings on Politics and Philosophy,* edited by Lewis S. Feuer (Anchor Books, 1959), p. 215.

19. *Ibid.,* p. 230.

20. For example, David McLellan, *Engels* (Fontana: William Collins and Sons, 1972), p. 62; Allen W. Wood, *Karl Marx* (London: Routledge and Kegan Paul, 1981), p. 112. But later, in the same book, Wood rejects his own suggestion that Engels believed in mechanistic determination of ideas. *Ibid.,* pp. 163–164.

21. Friedrich Engels, "Ludwig Feuerbach and the End of Classical German Philosophy," Karl Marx and Friedrich Engels, *Basic Writings on Politics and Philosophy,* p. 231.

22. Karl Marx, "The Eighteenth Brumaire of Louis Bonaparte," Karl Marx and Frederick Engels, *Selected Works,* Volume I, p. 272.

23. Friedrich Engels, "Ludwig Feuerbach and the End of Classi-

NOTES

cal German Philosophy," Karl Marx and Friedrich Engels, *Basic Writings on Politics and Philosophy,* p. 230.

24. Karl Marx and Frederick Engels, *Selected Correspondence,* p. 476.

25. Friedrich Engels, "Ludwig Feuerbach and the End of Classical German Philosophy," Karl Marx and Friedrich Engels, *Basic Writings on Politics and Philosophy,* p. 232.

26. Karl Marx and Frederick Engels, *Selected Correspondence,* p. 159.

27. Karl Marx, "The Eighteenth Brumaire of Louis Bonaparte," Karl Marx and Frederick Engels, *Selected Works,* Volume I, p. 275.

28. K. Marx and F. Engels, *On Religion* (Foreign Languages Publishing House, 1955), pp. 54–55.

29. *Ibid.,* p. 56.

30. Karl Marx, "The Eighteenth Brumaire of Louis Bonaparte," Karl Marx and Frederick Engels, *Selected Works,* Volume I, p. 247. See also *Ibid.,* pp. 250–251.

31. Frederick Engels, "The Housing Question," Karl Marx and Frederick Engels, *Selected Works,* Volume I, p. 623.

32. Karl Marx and Frederick Engels, "Manifesto of the Communist Party," Karl Marx and Frederick Engels, *Selected Works,* Volume I, pp. 49–50.

33. Karl Marx and Friedrich Engels, *The German Ideology,* p. 41.

34. Karl Marx, *A Contribution to the Critique of Political Economy,* p. 12.

35. Karl Marx and Friedrich Engels, *The German Ideology,* p. 43.

36. *Ibid.,* p. 30.

37. Karl Marx, *Capital,* Volume I, p. 94n.

38. *Ibid.*

39. For example, Joseph A. Schumpeter, *Capitalism, Socialism, and Democracy* (New York: Harper & Brothers, 1950), p. 11; J. A. Schumpeter, "The Communist Manifesto in Sociology and Economics," *Journal of Political Economy,* June 1949, p. 205n.

40. Frederick Engels, "Speech at the Graveside of Karl Marx," Karl Marx and Frederick Engels, *Selected Works,* Volume II, p. 167. This has been treated by J. A. Schumpeter as a

misstatement based on the emotionalism of the moment, but in fact Engels' graveside statement repeated almost verbatim what he had said six years earlier (*Ibid.*, p. 164), and which had not been corrected or modified by Marx. See J. A. Schumpeter, "The Communist Manifesto in Sociology and Economics," *Journal of Political Economy,* June 1949, p. 205n.

41. Karl Marx, *Capital,* Volume I, p. 94n.
42. Karl Marx and Frederick Engels, *Selected Correspondence,* pp. 483–484.
43. Karl Marx, "The Eighteenth Brumaire of Louis Bonaparte," Karl Marx and Frederick Engels, *Selected Works,* Volume I, p. 247.
44. Karl Marx & Frederick Engels, *Letters to Americans,* translated by Leonard E. Mins (International Publishers, 1953), p. 161.
45. Karl Marx, *Grundrisse,* translated by Martin Nicolaus (Vintage Books, 1973), p. 885.
46. Friedrich Engels, "Ludwig Feuerbach and the End of Classical German Philosophy," Karl Marx and Friedrich Engels, *Basic Writings on Politics and Philosophy,* pp. 240–241.
47. Karl Marx, "The Eighteenth Brumaire of Louis Bonaparte," Karl Marx and Frederick Engels, *Selected Works,* Volume I, p. 272.
48. Friedrich Engels, "Ludwig Feuerbach and the End of Classical German Philosophy," Karl Marx and Friedrich Engels, *Basic Writings on Politics and Philosophy,* pp. 237–238.
49. *Ibid.,* p. 235.
50. *Ibid.,* p. 237.
51. Karl Marx and Frederick Engels, *Selected Correspondence,* p. 481.
52. Karl Marx, "The Eighteenth Brumaire of Louis Bonaparte," Karl Marx and Frederick Engels, *Selected Works,* Volume I, p. 275.
53. *Ibid.*
54. J. A. Schumpeter, *Essays of J. A. Schumpeter,* edited by Richard V. Clemence (Addison-Wesley Press, Inc., 1951), p. 171.
55. Karl Marx and Friedrich Engels, "Manifesto of the Communist Party," Karl Marx and Friedrich Engels, *Basic Writings on Politics and Philosophy,* p. 26.
56. Karl Marx and Friedrich Engels, *The German Ideology,* p. 39.

NOTES

57. *Ibid.*, p. 40.

58. *Ibid.*, p. 49. See also Karl Marx, *The Poverty of Philosophy*, p. 123.

59. Karl Marx and Friedrich Engels, *The German Ideology*, p. 46.

60. *Ibid.*

61. Karl Marx, "The Eighteenth Brumaire of Louis Bonaparte," Karl Marx and Frederick Engels, *Selected Works*, Volume I, p. 334.

62. *Ibid.*, pp. 334–335.

63. Karl Marx and Frederick Engels, *Selected Correspondence*, p. 259.

64. Karl Marx and Friedrich Engels, "Manifesto of the Communist Party," Karl Marx and Friedrich Engels, *Basic Writings on Politics and Philosophy*, p. 26.

65. *Ibid.*, p. 20.

66. Karl Marx, *Capital*, Volume I, p. 13.

67. Karl Marx and Frederick Engels, *Selected Correspondence*, p. 310.

68. *Ibid.*, p. 353. See also Karl Marx, *Capital*, Volume I, p. 837.

69. Karl Marx and Frederick Engels, *Selected Correspondence*, p. 354.

70. *Ibid.*, pp. 85, 118, 144. David McLellan, *Karl Marx: His Life and Thought* (New York: Harper & Row, 1973), pp. 281–282.

71. Karl Marx and Frederick Engels, *Selected Correspondence*, p. 144.

72. *Ibid.*, p. 147.

CHAPTER 5
THE CAPITALIST ECONOMY

1. Karl Marx, *Capital*, Volume I (Charles H. Kerr & Company, 1919), pp. 163, 787.

2. Karl Marx, *A Contribution to the Critique of Political Economy* (International Library Publishing Co., 1904), pp. 269–270.

3. Karl Marx, *Grundrisse*, translated by Martin Nicolaus (Vintage Books, 1973), p. 258. See also *Ibid.*, p. 449.

4. Frederick Engels, *Herr Eugen Dühring's Revolution in Science* [*Anti-Dühring*] (International Publishers, 1939), p. 230.

5. Karl Marx, "Wage Labour and Capital," Karl Marx and Frederick Engels, *Selected Works,* Volume I (Foreign Languages Publishing House, 1955), p. 90.
6. Karl Marx, *Economic and Philosophic Manuscripts of 1844* (Foreign Languages Publishing House, 1961), p. 37.
7. Karl Marx, "Wage Labour and Capital," Karl Marx and Frederick Engels, *Selected Works,* Volume I, p. 103.
8. *Ibid.,* p. 90.
9. Karl Marx, *Capital,* Volume I, p. 562. See also *Ibid.,* p. 188.
10. *Ibid.,* p. 839.
11. Karl Marx, *Grundrisse,* p. 458.
12. Karl Marx, *Capital,* Volume I, p. 809.
13. See, for example, Karl Marx and Friedrich Engels, "Manifesto of the Communist Party," Karl Marx and Friedrich Engels, *Basic Writings on Politics and Philosophy,* edited by Lewis S. Feuer (Anchor Books, 1959), p. 30; Karl Marx, *Grundrisse,* p. 769; Friedrich Engels, *Engels on Capital,* translated & edited by Leonard E. Mins (International Publishers Co., Inc., 1937), pp. 6–7; Karl Marx, *Capital,* Volume I, pp. 89, 241, 259–260, 261.
14. Karl Marx, *Capital,* Volume I, p. 241.
15. *Ibid.,* p. 836.
16. *Ibid.,* p. 261.
17. *Ibid.,* p. 809.
18. Karl Marx, *Capital,* Volume III, p. 62.
19. *Ibid.,* p. 773.
20. Karl Marx, *Capital,* Volume I, p. 835.
21. *Ibid.,* p. 834.
22. *Ibid.,* p. 684. See also Frederick Engels, *Herr Eugen Dühring's Revolution in Science [Anti-Dühring],*
23. Karl Marx, *Capital,* Volume I, p. 837.
24. Friedrich Engels, "Socialism: Utopian and Scientific," Karl Marx and Friedrich Engels, *Basic Writings,* ed., Lewis S. Feuer (Garden City, N.Y.: Anchor Books, 1959), p. 92.
25. Karl Marx and Frederick Engels, *Selected Correspondence,* translated by Dona Torr (International Publishers, 1942), p. 58.

NOTES

26. Karl Marx and Friedrich Engels, "Manifesto of the Communist Party," *Basic Writings,* p. 12.
27. Karl Marx and Friedrich Engels, "Manifesto of the Communist Party," Karl Marx and Friedrich Engels, *Basic Writings on Politics and Philosophy,* p. 10.
28. *Ibid.,* pp. 10–11.
29. *Ibid.,* p. 38.
30. *Ibid.,* p. 11.
31. Frederick Engels, "Marx's Capital," Karl Marx and Frederick Engels, *Selected Works,* Volume I, pp. 468–469.
32. K. Marx and F. Engels, *On Religion* (Foreign Languages Publishing House, 1955), p. 272.
33. Friedrich Engels, "Socialism: Utopian and Scientific," Karl Marx and Friedrich Engels, *Basic Writings on Politics and Philosophy,* p. 107.
34. According to Hegel, "contradiction" was "the very moving principle of the world," rather than something which was "unthinkable." G.W.F. Hegel, *The Logic of Hegel,* translated by W. Wallace (Oxford: The Clarendon Press, 1892), p. 223.
35. "Letters and Essays on Political Sociology," Marx and Engels, *Basic Writings,* pp. 450–451, 480–481. A modern translator, apparently embarrassed by Marx's statements on this subject, declared blandly: "Marx's English in the above sentence has been altered to conform to modern usage." In short, he put his words in Marx's mouth, because Marx's words are politically embarrassing today. See Karl Marx, *Grundrisse,* translated by Martin Nicolaus (New York: Vintage Books, 1973), p. 798n.
36. Karl Marx and Friedrich Engels, "Manifesto of the Communist Party," *Basic Writings,* pp. 16–17.
37. Karl Marx, *Capital,* Volume I, p. 48.
38. Karl Marx, *Capital,* Volume I, pp. 390–391.
39. Karl Marx, *Theories of Surplus Value* (International Publishers, 1952), p. 385.
40. *Ibid.,* p. 368.
41. Karl Marx, "Wage Labour and Capital," Karl Marx and

Frederick Engels, *Selected Works,* Volume I, p. 87.

42. Karl Marx, *Capital,* Volume III, p. 140.

43. Karl Marx and Friedrich Engels, "Manifesto of the Communist Party," Karl Marx and Friedrich Engels, *Basic Writings on Politics and Philosophy,* p. 13.

44. Karl Marx, *Capital,* Volume I, pp. 686–687.

45. Karl Marx, *Capital,* Volume I, p. 836.

46. *Ibid.,* p. 837.

CHAPTER 6
MARXIAN ECONOMIC CRISES

1. Karl Marx, *A Contribution to the Critique of Political Economy* (International Library Publishing Co., 1904), pp. 269–270; Karl Marx, *The Poverty of Philosophy* (International Publishers, 1963), pp. 160, 186; Karl Marx, *Grundrisse,* translated by Martin Nicolaus (Vintage Books, 1973), pp. 85–87, 513, 832; Karl Marx and Frederick Engels, *Selected Correspondence,* translated by Dona Torr (International Publishers, 1942), p. 199.

2. Karl Marx, *Capital,* Volume III (Charles H. Kerr & Company, 1909), p. 568; Frederick Engels, *Herr Eugene Dühring's Revolution in Science [Anti-Dühring]* (International Publishers, 1939), p. 312; Karl Marx, *Theories of Surplus Value* (International Publishers, 1952), p. 394.

3. Karl Marx, *Grundrisse,* pp. 424, 433; Karl Marx, *Capital,* Volume II, p. 476; Frederick Engels, *Herr Eugen Dühring's Revolution in Science [Anti-Dühring],* p. 312.

4. Frederick Engels, *Herr Eugen Dühring's Revolution in Science [Anti-Dühring],* p. 312.

5. Karl Marx, *Capital,* Volume II, pp. 475–476.

6. Karl Marx, *Capital,* Volume III, p. 568.

7. Karl Marx, *Theories of Surplus Value,* p. 406.

8. Karl Marx, *Capital,* Volume III, p. 303.

9. Paul M. Sweezy, *The Theory of Capitalist Development* (Monthly Review Press, 1956), Chapters IX, X.

10. Karl Marx, *Capital,* Volume I, p. 694.

11. *Ibid.,* p. 128.

NOTES

12. Karl Marx, *Capital,* Volume III, p. 220.
13. Karl Marx, *A Contribution to the Critique of Political Economy,* pp. 29, 47, 64, 66, 81, 104–105, 106; Frederick Engels, *Herr Eugen Dühring's Revolution in Science [Anti-Dühring],* pp. 335, 338; Karl Marx, *Grundrisse,* p. 205; Karl Marx, *Capital,* Volume I, pp. 46, 106n; Karl Marx, *Theories of Surplus Value,* p. 381. For the same concept, in language not precisely identical, see also Karl Marx, *Capital,* Volume I, pp. 68, 82, 90.
14. Karl Marx, *A Contribution to the Critique of Political Economy,* p. 66; Karl Marx, *Capital,* Volume I, pp. 45, 53, 54, 58, 67, 73–74.
15. Karl Marx, *A Contribution to the Critique of Political Economy,* pp. 23, 33–34, 63–64, 81; Karl Marx, *Capital,* Volume I, pp. 45, 51, 59, 60, 67, 101, 102, 223; Karl Marx, *Theories of Surplus Value,* p. 381.
16. Karl Marx, *A Contribution to the Critique of Political Economy,* pp. 45, 47, 59, 81; Karl Marx, *Capital,* Volume I, p. 106n; Karl Marx, *Theories of Surplus Value,* p. 381; Frederick Engels, *Herr Eugen Dühring's Revolution in Science [Anti-Dühring],* pp. 335, 338.
17. Karl Marx, *Capital,* Volume III, p. 221. See also Frederick Engels, *Herr Eugen Dühring's Revolution in Science [Anti-Dühring],* p. 338.
18. Karl Marx, *Capital,* Volume I, p. 46.
19. Karl Marx, *Theories of Surplus Value,* p. 399.
20. Karl Marx, *Capital,* p. 120.
21. Karl Marx and Frederick Engels, *Selected Correspondence,* pp. 106, 232, 246; Karl Marx, *Capital,* Volume I, p. 45.
22. Karl Marx, *Capital,* Volume I, p. 185n.
23. *Ibid.,* p. 184.
24. Karl Marx, *Capital,* Volume III, p. 203.
25. "Their price is this exchange value of theirs, expressed in money." Karl Marx, *Grundrisse,* p. 137. When not expressed in money, exchange-value was simply the ratios at which goods exchanged for each other. See, for example, Karl Marx, *Capital,* Volume I, pp. 43, 56.

26. Karl Marx, *Capital,* Volume I, p. 95n. See also Karl Marx, *A Contribution to the Critique of Political Economy,* p. 29; Karl Marx, *The Poverty of Philosophy,* pp. 18–19.

27. Karl Marx, *Capital,* Volume I, p. 43.

28. *Ibid.,* p. 43. See also *Ibid.,* pp. 45, 70, 95n.

29. Karl Marx, *Capital,* Volume III, p. 745.

30. *Ibid.,* p. 1026.

31. Karl Marx and Frederick Engels, *Selected Correspondence,* p. 232. "Volume II" as originally conceived by Marx contained what was posthumously published as Volumes II and III, including the "transformation" of values into prices. See Karl Marx and Frederick Engels, *Selected Correspondence,* p. 215.

32. Karl Marx, *A Contribution to the Critique of Political Economy,* p. 13.

33. Frederick Engels, "Outlines of a Critique of Political Economy," Karl Marx, *Economic and Philosophic Manuscripts of 1844* (Foreign Languages Publishing House, 1961), p. 195.

34. *Ibid.,* p. 195.

35. *Ibid.,* pp. 195–196.

36. *Ibid.,* p. 196.

37. *Cf.* Paul M. Sweezy, *The Theory of Capitalist Development,* p. 190.

38. Karl Marx and Frederick Engels, "Manifesto of the Communist Party," Karl Marx and Friedrich Engels, *Basic Writings on Politics and Philosophy* (Anchor Books, 1959), p. 10.

39. For example, Martin Bronfenbrenner cites Paul M. Sweezy, who in turn cites a number of other economists—not including Karl Marx. Martin Bronfenbrenner, *"Das Kapital* for the Modern Man," *Science & Society,* Fall 1965, p. 419; Paul M. Sweezy, *The Theory of Capitalist Development,* Chapter XI.

40. See Thomas Sowell, *Say's Law: An Historical Analysis* (Princeton University Press, 1972), Chapters 2, 3.

41. David Ricardo, *The Works and Correspondence of David Ricardo,* ed. Piero Sraffa (Cambridge University Press, 1952), Volume VIII, p. 277.

42. Paul M. Sweezy, *The Theory of Capitalist Development,* Chapter XI.

NOTES

43. Karl Marx, *Capital*, Volume III, p. 568.
44. Karl Marx, *Grundrisse*, p. 750.
45. Friedrich Engels, "Letters on Historical Materialism," Karl Marx and Friedrich Engels, *Basic Writings on Politics and Philosophy*, p. 401.
46. Karl Marx, *Capital*, Volume III, p. 292.
47. Karl Marx, *Theories of Surplus Value*, p. 373n.
48. G.W.F. Hegel, "The Doctrine of Essence," *Hegel Selections*, ed. J. Loewenberg (Charles Scribner's Sons, 1929), p. 119.
49. Karl Marx, *Grundrisse*, pp. 147, 240, 351, 406, 410; Karl Marx, *Capital*, Volume I, p. 116. Perhaps the conclusive evidence is that Marx used the term "contradiction" when describing his own theories. Karl Marx, *Capital*, Volume I, p. 173; Karl Marx, *Capital*, Volume III, p. 282.
50. Quoted in Herbert Marcuse, *Reason and Revolution*, 2nd edition (The Humanities Press, 1954), p. 124.
51. Karl Marx, *Capital*, Volume I, p. 837.
52. Paul M. Sweezy, *The Theory of Capitalist Development*, p. 176.
53. Karl Marx, *Capital*, Volume III, p. 359.
54. Karl Marx and Frederick Engels, *Selected Correspondence*, p. 205.
55. *Ibid.*, p. 204.
56. Frederick Engels, Paul and Laura Lafargue, *Correspondence*, Volume I, translated by Yvonne Kapp (Foreign Languages Publishing House, 1959), p. 134.
57. Friedrich Engels, "Preface," Karl Marx, *Capital*, Volume II, p. 9.
58. Karl Marx, *Grundrisse*, p. 412.
59. Karl Marx, *Grundrisse*, p. 413. See also Karl Marx, *Theories of Surplus Value*, p. 368.
60. Karl Marx, "Wage Labour and Capital," Karl Marx and Frederick Engels, *Selected Works*, Volume I (Foreign Languages Publishing House, 1955), p. 86.
61. Karl Marx, *Economic and Philosophic Manuscripts of 1844*, p. 128. See also *Ibid.*, p. 119.
62. Thomas Sowell, *Say's Law*, Chapter 1.
63. Karl Marx, *Theories of Surplus Value*, p. 396.
64. *Ibid.*, p. 393.
65. *Ibid.*, p. 379.

66. *Ibid.*, p. 371.
67. *Ibid.*, pp. 203, 369.
68. *Ibid.*, p. 369.
69. Karl Marx, *Capital,* Volume III, p. 979n.
70. Karl Marx, *A Contribution to the Critique of Political Economy,* p. 232.
71. Karl Marx, *Theories of Surplus Value,* p. 370.
72. *Ibid.*, p. 408.
73. David Ricardo, *The Works and Correspondence of David Ricardo,* Volume II, 306; Volume VIII, 277; John Stuart Mill, *Principles of Political Economy,* ed. W. J. Ashley (Longmans, Green, and Co., 1909), p. 559.
74. James Mill, *Elements of Political Economy,* 3rd edition (Henry G. Bohn, 1844), pp. 228, 231, 237, 241; John Stuart Mill, *Principles of Political Economy,* p. 559; John Stuart Mill, *Collected Works* (University of Toronto Press, 1967), Volume IV, pp. 17–18, 42.
75. Karl Marx, *Capital,* Volume I, p. 136.
76. Karl Marx, *Theories of Surplus Value,* translated by Jack Cohen and S. W. Ryazanaskaya (Progress Publishers, 1971), Part III, p. 102. This is the only reference to this particular edition. All subsequent citations of *Theories of Surplus Value* refer to the edition already referred to in previous footnotes.
77. These and subsequent quotes from Sismondi are my translations. J.C.L. Simonde de Sismondi, *Nouveaux principes d' économie politique* (Edition Jeheber, 1971), Volume II, p. 247.
78. J.C.L. Simonde de Sismondi, *Études sur l'économie politique* (Chez Treuttel et Würtz, Libraires, 1887), Volume I, pp. 96–97.
79. J.C.L. Simonde de Sismondi, *Nouveaux principes d'économie politique,* Volume I, p. 251. See also *Idem, Études sur l'économie politique,* Volume I, p. 120; Volume II, p. 249.
80. See, for example, Thomas Sowell, "Sismondi: A Neglected Pioneer," *History of Political Economy,* Spring 1972, p. 88n.
81. *Ibid.*
82. Karl Marx, *Capital,* Volume II, Chapter XX.
83. *Ibid.*, Chapter XXI.
84. ". . . the increase of wealth . . . is implied in capitalist production." Karl Marx, *Capital,* Volume I, p. 337.

NOTES

85. Karl Marx, *Capital,* Volume II, p. 86.
86. *Ibid.,* pp. 86–87.
87. *Ibid.,* p. 578.
88. Thomas Sowell, "Sismondi: A Neglected Pioneer," *History of Political Economy,* Spring 1972, pp. 76–77.
89. J.C.L. Sismonde de Sismondi, *Nouveaux principes d'économie politique,* Volume II, p. 148.
90. Karl Marx, *Theories of Surplus Value,* p. 387.
91. *Ibid.,* p. 393.
92. Karl Marx, *Capital,* Volume I, p. 155n.
93. Karl Marx, *Theories of Surplus Value,* p. 380.
94. *Ibid.*
95. *Ibid.*
96. Karl Marx, *Theories of Surplus Value,* p. 379.
97. *Ibid.* The distinction between those factors which made crises possible and those that actually precipitated crises was made repeatedly by Marx. Karl Marx, *Theories of Surplus Value,* pp. 331, 383–384; Karl Marx, *Capital,* Volume I, p. 328.
98. Karl Marx, *Capital,* Volume I, p. 154.
99. *Ibid.,* p. 155.
100. Karl Marx, *Theories of Surplus Value,* p. 386.
101. *Ibid.,* p. 389.
102. Karl Marx, *Capital,* Volume III, p. 543. See also *Ibid.,* p. 602; Karl Marx, *A Contribution to the Critique of Political Economy,* p. 193.
103. Karl Marx, *Theories of Surplus Value,* p. 392.
104. *Ibid.,* p. 393.
105. *Ibid.,* pp. 390–391.
106. *Ibid.,* p. 401.
107. *Ibid.,* p. 408.
108. Robert Torrens, *An Essay on the Production of Wealth* (Augustus M. Kelley, 1965), p. 414.
109. *Ibid.,* p. 424.
110. Karl Marx, *Grundrisse,* p. 621.
111. Karl Marx, *Capital,* Volume I, p. 26n. See also *Ibid.,* p. 495; Karl Marx, "On Proudhon," Karl Marx and Frederick Engels, *Selected Works,* Volume I, p. 391.
112. Karl Marx, *Capital,* Volume I, p. 31; Frederick Engels, *The*

Condition of the Working-Class in England in 1844 (George Allen and Unwin Ltd., 1952), p. x.

113. Karl Marx, *Capital,* Volume I, p. 694. See also *Ibid.,* p. 699.
114. Karl Marx and Frederick Engels, *Selected Correspondence,* p. 422. See also Frederick Engels, *The Condition of the Working-Class in England in 1844.* pp. x–xi.
115. Frederick Engels, "An Outline of a Critique of Political Economy," Karl Marx, *Economic and Philosophic Manuscripts of 1844,* p. 195.
116. Karl Marx, *Capital,* Volume II, p. 211.
117. Karl Marx, *Capital,* Volume III, pp. 574n–575n; Frederick Engels, "Preface to the First German Edition," Karl Marx, *The Poverty of Philosophy,* p. 20n; Frederick Engels, *The Condition of the Working-Class in England in 1844,* p. xvi.

CHAPTER 7
MARXIAN VALUE

1. Karl Marx and Frederick Engels, *Selected Correspondence,* translated by Dona Torr (International Publishers, 1942), pp. 106, 232, 246; Karl Marx, *Capital,* Volume I (Charles H. Kerr & Company, 1919), p. 45.
2. Karl Marx, *Capital,* Volume I, p. 391.
3. Karl Marx and Frederick Engels, *Selected Correspondence,* p. 234.
4. *Ibid.,* p. 246.
5. *Ibid.,* p. 220. See also Friedrich Engels, *Engels on Capital,* translated and edited by Leonard E. Mins (International Publishers Co., Inc., 1937), p. 125.
6. Karl Marx and Frederick Engels, *Selected Correspondence,* p. 110.
7. *Ibid.,* p. 247; Karl Marx, *Capital,* Volume I, pp. 20n–21n.
8. Karl Marx and Frederick Engels, *Selected Correspondence,* p. 102.
9. Karl Marx and Frederick Engels, *Letters to Americans,* translated by Leonard E. Mins (International Publishers, 1953), p. 151.
10. David McLellan, *Karl Marx: His Life and Thought* (New York: Harper and Row, 1973), p. 310.

NOTES

11. Karl Marx and Frederick Engels, *Selected Correspondence*, p. 157.
12. *Ibid.*, 220.
13. Karl Marx, *Capital*, Volume I, pp. 238, 244n, 425n, 443n, 574, 619. See also Friedrich Engels, *Engels on Capital*, p. 126; Karl Marx and Frederick Engels, *Selected Correspondence*, p. 241; Karl Marx, *Capital*, Volume II, pp. 25, 28.
14. Friedrich Engels, *Engels on Capital*, p. 125.
15. *Ibid.*, p. 126.
16. *Ibid.*, p. 127.
17. Karl Marx and Frederick Engels, *Selected Correspondence*, p. 219.
18. See "Papers on the Marginal Revolution in Economics," *History of Political Economy*, Fall 1972.
19. Eugen von Bohm-Bawerk, *Karl Marx and the Close of His System*, translated by Alice M. Macdonald (New York: The MacMillan Co., 1898).
20. Karl Marx, *Theories of Surplus Value* (International Publishers, 1952), pp. 133, 212, 214, 221, 224, 232, 249, 250, 282. See also Karl Marx and Frederick Engels, *Selected Correspondence*, p. 243.
21. Eugen von Bohm-Bawerk, *Karl Marx and the Close of His System*, p. 63.
22. *Ibid.*, p. 131.
23. Karl Marx and Frederick Engels, *Selected Correspondence*, p. 246.
24. Frederick Engels, *Herr Eugen Dühring's Revolution in Science* [*Anti-Dühring*] (International Publishers, 1939), p. 147.
25. Karl Marx and Frederick Engels, *Selected Correspondence*, pp. 129–133. See also *Ibid.*, pp. 238–247.
26. Karl Marx, *Capital*, Volume I, p. 244n.
27. *Ibid.*, pp. 93n, 185n, 244n, 425n, 443n.
28. *Ibid.*, pp. 54–79, *passim*.
29. Karl Marx, *Grundrisse*, translated by Martin Nicolaus (Vintage Books, 1973), p. 137.
30. Karl Marx, *Capital*, Volume I, pp. 43, 95n; Karl Marx, *Theories of Surplus Value*, pp. 203, 261.

31. Karl Marx and Frederick Engels, *Selected Correspondence,* pp. 246–247.
32. *Ibid.,* p. 247.
33. Karl Marx, *Capital,* Volume I, p. 82. See also Karl Marx, *The Poverty of Philosophy* (International Publishers, 1963), p. 78.
34. Karl Marx, *Capital,* Volume I, p. 83.
35. *Ibid.,* p. 86.
36. *Ibid.,* pp. 81–96.
37. *Ibid.,* p. 84.
38. *Ibid.,* p. 85n.
39. *Ibid.,* p. 95n.
40. *Ibid.,* pp. 45, 55, 57n, 70, 76, 95.
41. *Ibid.,* pp. 43, 106, 114.
42. Karl Marx, *Theories of Surplus Value,* p. 261.
43. Karl Marx, *Capital,* Volume I, p. 55.
44. *Ibid.,* p. 95n.
45. *Ibid.,* p. 57n.
46. *Ibid.,* p. 82n.
47. *Ibid.,* p. 185n.
48. Karl Marx, *Capital,* Volume III, p. 56.
49. See Karl Marx, *Capital,* Volume I, pp. 235–244; Karl Marx, *Grundrisse,* p. 324.
50. Karl Marx, *Theories of Surplus Value,* p. 133.
51. *Ibid.*
52. Karl Marx, *Theories of Surplus Value,* p. 283.
53. Frederick Engels, "Preface," Karl Marx, *Capital,* Volume II, p. 18.
54. Karl Marx, *Capital,* Volume III, p. 38.
55. Karl Marx and Frederick Engels, *Selected Correspondence,* p. 245.
56. Karl Marx, *Capital,* Volume I, p. 93n.
57. Karl Marx, *Theories of Surplus Value,* p. 231.
58. *Ibid.,* p. 202.
59. Karl Marx and Frederick Engels, *Selected Correspondence,* p. 227.
60. Karl Marx, *A Contribution to the Critique of Political Economy* (International Library Publishing Co., 1904), pp. 293–294.

NOTES

61. Karl Marx, *Capital,* translated by Ben Fowkes (New York: Vintage Books, 1977), Vol. I, p. 104. All other references to *Capital* are to the standard Kerr edition.
62. Karl Marx, *Capital,* Volume I, Chapter VI.
63. *Ibid.,* p. 164.
64. *Ibid.,* p. 108.
65. *Ibid.,* p. 233.
66. *Ibid.,* p. 232.
67. Adam Smith, *The Wealth of Nations* (Modern Library, 1937), p. lvii.
68. See Thomas Sowell, *Classical Economics Reconsidered* (Princeton: Princeton University Press, 1974), pp. 38–42, 51, 121.
69. Karl Marx, *Capital,* Volume I, pp. 257, 265–290, 294, 308, 718–783.
70. Karl Marx and Frederick Engels, *Selected Correspondence,* p. 172.
71. Frederick Engels, "Preface to the First German Edition," Karl Marx, *The Poverty of Philosophy,* p. 11.
72. Karl Marx, *Capital,* Volume I, p. 14. See also Karl Marx, *Capital,* Volume III, p. 62.
73. Karl Marx, *Capital,* Volume I, p. 171.
74. *Ibid.,* p. 337.
75. Karl Marx, "Wage Labour and Capital," Karl Marx and Frederick Engels, *Selected Works* (Moscow: Foreign Languages Publishing House, 1955), Volume I, pp. 99–100; Karl Marx, *Capital,* Volume III, pp. 310–311.
76. Karl Marx, *Capital,* Volume I, pp. 552–553.
77. Karl Marx, *Capital,* Volume II, p. 40.
78. *Ibid.,* p. 44.
79. "The value of every commodity produced by capitalist methods is represented by the formula: $C = c + v + s$." Karl Marx, *Capital,* Volume III, p. 38.
80. Karl Marx, *Capital,* Volume I, p. 236.
81. *Ibid.,* p. 237.
82. *Ibid.,* p. 239.
83. *Ibid.,* pp. 241, 334.
84. *Ibid.,* p. 242.

85. *Ibid.*

86. *Ibid.*, p. 238.

87. Karl Marx, *Capital,* Volume I, pp. 568–581, 586–617, 671–711.

88. *Ibid.*, pp. 619–783.

89. *Ibid.*, pp. 784–848.

90. Karl Marx, *Capital,* Volume II, p. 32.

91. *Ibid.*, p. 155.

92. Karl Marx, *Capital,* Volume II, pp. 178–207.

93. *Ibid.*, pp. 173–177.

94. *Ibid.*, p. 455.

95. Karl Marx, *Capital,* Volume III, p. 55.

96. *Ibid.*, Volume II, p. 28; Karl Marx and Frederick Engels, *Selected Correspondence,* p. 129; Karl Marx, *The Poverty of Philosophy* (New York: International Publishers, 1963), p. 98; Karl Marx, *Grundrisse,* pp. 435–436.

97. Karl Marx and Frederick Engels, *Selected Correspondence,* p. 130.

98. Karl Marx and Frederick Engels, *Selected Correspondence,* pp. 131, 241, 243; Karl Marx, *Capital,* Volume III, pp. 38–39.

99. See, for example, Karl Marx, *Selected Correspondence,* pp. 129–130; Karl Marx, *Theories of Surplus Value-Selections* (New York: International Publishers, 1952), pp. 212–214, 221–224; Karl Marx, *Capital,* Volume III, p. 181.

100. Karl Marx and Frederick Engels, *Selected Correspondence,* p. 129.

101. Otherwise, capitals earning less than the average profit would transfer into industries with above average profit rates, their increased competition in the industries they entered driving down the latter's profit rate. Conversely, the reduced competition in the industry they left would raise the profit rate there. The process of transfer would continue as long as the differences in profit rates continued—which is to say the transfers would tend to equalize the profit rates.

102. Karl Marx, *Capital,* Volume I, p. 671; Karl Marx and Frederick Engels, *Selected Correspondence,* p. 130.

103. Karl Marx and Frederick Engels, *Selected Correspondence,* p. 131.

104. Karl Marx, *Theories of Surplus Value,* p. 231.

NOTES

105. Karl Marx, *Capital*, Volume III, p. 85; Karl Marx, *Capital*, Volume II, p. 338.
106. Karl Marx, *Capital*, Volume III, p. 64.
107. *Ibid.*, pp. 44–45.
108. *Ibid.*, p. 49. See also *Ibid.*, p. 208.
109. See Paul Sweezy, *The Theory of Capitalist Development* (New York: Monthly Review Press, 1956), Chapter VII.
110. Karl Marx, *Grundrisse*, pp. 137–138; Karl Marx, "Wage Labour and Capital," Marx and Engels, *Selected Works*, Volume I, p. 87; Karl Marx, *Capital*, Volume III, p. 223.
111. See F. Seton "The 'Transformation Problem,' " *Review of Economic Studies*, Volume 24 (1957), pp. 149–160. Seton claims that Marx assumes equal rates of surplus value ("exploitation") in all sectors—not simply as a postulate in the first approximation, but as an empirical assumption. Nowhere does Seton document this repeated assertion.
112. For example, Paul M. Sweezy, "Editor's Introduction," Eugen von Böhm-Bawerk and Rudolf Hilferding, *Karl Marx and the Close of His System & Böhm-Bawerk's Criticism of Marx* (New York: Augustus M. Kelley, 1949), p. xxiv. But compare Ronald L. Meek, *Studies in the Labour Theory of Value*, 2nd edition (New York: Monthly Review Press, 1956), p. 197.
113. Karl Marx, *Capital*, Volume III, p. 84n.
114. *Ibid.*, p. 56.
115. *Ibid.*, p. 54.
116. Karl Marx, *Capital*, Volume III, p. 206.
117. Karl Marx, *The Poverty of Philosophy*, pp. 60–61.
118. Karl Marx, *A Contribution to the Critique of Political Economy*, p. 107.
119. Frederick Engels, "Preface to the First German Edition," Karl Marx, *The Poverty of Philosophy*, p. 18.
120. *Ibid.*, p. 19.
121. Karl Marx, *Grundrisse*, p. 171.
122. Karl Marx, *A Contribution to the Critique of Political Economy*, p. 105.
123. *Ibid.*, p. 106.
124. Karl Marx, *Grundrisse*, pp. 138, 153, 207; Karl Marx, *Capital*, Volume I, p. 106n. This is contrary to a modern Marxist

interpretation. Marxian economics provides an "objective basis, independent of the market" for determining value. Don J. Harris, "On Marx's Scheme of Reproduction and Accumulation," *Journal of Political Economy,* May/June 1972, p. 507.

125. John Weeks, *Capital and Exploitation* (Princeton: Princeton University Press, 1981), p. 28.

126. Frederick Engels, *Herr Eugen Dühring's Revolution in Science* [*Anti-Dühring*], pp. 339–340.

127. Karl Marx, *The Poverty of Philosophy,* p. 21.

128. Karl Marx, "Critique of the Gotha Program," Karl Marx and Friedrich Engels, *Basic Writings on Politics and Philosophy,* edited by Lewis S. Feuer (Anchor Books, 1959), p. 116.

129. Karl Marx, *Capital,* Volume III, p. 221.

130. Karl Marx, *Capital,* Volume I, p. 92.

131. Frederick Engels, *Herr Eugen Dühring's Revolution in Science* [*Anti-Dühring*], p. 338.

132. John Robinson, *An Essay on Marxian Economics* (Macmillan & Co., Ltd., 1957), p. 23.

133. Thomas Sowell, *Classical Economics Reconsidered* (Princeton University Press, 1974), pp. 132–136.

134. *Ibid.,* pp. 132–133.

135. Karl Marx, *Capital,* Volume I, p. 282.

136. *Ibid.,* p. 297.

137. *Ibid.,* p. 658.

138. Karl Marx, *Capital,* Volume III, p. 272.

139. *Ibid.*

140. Karl Marx, *Capital,* Volume III, p. 275.

141. *Ibid.,* p. 248.

142. *Ibid.*

143. Karl Marx, *Capital,* Volume III, p. 249.

144. For example, Paul M. Sweezy, *The Theory of Capitalist Development,* Chapter IX.

145. Karl Marx, *Capital,* Volume III, pp. 292–293.

146. *Ibid.,* p. 283.

147. *Ibid.*

148. *Ibid.,* p. 294.

NOTES

149. David Ricardo, *The Works and Correspondence of David Ricardo,* ed. Piero Sraffa (Cambridge University Press, 1951), Vol. I, p. 50.
150. *Ibid.*
151. John Stuart Mill, *Essays on Some Unsettled Questions of Political Economy* (John W. Parker, 1844), p. 96.
152. *Ibid.*, pp. 96–97.
153. Karl Marx, *Theories of Surplus Value,* p. 320.
154. David Ricardo, *The Works and Correspondence of David Ricardo,* Volume II, pp. 249–250.
155. Karl Marx, "Wage Labour and Capital," Karl Marx and Frederick Engels, *Selected Works,* Volume I (Foreign Languages Publishing House, 1955), p. 94.
156. *Ibid.*, p. 96.
157. *Ibid.*, p. 98.
158. Marx usually—but not invariably—used the expression "real wages" to mean the quantity of goods and services purchasable with the worker's earnings. Karl Marx, "Wage Labour and Capital," Karl Marx and Frederick Engels, *Selected Works,* Volume I, pp. 95, 96, 97; Karl Marx, *Capital,* Volume I, p. 579, 594, 662. This is distinguished from "real wages" in the Ricardian sense of labor's relative share of output. Karl Marx, *Theories of Surplus Value-Selections,* p. 318.
159. Karl Marx, *The Poverty of Philosophy,* pp. 213, 215–216, 221; Karl Marx, "Wage Labour and Capital," Karl Marx and Frederick Engels, *Selected Works,* Volume I, pp. 96–105, *passim;* Karl Marx, *Economic and Philosophic Manuscripts of 1844* (Foreign Languages Publishing House, 1961), pp. 20–28, *passim.*
160. Karl Marx and Frederick Engels, *Collected Works* (International Publishers, 1976), Volume 6, p. 426.
161. Karl Marx and Friedrich Engels, "Manifesto of the Communist Party," Karl Marx and Friedrich Engels, *Basic Writings on Politics and Philosophy,* p. 19.
162. Karl Marx, *The Poverty of Philosophy,* p. 51.
163. *Ibid.*, p. 51n.

164. Karl Marx and Frederick Engels, *Selected Correspondence*, p. 325.
165. *Ibid.*, p. 157.
166. Karl Marx, "Critique of the Gotha Program," Karl Marx and Friedrich Engels, *Basic Writings on Politics and Philosophy*, p. 124.
167. Karl Marx and Frederick Engels, *Selected Correspondence*, p. 325.
168. Karl Marx, *Capital*, Volume I, p. 190.
169. Karl Marx, *Capital*, Volume III, p. 956.
170. Paul A. Samuelson, "Wages and Interest: A Dissection of Marxian Economic Models," *American Economic Review*, December 1957, pp. 908–911, especially 910n.
171. Karl Marx, *Capital*, Volume I, p. 573.
172. *Ibid.*, p. 570.
173. *Ibid.*, p. 571.
174. Fred M. Gottheil, *Marx's Economic Predictions* (Northwestern University Press, 1966), pp. 158–159.
175. Ronald L. Meek, "Marx's 'Doctrine of Increasing Misery,'" *Science & Society*, Fall 1962, p. 428n.
176. Karl Marx, *Capital*, Volume I, p. 700.
177. Karl Marx, "Wages, Price and Profit," Karl Marx and Friedrich Engels, *Selected Works*, Volume I, p. 407.
178. Frederick Engels, *The Condition of the Working-Class in England in 1844* (George Allen and Unwin Ltd., 1952), p. xiv. Even a twentieth-century Marxist economist quotes a contemporary observation in a working-class neighborhood: "If these neighbors of mine are the end-product of a long historical process of 'impoverishment', then all I can say is that their grandfathers and great-grandfathers must have been bloody rich men." Ronald L. Meek, *op. cit.*, p. 435.
179. Karl Marx, "Critique of the Gotha Program," Karl Marx and Friedrich Engels, *Basic Writings on Politics and Philosophy*, p. 124. See also Karl Marx, *Capital*, Volume I, pp. 708–709.
180. Karl Marx, *Selected Writings in Sociology and Social Philosophy*, edited by T. B. Bottomore and Maximilien Rubel (London: Watts 1956), p. 246.

NOTES

181. Karl Marx, *Writings of the Young Marx on Philosophy and Society,* edited and translated by Loyd D. Easton and Kurt H. Guddat (Doubleday and Company, Inc., 1967), p. 281; Karl Marx, *Economic and Philosophic Manuscripts of 1844,* p. 75; Karl Marx, *Grundrisse,* p. 712.
182. Karl Marx, *Capital,* Volume I, p. 399.
183. *Ibid.,* p. 396.
184. *Ibid.,* p. 708.
185. *Ibid.,* p. 534.
186. *Ibid.,* pp. 708–709.
187. John Robinson, *An Essay on Marxian Economics,* p. 36; Paul A. Samuelson, *op. cit.,* pp. 892–895.
188. Karl Marx, *Capital,* Volume III, p. 288.

CHAPTER 8
POLITICAL SYSTEMS AND REVOLUTION

1. Frederick Engels, "The Civil War in France," Karl Marx and Frederick Engels, *Selected Works,* Volume I (Foreign Languages Publishing House, 1955), p. 485.
2. Karl Marx and Friedrich Engels, "Manifesto of the Communist Party," Karl Marx and Friedrich Engels, *Basic Writings on Politics and Philosophy,* edited by Lewis S. Feuer (Anchor Books, 1959), p. 9.
3. *Ibid.,* p. 10.
4. Frederick Engels, *Herr Eugen Dühring's Revolution in Science* [*Anti-Dühring*] (International Publishers, 1939), p. 304.
5. Friedrich Engels, "Socialism: Utopian and Scientific," Karl Marx and Friedrich Engels, *Basic Writings on Politics and Philosophy,* p. 102.
6. Karl Marx and Frederick Engels, "Letters," Karl Marx and Frederick Engels, *Selected Works,* Volume II, p. 485.
7. Karl Marx, "The Civil War in France," Karl Marx and Frederick Engels, *Selected Works,* Volume I, p. 520.
8. *Ibid.,* p. 497.
9. Karl Marx, "The Class Struggles in France 1848 to 1850,"

MARXISM

Karl Marx and Frederick Engels, *Selected Works,* Volume I, p. 130.

10. Karl Marx, *Capital,* Volume I (Charles H. Kerr & Company, 1919), p. 447.
11. K. Marx and F. Engels, *The Holy Family* (Foreign Languages Publishing House, 1956), pp. 118, 128.
12. *Ibid.,* p. 176.
13. *Ibid.,* p. 127.
14. *Ibid.,* p. 157.
15. Karl Marx, *Capital,* Volume I, p. 297.
16. Karl Marx and Friedrich Engels, "Manifesto of the Communist Party," Karl Marx and Friedrich Engels, *Basic Writings on Politics and Philosophy,* p. 28.
17. Karl Marx and Frederick Engels, *Collected Works* (International Publishers, 1976), Volume 6, p. 350.
18. Karl Marx, "Critique of the Gotha Program," Karl Marx and Friedrich Engels, *Basic Writings on Politics and Philosophy,* p. 127.
19. Karl Marx and Frederick Engels, *Selected Correspondence,* translated by Dona Torr (International Publishers, 1942), p. 57.
20. *Ibid.,* p. 486.
21. Frederick Engels, "Origin of Family, Private Property and State," Karl Marx and Frederick Engels, *Selected Works,* Volume II, p. 320.
22. John Stuart Mill, "Considerations on Representative Government," *Collected Works of John Stuart Mill,* Volume XIX, p. 467.
23. Karl Marx, "The Civil War in France," Karl Marx and Friedrich Engels, *Basic Writings on Politics and Philosophy,* p. 362.
24. Karl Marx, "The Civil War in France," Karl Marx and Frederick Engels, *Selected Works,* Volume I, p. 519.
25. *Ibid.,* p. 521.
26. *Ibid.,* p. 528.
27. *Ibid.,* p. 525. In a similar vein, Engels denounced a contemporary socialist writer who "incited his gendarmes of the future to attack religion, and thereby helps it to martyrdom and a prolonged lease of life." Frederick Engels, *Herr Eugen Dühring's Revolution in Science [Anti-Dühring],* p. 355.

NOTES

28. Karl Marx, "The Civil War in France," Karl Marx and Frederick Engels, *Selected Works,* Volume I, p. 527. Engels declared that militarism "carries in itself the seeds of its own destruction." Frederick Engels, *Herr Eugen Dühring's Revolution in Science [Anti-Dühring],* p. 194.

29. Karl Marx, "The Civil War in France," Karl Marx and Frederick Engels, *Selected Works,* Volume I, p. 527.

30. Joseph A. Schumpeter, *Capitalism, Socialism and Democracy* (Harper and Brothers, 1950), p. 313.

31. Karl Marx and Friedrich Engels, "Letters and Essays on Political Sociology," Karl Marx and Friedrich Engels, *Basic Writings on Politics and Philosophy,* p. 484. See also Karl Marx and Frederick Engels, *Selected Correspondence,* p. 320.

32. Karl Marx and Friedrich Engels, "Letters and Essays on Political Sociology," Karl Marx and Friedrich Engels, *Basic Writings on Politics and Philosophy,* p. 484.

33. Karl Marx and Frederick Engels, *Selected Correspondence,* p. 320.

34. See Lewis S. Feuer's editorial comment, Karl Marx and Friedrich Engels, *Basic Writings on Politics and Philosophy,* p. 481.

35. Friedrich Engels, "Socialism: Utopian and Scientific," Karl Marx and Friedrich Engels, *Basic Writings,* pp. 75–76.

36. Frederick Engels, *Herr Eugen Dühring's Revolution in Science [Anti-Dühring],* p. 306. See also Frederick Engels, "Origin of Family, Private Property and State," Karl Marx and Frederick Engels, *Selected Works,* Volume II, p. 321.

37. Frederick Engels, *Herr Eugen Dühring's Revolution in Science [Anti-Dühring],* p. 307; Karl Marx and Frederick Engels, *Selected Correspondence,* p. 337.

38. Karl Marx and Frederick Engels, *Selected Correspondence,* p. 337.

39. Karl Marx and Friedrich Engels, "Letters and Essays on Political Sociology," Karl Marx and Friedrich Engels, *Basic Writings on Politics and Philosophy,* p. 485.

40. For example, Shlomo Avineri, *The Social and Political Thought of Karl Marx* (Cambridge: Cambridge University Press, 1978), pp. 202–203.

41. Karl Marx, *Grundrisse,* translated by Martin Nicolaus (Vintage Books, 1973), p. 105.

MARXISM

42. Karl Marx, *Letters to Dr. Kugelmann* (International Publishers, 1934), p. 77.
43. Karl Marx and Frederick Engels, *Letters to Americans,* translated by Leonard E. Mins (International Publishers, 1953), p. 108.
44. Karl Marx, *Letters to Dr. Kugelmann* (International Publishers, 1934), p. 77.
45. Karl Marx and Frederick Engels, *Selected Correspondence,* p. 320.
46. Karl Marx, "The Class Struggles in France 1848 to 1850," Karl Marx and Frederick Engels, *Selected Works,* Volume I, p. 130.
47. *Ibid.*
48. Karl Marx, "The Class Struggles in France 1848 to 1850," Karl Marx and Frederick Engels, *Selected Works,* Volume I, p. 136.
49. *Ibid.,* p. 224.
50. Karl Marx and Frederick Engels, *Selected Correspondence,* p. 429.
51. Karl Marx, *Capital,* Volume I, p. 32.
52. *Ibid.,* p. 837.
53. Karl Marx, "The Eighteenth Brumaire of Louis Bonaparte," Karl Marx and Frederick Engels, *Selected Works,* Volume I, p. 288.
54. Karl Marx and Frederick Engels, *Selected Correspondence,* p. 291.
55. Frederick Engels, "On the History of the Communist League," Karl Marx and Frederick Engels, *Selected Works,* Volume II, p. 347.
56. Karl Marx and Frederick Engels, *Selected Correspondence,* p. 437.
57. Frederick Engels, "The Civil War in France," Karl Marx and Frederick Engels, *Selected Works,* Volume I, p. 482.
58. Karl Marx and Frederick Engels, *Selected Correspondence,* p. 92.
59. Karl Marx and Frederick Engels, *Selected Correspondence,* pp. 92, 453, 464, 474; Karl Marx and Frederick Engels, *Letters to*

Americans (New York: International Publishers, 1953), pp. 161, 225; Karl Marx and Frederick Engels, "Manifesto of the Communist Party," *Selected Works*, Volume I, p. 31.

60. K. Marx and F. Engels, *The Holy Family* (Moscow: Foreign Languages Publishing House, 1956), p. 52.

61. Karl Marx, "The Eighteenth Brumaire of Louis Bonaparte," Karl Marx and Frederick Engels, *Selected Works*, Volume I, pp. 250–251.

62. Karl Marx, "The Class Struggles in France 1848 to 1850," Karl Marx and Frederick Engels, *Selected Works*, Volume I, p. 134.

63. Karl Marx and Frederick Engels, *Selected Correspondence*, p. 433.

64. *Ibid.*, p. 434.

65. Karl Marx, "The Civil War in France," Karl Marx and Frederick Engels, *Selected Works*, Volume I, p. 539.

66. Karl Marx and Frederick Engels, "Address of the Central Committee to the Communist League," Karl Marx and Frederick Engels, *Selected Works*, Volume I, p. 112.

67. Karl Marx and Frederick Engels, *Selected Correspondence*, p. 303.

68. Karl Marx and Friedrich Engels, "Manifesto of the Communist Party," Karl Marx and Friedrich Engels, *Basic Writings on Politics and Philosophy*, pp. 26, 67; Karl Marx and Frederick Engels, *Selected Correspondence*, p. 118; Frederick Engels, "Origin of Family, Private Property and State," Karl Marx and Frederick Engels, *Selected Works*, Volume II, p. 314; Frederick Engels, Paul and Laura Lafargue, *Correspondence: Volume II*, translated by Yvonne Kapp (Foreign Languages Publishing House, 1960), p. 424.

69. Karl Marx and Friedrich Engels, "Manifesto of the Communist Party," Karl Marx and Friedrich Engels, *Basic Writings on Politics and Philosophy*, p. 3.

70. K. Marx and F. Engels, *The Holy Family* (Foreign Languages Publishing House, 1956), p. 205; Karl Marx and Friedrich Engels, *The German Ideology* (International Publishers, 1947), pp. 189–190.

MARXISM

71. Karl Marx and Friedrich Engels, "Manifesto of the Communist Party," Karl Marx and Friedrich Engels, *Basic Writings on Politics and Philosophy,* p. 4.
72. Karl Marx and Frederick Engels, "Manifesto of the Communist Party," Karl Marx and Frederick Engels, *Selected Works,* Volume I, p. 31.
73. Karl Marx and Friedrich Engels, "Letters and Essays on Political Sociology," Karl Marx and Friedrich Engels, *Basic Writings on Politics and Philosophy,* p. 493.
74. Karl Marx and Friedrich Engels, *The German Ideology,* p. 89.
75. V. I. Lenin, "The State and Revolution," *Selected Works* (Moscow: Foreign Languages Publishing House, 1952), Volume II, Part 1, pp. 301–302.
76. Robert Owen, *A New View of Society* (Everyman's Library, 1963), p. 24.
77. *Ibid.,* p. 37.
78. *Ibid.,* p. 129.
79. *Ibid.,* p. 263.
80. *Ibid.,* p. 269.
81. *Ibid.,* p. 271.
82. *Ibid.,* p. 272.
83. *Ibid.,* pp. 264–298.
84. Karl Marx, *Writings of the Young Marx on Philosophy and Society,* edited and translated by Loyd D. Easton and Kurt H. Guddat (Doubleday and Company, Inc., 1967), p. 212.
85. *Ibid.,* p. 314.
86. Karl Marx and Frederick Engels, *Selected Correspondence,* p. 473.
87. Karl Marx, *The Poverty of Philosophy* (International Publishers, 1963), p. 175.
88. Frederick Engels, *The Condition of the Working-Class in England in 1844* (George Allen and Unwin Ltd., 1952), p. 297.
89. *Ibid.,* p. x.
90. Friedrich Engels, "Socialism: Utopian and Scientific," Karl Marx and Friedrich Engels, *Basic Writings on Politics and Philosophy,* p. 73.
91. *Ibid.,* p. 70.
92. *Ibid.,* p. 71.
93. *Ibid.*

94. Karl Marx and Frederick Engels, *Selected Correspondence,* p. 518.

95. Friedrich Engels, "Socialism: Utopian and Scientific," Karl Marx and Friedrich Engels, *Basic Writings,* p. 95.

96. Karl Marx, "Critique of the Gotha Programme," Karl Marx and Friedrich Engels, *Basic Writings on Politics and Philosophy,* ed. Lewis S. Feuer, pp. 115–116.

97. *Ibid.,* pp. 114, 116; Frederick Engels, *Herr Eugen Duhring's Revolution in Science Anti-Duhring* (New York: International Publishers, 1939), pp. 339–340; Frederick Engels, "Preface," Karl Marx, *The Poverty of Philosophy* (New York: International Publishers, 1963), p. 21; Frederick Engels, "The Housing Question," Karl Marx and Frederick Engels, *Selected Works* (Moscow: Foreign Languages Publishing House, 1955), Volume I, p. 566.

98. Karl Marx, *The Poverty of Philosophy* (New York: International Publishers, 1947), p. 101.

99. See Chapter 7, pp. 126–129.

100. Karl Marx, "Critique of the Gotha Programme," Karl Marx and Friedrich Engels, *Basic Writings,* p. 117.

101. *Ibid.,* p. 119.

102. *Ibid.*

103. Karl Marx, *Capital,* Volume I, p. 21.

CHAPTER 9
MARX THE MAN

1. David McLellan, *Karl Marx: His Life and Thought* (Harper Colophon Books, 1973), p. 15n. Baron von Westphalen did not live next door, however, as sometimes stated.

2. Robert Payne, *Marx* (Simon and Schuster, 1968), p. 21.

3. *Ibid.,* p. 20.

4. Karl Marx, *The Letters of Karl Marx* (Englewood Cliffs: Prentice-Hall, Inc., 1979), p. 171. See also Robert Payne, *Marx: A Biography* (New York: Simon and Schuster, 1968), pp. 316, 345.

5. David McLellan, *Karl Marx: His Life and Thought,* p. 15.

6. *Ibid.,* p. 17.

7. David McLellan, *Karl Marx: His Life and Thought* (New York: Harper & Row, 1973), p. 33.

8. Karl Marx, *The Letters of Karl Marx,* translated by Saul K. Padover, pp. 490–511, *passim.*
9. David McLellan, *Karl Marx: His Life and Thought,* p. 22.
10. Robert Payne, *Marx,* pp. 59–74, *passim.*
11. *Ibid.,* p. 62.
12. *Ibid.,* p. 63.
13. David McLellan, *Karl Marx: His Life and Thought,* pp. 32–33.
14. *Ibid.,* p. 31.
15. *Ibid.,* p. 34.
16. Robert Payne, *Marx,* p. 77.
17. *Ibid.,* p. 79.
18. David McLellan, *Karl Marx: His Life and Thought,* p. 40.
19. *Ibid.,* p. 53.
20. *Ibid.*
21. David McLellan, *Karl Marx: His Life and Thought,* p. 59. Franz Mehring, *Karl Marx: The Story of His Life* (George Allen & Unwin Ltd., 1966), p. 51.
22. David McLellan, *Karl Marx: His Life and Thought,* pp. 51–53, 53.
23. *Ibid.,* p. 55.
24. Robert Payne, *Marx,* p. 85.
25. *Ibid.,* p. 88.
26. Saul K. Padover, *Karl Marx* (New American Library, 1980), p. 76.
27. Robert Payne, *Marx,* p. 117; Saul K. Padover, *Karl Marx,* p. 89.
28. Saul K. Padover, *Karl Marx,* p. 89.
29. Gustav Mayer, *Friedrich Engels: A Biography* (Alfred A. Knopf, Inc., 1936), p. 4.
30. Saul K. Padover, *Karl Marx,* p. 94.
31. Gustav Mayer, *Friedrich Engels: A Biography,* p. 9.
32. David McLellan, *Engels* (William Collins Sons & Company Ltd., 1977), p. 16.
33. K. Marx and F. Engels, *The Holy Family* (Foreign Languages Publishing House, 1956), p. 16.
34. Faith Evans, translator, *The Daughters of Karl Marx* (New York: Harcourt Brace Jovanovich, 1970), p. 281n. See also David McLellan, *Karl Marx,* pp. 285–286.
35. Robert Payne, *Marx,* p. 160.

NOTES

36. *Ibid.,* p. 161.
37. Saul K. Padover, *Karl Marx,* p. 115.
38. Karl Marx and Frederick Engels, *Collected Works* (International Publishers, 1982), Volume, p. 143.
39. Robert Payne, *Marx,* p. 183.
40. David McLellan, *Engels,* p. 19.
41. *Ibid.,* p. 66.
42. Karl Marx and Frederick Engels, *Collected Works,* Volume 38, p. 153.
43. *Ibid.*
44. *Ibid.,* p. 115.
45. David McLellan, *Karl Marx,* pp. 222–223.
46. Robert Payne, *Marx,* p. 338.
47. Saul K. Padover, *Karl Marx: An Intimate Biography* (New York: New American Library, 1978), p. 132.
48. Karl Marx and Frederick Engels, *Collected Works,* Volume 38, p. 30.
49. David McLellan, *Engels,* p. 17.
50. *Ibid.,* p. 20.
51. Karl Marx and Friedrich Engels, *Selected Letters,* edited by Fritz J. Raddatz (Little, Brown & Company, 1980), p. 23.
52. See David McLellan, *Karl Marx: His Life and Thought,* pp. 264, 357n.
53. *Ibid.,* p. 264.
54. Saul K. Padover, *Karl Marx,* p. 182.
55. *Ibid.,* p. 184.
56. *Ibid.,* p. 264. Marx himself confessed to Engels that "I live too expensively for my circumstances," Karl Marx and Friedrich Engels, *Selected Letters,* p. 112.
57. See Boris Nicolaievsky and Otto Maenchen-Helfen, *Karl Marx: Man and Fighter* (Philadelphia: J. B. Lippincott Company, 1936), p. 239; Robert Payne, *Marx,* pp. 349–350.
58. See, for example, Karl Marx and Frederick Engels, *Collected Works* (New York: International Publishers, 1983), Volume 38, p. 227; Volume 39, p. 85.
59. Robert Payne, *Marx,* p. 266.
60. *Ibid.,* pp. 537–538;
61. Robert Payne, *Marx,* p. 534.
62. Karl Marx and Friedrich Engels, *Selected Letters,* p. 95.

63. *Ibid.,* p. 27.
64. Karl Marx and Frederick Engels, *Collected Works,* Volume 38, p. 323.
65. Karl Marx and Friedrich Engels, *Selected Letters,* p. 108.
66. *Ibid.,* p. 44.
67. *Ibid.,* p. 68.
68. *Ibid.,* p. 66.
69. *Ibid.,* p. 81.
70. *Ibid.,* p. 82.
71. Robert Payne, *Marx,* p. 71.
72. *Ibid.,* p. 72.
73. As is done by Dagobert D. Runes, "Introduction." Karl Marx, *A World Without Jews* (New York: Philosophical Library, 1960), p. xi.
74. K. Marx and F. Engels, *The Holy Family,* pp. 117–121, 127–133, 143–159.
75. *Ibid.,* p. 148.
76. Karl Marx and Frederick Engels, *Letters to Americans* (New York: International Publishers, 1953), pp. 65–66.
77. See Karl Marx, *Letters of Karl Marx,* pp. 197, 214–216.
78. Karl Marx and Frederick Engels, *Collected Works,* Volume 38, p. 372.
79. See, for example, Robert Payne, *Marx,* p. 426; Saul K. Padover, *Karl Marx,* pp. 216–221.
80. There is not one reference to Marx in all of Mill's voluminous writings, nor in his voluminous correspondence.
81. Franz Mehring, *Karl Marx: The Story of His Life,* p. 323.
82. Robert Payne, *Marx,* p. 366.
83. *Ibid.,* p. 369.
84. *Ibid.*
85. Robert Payne, *Marx,* pp. 369, 372.
86. *Ibid.,* p. 373.
87. Karl Marx and Frederick Engels, *Selected Correspondence,* translated by Dona Torr (International Publishers, 1942), p. 330.
88. David McLellan, *Karl Marx: His Life and Thought,* p. 422.
89. *Ibid.*

NOTES

90. Karl Marx–Friedrich Engels, *Selected Letters,* p. 9.
91. David McLellan, *Karl Marx,* p. 353.
92. Robert Payne, *Marx,* p. 426.
93. *Ibid.,* p. 327.
94. *Ibid.,* p. 355.
95. Saul K. Padover, *Karl Marx,* p. 271.
96. *Ibid.,* pp. 270–271.
97. Karl Marx and Friedrich Engels, *Selected Letters,* p. 52.
98. *Ibid.,* p. 81.
99. *Ibid.,* p. 98.
100. Saul K. Padover, *Karl Marx,* p. 277.
101. See, for example, Frederick Engels, Paul and Laura Lafargue, *Correspondence* (Moscow: Foreign Languages Publishing House), Volume I, pp. 49, 50, 51, 52, 54, 55, 57, 60, 62, 68, 104, 110, 119, 131, 133, 136, 174, 185, 214, 245, 255, 257, 295, 309, 316, 345, 367. There are two additional volumes of their correspondence, for others to explore.
102. Robert Payne, *Marx,* pp. 522–531.
103. Boris Nicolaievsky and Otto Maenchen-Halfen, *Karl Marx: Man and Fighter,* pp. 243–245.
104. Karl Marx, *Letters of Karl Marx,* p. 414.
105. Robert Payne, *Marx,* p. 295.
106. Maximilien Rubel and Margaret Manale, *Marx Without Myth: A Chronological Study of His Life and Work* (Harper & Row, Publishers, 1975), p. 14.
107. Robert Payne, *Marx,* p. 321.
108. *Ibid.,* p. 143.
109. *Ibid.,* pp. 155–156.
110. Karl Marx and Friedrich Engels, *Selected Letters,* p. 106.
111. Karl Marx, *The Letters of Karl Marx,* pp. 163–166.
112. Karl Marx and Friedrich Engels, *The German Ideology* (New York: International Publishers, 1947), pp. 100–101; K. Marx and F. Engels, *The Holy Family* (Moscow: Foreign Languages Publishing House), pp. 78–80, 144.
113. Karl Marx and Frederick Engels, *Collected Works,* Volume 6, p. 350.
114. *Ibid.,* p. 354.

115. Robert Payne, *Marx*, p. 192.
116. Graeme Duncan, *Marx and Mill* (Cambridge University Press, 1973), p. ix.
117. Karl Marx and Frederick Engels, *Selected Correspondence,* pp. 48–52.
118. *Ibid.,* pp. 48–52.
119. Frederick Engels, "Speech at the Graveside of Karl Marx," Karl Marx and Frederick Engels, *Selected Works,* Volume II (Foreign Languages Publishing House, 1955), p. 167.
120. *Ibid.,* pp. 168–169.
121. Frederick Engels, "Speech at the Graveside of Karl Marx," Karl Marx and Frederick Engels, *Selected Works,* Volume II, p. 169.
122. Franz Mehring, *Karl Marx: The Story of His Life* (George Allen & Unwin Ltd., 1966), p. xii.

CHAPTER 10
THE LEGACY OF MARX

1. See, for example, Thomas Sowell, "The 'Evolutionary' Economics of Thorstein Veblen," *Oxford Economic Papers,* July 1967, pp. 177–198, esp. 182–185.
2. See Herbert von Beckerath, "Joseph A. Schumpeter as a Sociologist," *Schumpeter, Social Scientist,* ed. Seymour E. Harris (Harvard University Press, 1951), pp. 112–113.
3. Max Weber, *The Protestant Ethic and the Spirit of Capitalism,* translated by Talcott Parsons (Charles Scribner's Sons, 1958), especially, pp. 24–25, 55–56, 74–75, 90–91, 183, 277–278.
4. Sidney Hook, "Spectral Marxism," *American Scholar,* Spring 1980, p. 271.
5. For example, Marx referred to Ricardo's "scientific impartiality and love of truth" as "characteristic of him." Karl Marx, *Capital,* Volume I (Charles H. Kerr & Company, 1919), p. 478n. See also Karl Marx, *A Contribution to the Critique of Political Economy* (International Library Publishing Co., 1904), pp. 70–71; Karl Marx, *The Poverty of Philosophy* (International Publishers, 1963), p. 213; Karl Marx and Frederick Engels, *Selected Correspondence,* translated by Dona

NOTES

Torr (International Publishers, 1942), p. 31; Karl Marx, *Grundrisse,* translated by Martin Nicolaus (Vintage Books, 1973), pp. 252, 326, 651.

6. Karl Marx, *Capital,* Volume I, p. 25; Karl Marx and Frederick Engels, *Selected Correspondence,* p. 102.

7. Edmund Wilson, *To the Finland Station* (Harcourt, Brace and Co., 1940), p. 292.

8. Karl Marx and Frederick Engels, *Selected Correspondence,* pp. 226–227, 232; Karl Marx, *Capital,* Volume II (Charles H. Kerr & Company, 1913), pp. 23, 24, 25; Friedrich Engels, "Socialism: Utopian and Scientific," Karl Marx and Friedrich Engels, *Basic Writings on Politics and Philosophy,* edited by Lewis S. Feuer (Anchor Books, 1959), pp. 89–90; Karl Marx, *Grundrisse,* translated by Martin Nicolaus, p. 684.

9. Karl Marx, *Capital,* Volume I, p. 168.

10. "The annual labour of every nation is the fund which originally supplies it with all the necessaries and conveniences of life which it annually consumes, and which consist always either in the immediate produce of that labour, or in what is purchased with that produce." Adam Smith, *The Wealth of Nations* (Modern Library, 1937), p. lvii.

11. Thomas Sowell, *Knowledge and Decisions* (Basic Books, 1980), p. 226.

12. "Capital is a collective product, and only by the united action of many members, nay, in the last resort only by the united actions of all members of society, can it be set in motion." Friedrich Engels, "Manifesto of the Communist Party," Karl Marx and Friedrich Engels, *Basic Writings on Politics and Philosophy,* p. 21. See also Karl Marx, *Capital,* Volume I, p. 684; Karl Marx, *Grundrisse,* p. 589.

13. Karl Marx, *Capital,* Volume I, p. 637.

14. *Ibid.,* p. 638.

15. Karl Marx, *Capital,* Volume II, p. 439.

16. Frederick Engels, "The Origin of the Family, Private Property and the State," Karl Marx and Frederick Engels, *Selected Works,* Volume II (Foreign Languages Publishing House, 1955), p. 314.

17. See, for example, Thomas Sowell, *The Economics and Politics of Race* (William Morrow, 1983), Chapters 2, 3, *passim.*
18. David Granick, *The Red Executive* (Doubleday & Co., 1961), Chapter 3.
19. Thomas Sowell, *The Economics and Politics of Race, passim.*
20. Thomas Sowell, *"Weber* and *Bakke* and the Presuppositions of 'Affirmative Action,' " *Wayne Law Review,* July 1980, p. 1316n.
21. Karl Marx, *Capital,* Volume I, Chapters XXVI–XXIX.
22. Karl Marx, "The Eighteenth Brumaire of Louis Bonaparte," Karl Marx and Frederick Engels, *Selected Works,* Volume I, pp. 272–273; Karl Marx, *Capital,* Volume I, pp. 85, 213, 346–347, 837n; Karl Marx, *Capital,* Volume II, p. 22; Karl Marx, *Theories of Surplus Value* (International Publishers, 1952), p. 380; Karl Marx and Frederick Engels, *Selected Correspondence,* pp. 437–438, 476; Frederick Engels, *Dialectics of Nature* (Progress Publishers, 1964), p. 35; Friedrich Engels, "Ludwig Feuerbach and the End of Classical German Philosophy," Karl Marx and Friedrich Engels, *Basic Writings on Politics and Philosophy,* pp. 230, 231, 232; Frederick Engels, Paul and Laura Lafargue, *Correspondence,* Volume I, translated by Yvonne Kapp (Foreign Languages Publishing House, 1959), p. 313; Friedrich Engels, *Engels on Capital,* translated & edited by·Leonard E. Mins (International Publishers Co., Inc., 1937), p. 8.
23. Karl Marx, *Capital,* Volume I, p. 213.
24. *Ibid.,* p. 289n.
25. Karl Marx and Frederick Engels, *Selected Correspondence,* p. 476.
26. Karl Marx, "Wage Labour and Capital," Karl Marx and Frederick Engels, *Selected Works,* Volume I, pp. 99–101.
27. Joseph S. Berliner, "Prospects for Technological Progress," *Soviet Economy in a New Perspective,* Joint Economic Committee, Congress of the United States (U.S. Government Printing Office, 1976), pp. 436–442.
28. *Ibid.,* p. 437.
29. Karl Marx, *Capital,* Volume III, p. 124.

NOTES

30. Karl Marx, *Capital,* Volume I, p. 827; Karl Marx, *Capital,* Volume II, p. 362.
31. Karl Marx, *Capital,* Volume II, p. 415.
32. Thomas Sowell, *Knowledge and Decisions,* Chapters 3, 8.
33. Milton Friedman and Anna J. Schwartz, *A Monetary History of the United States, 1876–1960* (Princeton University Press, 1963), Chapter 7, especially pp. 407–419.
34. See, for example, Murray Rothbard, *America's Great Depression* (Kansas City: Sheed and Ward, Inc., 1972), pp. 213–215.
35. Karl Marx and Frederick Engels, *Collected Works* (International Publishers, 1982), Volume 38, p. 275.
36. Peter F. Drucker, "Pension Fund 'Socialism,' " *The Public Interest,* Winter 1976, p. 4.
37. See, for example, Thomas Sowell, *Knowledge and Decisions,* pp. 354–355.
38. Thomas Sowell, *Knowledge and Decisions,* pp. 6–8.
39. Karl Marx and Frederick Engels, *Selected Correspondence,* p. 472. See also *Ibid.,* p. 355.
40. Karl Polanyi, *The Great Transformation* (Beacon Press, 1948), p. 45.
41. Friedrich Engels, "Socialism: Utopian and Scientific," Karl Marx and Friedrich Engels, *Basic Writings on Politics and Philosophy,* p. 109.
42. Karl Marx, "Theses on Feuerbach," Karl Marx and Friedrich Engels, *Basic Writings on Politics and Philosophy,* p. 244.
43. See, for example, Peter T. Bauer, *Equality, the Third World, and Economic Delusion* (Harvard University Press, 1981), Chapters 5–7, 14.
44. "Who can refute a sneer?" by William Paley, in John Bartlett, *Familiar Quotations* (Boston: Little, Brown and Co., 1968), p. 474.
45. V. I. Lenin, "What is to be Done?" *Selected Works* (Foreign Publishing Office, 1952), Volume I, Part 1, p. 233.
46. *Ibid.,* p. 242.
47. *Ibid.,* p. 237.
48. *Ibid.,* p. 317.

49. *Ibid.,* p. 351.
50. *Ibid.* p. 352.
51. *Ibid.,* p. 392.
52. *Ibid.,* p. 277. See also V.I. Lenin, "The Three Sources and Three Component Parts of Marxism," *Selected Works,* Volume I, Part 1, p. 80.
53. V. I. Lenin, "The State and Revolution," *Selected Works,* Volume II, Part 1, p. 227.
54. V. I. Lenin, "What is to be Done?" *Selected Works,* Volume I, Part 1, p. 234.
55. V. I. Lenin, "The State and Revolution," *Selected Works,* Volume II, Part 1, p. 272.
56. *Ibid.,* p. 203.
57. V. I. Lenin, "The Proletarian Revolution and the Renegade Kautsky," *Selected Works,* Volume II, Part 2, p. 41.
58. V. I. Lenin, "The State and Revolution," *Selected Works,* Volume II, Part I, pp. 205, 220.
59. *Ibid.,* p. 237.
60. V. I. Lenin, "Imperialism, the Highest Stage of Capitalism," *Selected Works,* Volume I, Part 2, p. 448.
61. *Ibid.,* p. 450.
62. V. I. Lenin, *Imperialism* (International Publishers, 1939), p. 13.
63. *Ibid.,* p. 29.
64. *Ibid.,* p. 63.
65. *Ibid.*
66. *Ibid.,* p. 76.
67. *Ibid.,* p. 13.
68. *Ibid.,* p. 63.
69. *Ibid.,* p. 97.
70. *Ibid.,* p. 38.
71. *Ibid.,* p. 64.
72. U.S. Bureau of the Census, *Historical Statistics of the United States, Colonial Times to 1970* (U.S. Government Printing Office, 1975), p. 870.
73. V. I. Lenin, *Imperialism* (International Publishers, 1939), p. 64.

NOTES

74. V. I. Lenin, "The Impending Catastrophe and How to Combat It," *Selected Works,* Volume II, Part 1, p. 120.
75. V. I. Lenin, "The State and Revolution," *Selected Works,* Volume II, Part 1, pp. 243–244.
76. *Ibid.,* p. 249.
77. *Ibid.,* p. 251.
78. *Ibid.,* pp. 304–305.
79. *Ibid.,* p. 320. See also *ibid.* p. 244.
80. V. I. Lenin, "The Fight to Overcome the Fuel Crisis," *Selected Works,* Volume II, Part 2, p. 290.
81. V. I. Lenin, "The Role and Functions of Trade Unions Under the New Economic Policy," *Selected Works,* Volume II, Part 2, p. 618.
82. V. I. Lenin, "Five Years of the Russian Revolution and the Prospects of the World Revolution," *Selected Works,* Volume II, Part 2, p. 695.
83. Robert Payne, *The Life and Death of Lenin* (Simon and Schuster, 1964), p. 531.
84. *Ibid.,* p. 531.
85. *Ibid.,* p. 535.
86. V. I. Lenin, "Ninth Congress of the Russian Communist Party (Bolsheviks)," *Selected Works,* Volume II, Part 2, p. 333.
87. V. I. Lenin, "The Role and Functions of Trade Unions Under the New Economic Policy," *Selected Works,* Volume II, Part 2, p. 618.
88. *Ibid.*
89. V. I. Lenin, The Role and Functions of Trade Unions Under the New Economic Policy," *Selected Works,* Volume II, Part 2, p. 616.
90. *Ibid.,* p. 617.
91. V. I. Lenin, "Ninth Congress of the Russian Communist Party (Bolsheviks)," *Selected Works,* Volume II, Part 2, p. 333.
92. "Whilst in ordinary life every shopkeeper is very well able to distinguish between what somebody professes to be and what he really is, our historians have not yet won even this trivial insight." Karl Marx and Friedrich Engels, *The German Ideology,* p. 43. "Just as our opinion of an individual is not

based on what he thinks of himself, so can we not judge such a period of transformation by its own consciousness. . . ." Karl Marx, *A Contribution to the Critique of Political Economy,* p. 12.

93. See, for example, Karl Marx, *Capital,* Volume I, p. 446; Karl Marx, *Grundrisse,* p. 652. See also Frederick Engels, Paul and Laura Lafargue, *Correspondence,* Volume II, p. 82.

94. Karl Marx and Friedrich Engels, "Manifesto of the Communist Party," Karl Marx and Friedrich Engels, *Basic Writings on Politics and Philosophy,* p. 11.

95. Svetozar Pejovich, "The End of Planning: The Soviet Union and East European Experience," *The Politics of Planning* (Institute for Contemporary Studies, 1976), p. 109.

INDEX

INDEX

275

INDEX

277

INDEX

MARXISM

Schumpeter, Joseph A., 13, 187, 235 (note 40)
Schurz, Carl, 183
Science, 18, 19, 21, 32, 35, 37, 38, 39, 45, 78, 107, 204
Self-Interest. *See* Motives.
Seton, F., 251 (note 111)
Shaw, George Bernard, 221
Simonde de Sismondi, J.C.L., 97
Slavery, 23, 54, 117, 139, 203
Smith, Adam, 12, 20, 23–24, 88, 113, 116, 117, 130, 190, 267 (note 10)
Socialism, 53, 72, 76, 82, 94, 126–129, 144, 148, 196–197, 200
  and communism, 156–162
  pre-Marxian, 158–160
Socialism: Utopian and Scientific, 185–186
Socially Necessary Labor. *See* Value.
"solution" creates "problem." *See* History.
Solzhenitsyn, Aleksandr I., 207
Soviet Union, 145, 150, 188, 193, 194, 216–217, 218, 220, 221
Speculation, 131, 198–199
Stalin, Josef V., 184, 188, 193, 207, 212, 220, 221
State, 143–144, 162
  capitalist, 79, 143, 162
  definition, 149
  democratic, 149–150
  "withering away," 146, 148–149, 161, 162

Subsistence, 137
Successive Approximations, 19, 35, 89, 115, 119
Surplus Value, 113. *See also* Exploitation.
Sweezy, Paul M., 6, 94, 242 (note 39)

Technology, 54, 56, 58, 67, 70, 118
Tendencies, 129–130, 132
Theories of Surplus Value, 97, 133, 180
Thesis-Antithesis-Synthesis. *See* Jargon.
Timeless Analysis, 77, 78, 117, 158, 160
Torrens, Robert, 102
Transformation Problem. *See* Value.
Trier, 164

Underconsumption. *See* Business Cycles.
United States of America, 45, 64, 150–151, 178, 179, 215
University of Berlin, 165, 167
University of Bonn, 165
University of Jena, 167
Utopian Socialism, 24, 25, 158, 159–160, 161

Value, 13, 20, 89–90, 106–142, 198, 199, 249 (note 79)
  concept versus theory, 88–89, 106, 107

280

INDEX